The Gospel and the Law in Galatia

Paul's Response to Jewish-Christian Separatism and the Threat of Galatian Apostasy

Vincent M. Smiles

A Michael Glazier Book
THE LITURGICAL PRESS
Collegeville, Minnesota

A Michael Glazier Book published by The Liturgical Press

Cover design by David Manahan, O.S.B. Mosaic detail: St. Paul and apostles, 13th century, Monreale Cathedral, Sicily.

Unless cited otherwise, the Scripture passages in this book are the author's translation.

1   2   3   4   5   6   7   8   9

Library of Congress Cataloging-in-Publication Data

Smiles, Vincent M., 1949–
      The Gospel and the law in Galatia : Paul's response to Jewish
   Christian separatism and the threat of Galatian apostasy / Vincent M.
   Smiles.
          p.   cm.
      "A Michael Glazier book."
      Includes bibliographical references and indexes.
      ISBN 0-8146-5868-7 (alk. paper)
      1. Bible. N.T. Galatians—Theology. 2. Law and gospel—Biblical
   teaching. 3. Paul, the Apostle, Saint—Views on Jewish law. I. Title.
   BS2685.6.L34S65   1998
   227'.406—dc21   98-21271
                                                                        CIP

For Ingrid
Sine Qua Non
and
Matthew, Aaron, and Daniel

יְקַרְתֶּם בְּעֵינַי

Contents

Preface

This book began life as my Ph.D. dissertation for Fordham University which I completed in 1988. Pauline studies, of course, have not stood still in the last ten years. In fact, the number of articles, commentaries, and major monographs is daunting, particularly when one's writing endeavors take place in the midst of a very full teaching schedule. Nevertheless, I have done my best to take into account recent scholarship in the field—too much so, some might think, when surveying the plethora of footnotes! Even so, I am vividly aware of not having done justice to the excellent work of Hendrikus Boers, Richard Longenecker, Moisés Silva, and others. I can only regret my shortcomings.

About the footnotes—they are often lengthy and detailed, and many readers will properly want to skip over them. The argument of the book can be followed well enough without their aid. My hope is that they might serve both as a resource for further investigation of particular issues, and that they will clarify the book's debate with E. P. Sanders, James D. G. Dunn, and others. Though my disagreements with these scholars are sometimes extensive, so also is my indebtedness to them.

I owe a deep debt of thanks to Michael Naughton and Mark Twomey of The Liturgical Press who remained patient and encouraging, even though the manuscript was long overdue. My thanks also to my colleagues in the Department and School of Theology at the College of St. Benedict and St. John's University for their kindness, support, and lively discussion. I owe an incalculable debt to Richard J. Dillon of Fordham University whose inspiring teaching and rigorous scholarship first made me an enthusiast for the Scriptures in general and Paul in particular. I am grateful not only for his expert guidance, but for his great generosity and warm friendship. The book's dedication to my wife and three sons reflects love and gratitude I cannot put into words. To say "You are precious in my eyes" is an understatement.

May 24, 1998

I

Introduction

The Contingency of Paul's Letters

Paul's letter to the churches of Galatia is just that, a letter, addressed in a specific situation to a specific audience.[1] It is in the nature of genuine letters, as opposed to treatises in letter form (e.g., Ephesians), that they speak within the context of a specific set of relationships and circumstances that give rise to the letter. As outsiders to the correspondence between Paul and his churches modern readers are at a disadvantage, parties only to one side of the conversation. And yet knowledge of that situation is crucial to interpretation of the given letter. Of course, it is possible to interpret Paul, or any writer for that matter, in comparative abstraction. Within much recent critical scholarship, in fact,

---

1. The locale of these churches and the date of the letter are not decisive for this study, but locale and date are closely related questions. On the question of locale I am more persuaded by the "North Galatian" ("territory") than by the "South Galatian" ("province") hypothesis. For example, see Kümmel, *Introduction to the New Testament,* 296–98; Schlier, *Galater,* 15–16. The province hypothesis has been argued for extensively by Bruce, *Epistle to the Galatians,* 5–18; see also Dunn, *Epistle to the Galatians,* 5–19. In line with the territory hypothesis, I prefer a later date. Kümmel, *Introduction to the New Testament,* 304, suggests about "54 or 55 in Ephesus or Macedonia." An even later dating, "from Macedonia or Achaia, in the winter or spring of the years 57, 58 A.D.," is argued by Lightfoot, *Galatians,* 40.

1

Paul's letters are often conflated and mined for their rich veins of theological thought but not taken seriously as individual letters to particular communities. Such study has by no means been fruitless (e.g., Rudolf Bultmann on Paul!), but the concerns and nuances of each letter can hardly be appreciated with such an approach, and they may indeed be distorted.[2]

The relationship, therefore, between the "contingency" of the letter situation and the "coherence" of the gospel, as Paul understood it, is fundamental. This vocabulary of "contingency" and "coherence" derives from J. Christiaan Beker, who maintains that Paul's theologizing is characterized by a constant interplay between the gospel's coherent center and the contingencies of the letter situation. In each letter Paul attempts to articulate the gospel as "a word on target" according to the needs of the community or communities in view.[3] Thus the gospel is "never an abstraction removed from its 'address' and audience."[4] It transcends formulaic articulation because it is "the power of God" (Rom 1:16) and "the word of God," made available by but by no means captured within "human words" (1 Thess 2:13). Ultimately the gospel is God's deed, present in the world as grace before both Christ and Abraham (Gal 3:8; Rom 1:2). It is not, then, pace Beker, a future reality, "the imminent cosmic triumph of God," which is the "primary language" of Paul's gospel.[5] As I see it, it is God's "justify-

2. This point is well made by Beker, *Paul the Apostle,* 35–36, 40–41. This study presupposes seven letters as deriving from Paul himself: Romans, 1 and 2 Corinthians, Galatians, Philippians, 1 Thessalonians, Philemon.

3. Ibid., 12; see also 24 and 352.

4. Ibid., 24; see also 34 and 352. See also Beker's more recent discussion of the method in "Recasting Pauline Theology," *Pauline Theology I,* ed. J. M.Bassler, 15–24.

5. Beker, *Paul the Apostle,* 19 and 16 respectively. Paul's apocalyptic worldview is indeed a foundational component in his thought and in his articulation of the gospel (see Keck, "Paul as Thinker," 27–38, especially 29–33). Beker (see xix and 58) himself recognizes the difficulties in this view for the interpretation of Galatians and somewhat modifies it but continues to see "the imminent apocalyptic triumph of God" as the "ultimate point of reference" for Paul's gospel assertions ("Recasting Pauline Theology," 18). In my view the "ultimate point of reference" for Paul is the event

ing the ungodly" (Rom 4:5; cf. 4:17), in other words, the past and ongoing reality of grace, which is the "coherent center" of Paul's gospel. But though I disagree with Beker on Paul's "primary language," I agree with him regarding method. Paul's gospel can only be known "in its particularity."[6] I attempt here to understand Galatians as Paul's passionate but also *reasoned* articulation of the gospel in accordance with the needs of a particular situation.[7] This means that in what follows two questions dominate the examination of the letter to Galatia: (1) what is the historical and theological situation Paul envisages as he dictates this letter? and (2) what is "the gospel" in this context? In other words, what does Paul believe the Galatians need to understand and take to heart in order to make the right decisions in the crisis that has arisen?

---

and ongoing reality of "grace" (see chap. 2, "Paul as Paradigm of the Gospel for the Galatians").

6. Beker, *Paul the Apostle,* 352. "Therefore, the letter must be bent toward the oral, dialogical nature of the gospel. The coherent center of the gospel . . . cannot be a *depositum fidei* or doctrinal abstraction that as a universal, timeless substance is to be poured into every conceivable situation regardless of historical circumstance. . . . Particularity and occasionality do not represent a contamination of Paul's 'pure thought'; rather, they serve to make the truth of the gospel the effective word of God" (24).

7. Eckert, *Verkündigung,* 22–26, also stresses the importance of the historical situation for understanding the letter. See also the excellent discussion by Furnish, "Putting Paul in His Place," 3–17, particularly his insistence that the "place for understanding Paul" is "in his letters, read critically and *in context.*" Thus "two tasks are fundamental, the historical and the theological," each of which "demands the other" (12, my emphasis). This means taking seriously Paul's overriding concern for "his congregations to understand the truth of the gospel" and thus recognize that "in a *deliberate and reasoned way*" Paul reflects in his letters "about some particular aspects or implications of his gospel" (15, my emphasis). Furnish is properly reacting here against a number of scholars who "have been reluctant to take Paul's theological statements very seriously, judging his thought to be more 'intuitive' than deliberate" (14; see also relevant footnotes), whereas Paul's contextual theology is conducted "with considerable care" (15). See also note 27 below, on Haenchen's interpretation of Gal 2:1-10, and Lührmann on 2:11-14.

The Contingency of Galatians: Observations on Method

THE IMPORTANCE OF THE OTHER LETTERS AND OF ACTS

How Paul envisaged the situation as he wrote the letter must remain primary,[8] but this is not the same thing as being pessimistic about our ability to know the essential contours of the actual situation. A combination of Galatians itself and Paul's other letters (notably Romans and Philippians 3) along with Acts (particularly Acts 15),[9] James 1–2, and information gleaned from the Gospels (e.g., Mark 2:1–3:6; Matt 5:17-19; 23:1-8) is sufficient to show that the early churches engaged in vigorous debates on the relationship between the gospel and the law.[10] More particularly, the virtual certainty that Gal 2:1-10 and Acts 15:1-29 are, respectively, primary and secondary accounts of the same Jerusalem conference[11] represents a coincidence of historical sources that is not to be ignored. Of course, they are both tendentious accounts,

8. This point is properly emphasized by Cosgrove, *Cross and the Spirit,* 16, and see 45 and 87; also see Stanley, "Under a Curse," 488; Verseput, "Paul's Gentile Mission," 36.

9. Acts is a secondary source but is not without its value. Certainly it cannot be dismissed from the discussion, as it is by Schmithals, *Paul and James,* 38–39, and by Cosgrove and Lyons (n. 11, below). Haenchen, *Acts of the Apostles,* 464, maintains that Luke's version of the council "does not possess historical value"; nevertheless, he vindicates Acts' portrait of Paul as a delegate of Antioch (465; see also Haenchen, "Petrus-Probleme," 193) against Paul's own implication that he was an independent missionary (see also n. 11, below).

10. See Dunn, *Unity and Diversity,* 245–57; idem, "Bridge Between Jesus and Paul," *Jesus,* 10–31; idem, *Partings of the Ways,* 117–35.

11. There is, of course, no consensus on this matter, but it is reasonable to say that most share this view. See the discussions in Haenchen, *Acts of the Apostles,* 462–68; and Walker, "Why Paul Went to Jerusalem," 506–7, and his note 14. I disagree strongly, therefore, with the principle enunciated by Betz, "Geist," 78, and espoused by Lyons, *Pauline Autobiography,* 103 (see also Cosgrove, *Cross and the Spirit,* 23), that "everything we want to know" about the situation of the letter "must be reconstructed on the basis of the letter itself, with help from no other source." Galatians is the primary, but not the only, source.

and Acts 15 of itself tells us nothing of the Galatian situation. It does, however, corroborate Gal 2:3 and 6:12, from which we learn that the issue of the circumcision of Gentile believers was a primary question in that larger gospel-law debate. Acts 15 also confirms what most scholars have taken to be central to the Galatians debate itself, that the demand for Gentile obedience to the Law had to do with concern for their salvation: "Unless you are circumcised according to the law of Moses, you cannot be saved" (Acts 15:1, see v. 5).[12]

It is essential to situate Galatians within the history of the church's earliest decades, particularly within the context of the gospel-law debate of which Paul was a part. To fail to do so is not only to lose invaluable aids to interpretation but may also lead to unnecessary perplexities. Charles Cosgrove, for instance, insists that the Galatians' status as "sons" and "heirs" was not disputed by Paul's opponents; they advocated "'works of law' for the *increase* of life in the Spirit." Cosgrove's analysis of Galatians, in my view, fails to sustain this thesis, but it is also suspect in that it does not account for Acts 15.[13] The latter criticism also applies to the analysis of George Lyons, who uses rhetorical analysis to identify the letter as "deliberative." For Lyons, the denials as well as the affirmations have to do with Paul's concern to establish "his divinely determined ethos, not [with] defending his personal or official credentials." In other words, the opponents are not to be seen as having made claims and accusations against Paul. In the autobiography of Galatians 1–2 the emphasis falls, says Lyons, "on [Paul's] positive claim—'from God,' not its negative counterpart."[14] But there is no either-or here. Paul is as emphatic

---

12. On this, see Böttger, "Paulus," 77–100, especially 81, 83–88, and see chapter 3, below. For a contrary view see Cosgrove (following note), and Räisänen, "Legalism and Salvation," 75, note 68.

13. Cosgrove, *Cross and the Spirit,* 118 (my emphasis); see also 44, 115, 137. Acts 15 is discussed nowhere in his study.

14. Lyons, *Pauline Autobiography,* 112–21, 170–76, on the rhetorical form of the letter. Both quotes are on 133. Cosgrove, *Cross and the Spirit,* 124, agrees with Lyons on this (see below for further discussion of this issue). Against Schmithals and Marxsen (see n. 24, below), Lyons recognizes that Paul probably understood "his opponents and their charges" (99)

as to what is *not true* about himself in this letter as he is about anything else. What Lyons *affirms* about Galatians as "deliberative oratory" that aims at "persuasion" is, in my view, an important contribution to understanding the letter, but his attempt to rule out "apology" as an aspect of the letter—the two types are hardly watertight (see below)—fails to account for the letter's repeated denials and, again, leaves out of account valuable corroborative evidence from Acts and Paul's other letters.[15]

In attempting to understand the opponents' side of the debate, various precautions are, of course, necessary. I have already indicated that it is crucial to be guided, as Cosgrove properly says, not primarily by the "historical Galatians" but by the "epistolary Galatians."[16] In other words, the primary concern has to remain with the letter itself and with the issues it addresses. Second, with Hans Dieter Betz, it has to be admitted that "not everything that Paul denies is necessarily an accusation by his opposition."[17] Nevertheless, denials emphasized by repetition (e.g., 1:1 with 1:11-12 and 1:16c-19) and assertions repeated in different terms (e.g., the "truth" of Paul's gospel in 1:11-12; 2:5-6, 14; 3:3; 4:16) are important possible indicators of the situation Paul faced. In

---

quite well; they were "pressing circumcision" upon the Galatians. Yet Paul, in Lyons' view, remains clueless as to their motives; "he can conceive of only malevolent or unworthy ones (4:17; 6:12-13)" (129). Those texts are, to be sure, part of Paul's rhetoric impugning the opponents' personal motives (see also 1:7, "They want to pervert the gospel"). But ignoring the wider context, Lyons cannot see that Paul knows their real theological motives well enough. He responds to their views on the law from the perspective of a shared tradition (1:13-14; 2:15, "We Jews by birth"). And just as his disagreements with their theology led to *ad hominem* attacks, so also, we can assume, did their disagreements with Paul's theology.

15. See Lyons, *Pauline Autobiography,* 170–76. On Galatians as primarily "deliberative" rather than "apologetic," see also Kennedy, *Interpretation Through Rhetorical Criticism,* 144–52, who criticizes Betz's analysis of the letter (see also n. 31 and further discussion, below).

16. Cosgrove, *Cross and the Spirit,* 87 (see also 16 and 45).

17. Betz, *Galatians,* 6; see also 56, note 115. Betz, however, is criticized by Lyons, *Pauline Autobiography,* 99–105, for "mirror reading" (see following note).

other words, "mirror-reading" is far from mere speculation; used carefully, with checks and balances from the other letters and Acts, it can yield important clues.[18] Lyons insists: "There is no textual reason requiring the presumption of charges underlying Paul's autobiographical remarks, and certainly nothing requiring those of the consensus view." The selection of "which of Paul's denials are presumed to respond to opposing accusations" is, in Lyon's view, "almost totally arbitrary."[19] But Lyons can only come to this position because he ignores the evidence of Paul's other letters and of Acts. They, in fact, are the "textual reason," which, in addition to the repetitions and emphases of Galatians itself, enable a responsible reconstruction of the letter situation.

DETERMINING THE NATURE OF THE OPPONENTS' POSITION

From Galatians (2:3; 6:12) as well as Acts (15:1-5) we know of the demand that Gentile believers obey the law, including the law of circumcision, and that Paul and Barnabas went to Jerusalem and opposed this demand.[20] Indeed, it seems that they went *specifically* to oppose this demand, and Paul's other discussions of the law in Romans and Philippians 3 confirm that, at least from Paul's side, the debate was strongly polemical. Who were the

18. See Barclay, "Mirror Reading," 247–67, in which he responds to Lyons, *Pauline Autobiography,* arguing that carefully applied, "mirror reading" can be fruitful (see 260 and n. 38). On the "abruptness" of Paul's denials in 1:1 and the likelihood that they indicate his reaction to claims of his opponents, see Dunn, *Epistle to the Galatians,* 25–26.

19. Lyons, *Pauline Autobiography,* 95. A large part of Lyons' case rests on his analysis of Paul's "antithetical constructions" (107–12). He properly describes these as rhetorical features that have affinities with the Wisdom tradition, including the teaching of Jesus (107), and that "need not be assumed to reply to charges" (110). Of course that is true. But several of the examples he cites (110, n. 147) were written in polemical situations to overturn the opposite of what Paul wanted to assert. Romans 9:12, for instance, contradicts opponents who, as Lyons knows (see n. 21, below), required law observance of Gentile converts. Similarly, in Rom 9:16; 4:10; 1 Cor 6:5-6; and Phil 3:9, Paul's antithesis is a direct response to an opposing view.

20. For a thorough survey of the issue of circumcision in the New Testament period, see Horn, "Verzicht," 479–505.

opponents in Jerusalem? Acts calls them "believers from the party of the Pharisees" (15:5); Paul calls them "false brothers who sneaked in to spy out our freedom" (Gal 2:4). Given the way Paul describes this conflict, and the one in Antioch, *for the Galatians* (see below) the natural assumption is that those who were "troubling" (1:7) the Galatians shared a viewpoint similar to that of Paul's opponents in Jerusalem and Antioch.[21] From Rom 3:8 we learn that "some" accused Paul of preaching a gospel of cheap grace, an accusation he answers in detail in Romans 6 (cf. Gal 2:17). Is it, then, "purely conjectural,"[22] faced with Paul's vigorous and repeated denials in Galatians 1, to believe that they represent his response to claims and accusations from those who opposed him in Galatia? Are we to believe that Paul was the only one who treated this as a polemical encounter? Was he the only one to make accusations? The burden of proof, it seems to me, lies with those who wish to make that case. And that burden will become all the more difficult once the polemics of the Antioch incident (Gal 2:11-14) are considered, not to mention the evidence of accusations being leveled against Paul in Corinth (e.g., 2 Cor 10:2).[23] Even Luke confesses that both in Antioch and Jerusalem

21. Contra Lyons, *Pauline Autobiography,* 162–63. Although Lyons rejects this assumption, he himself (129) says that in Galatia "Paul vigorously opposes those, who . . . are pressing circumcision upon his converts," the precise problem in Antioch and Jerusalem, according to Acts 15:1-5 (cf. Gal 2:1-3). Further, the usual understanding of Galatians does not have to assume, as Lyons (163) thinks, that the Galatian opponents are "from Jerusalem," even though it is probable that they appealed to the authoritative tradition of Jerusalem. It is impossible to tell where they were from, but as I shall explain below, it seems more likely that they were from the Diaspora.

22. Lyons, *Pauline Autobiography,* 95.

23. Lyons, *Pauline Autobiography,* 125–30, refers to those who preach "the other gospel" in Galatia as "troublemakers" and seems to regard them as not dissimilar from the opponents in Corinth (2 Corinthians 10–13) in that they "accepted Paul's kerygma but promptly departed from Paul's understanding of it" (128, n. 20; quoting Koester). Presumably Lyons would disagree, but the evidence that the opponents in Corinth leveled derogatory claims against Paul seems quite explicit (e.g., 10:2, 10 with 11:4-6 and 12:11-13).

there was "no small disagreement and debate" with those who advocated circumcision (Acts 15:2, cf. v. 7).

Given the wide-ranging nature of the gospel-law debate, and that Paul was one of its main protagonists, it is quite reasonable to presume that the apostle was sufficiently informed about the circumstances in Galatia so that the major sections of the letter can be viewed as his response to a real situation. The fatal weakness in the position of Walter Schmithals is his presupposition (his word) "that Paul was only meagerly informed about goings-on in Galatia."[24] How can the interpreter presume to know more about the situation than Paul himself? This is an evasion, not a solution, of the letter's difficulties and, once again, fails to recognize agreement among historical sources. The "rhetorical-situation," Paul's desire and need to be persuasive, demanded that he be well informed.[25] How could he hope to persuade the Galatians of his point of view if he could not even speak accurately to the situation they were in? There were some who were insisting that the Galatians should accept the Jewish law, particularly circumcision, as a condition for being "in right relationship with God" (3:11). Thus also, it is not necessary to posit Gnosticism as a major feature of the opponents' theology;[26] they are probably best characterized as Jewish Christians who attempted to "compel" (6:12; cf. 2:3, 14) the Galatians to conform to requirements of the Jewish law.

---

24. Schmithals, *Paul and the Gnostics,* 18. Also of the view that Paul was poorly informed is Marxsen, *Introduction to the New Testament,* 55. See responses to this view by Lyons, *Pauline Autobiography,* 98–99; Bruce, *Epistle to the Galatians,* 25.

25. "Rhetorical situation" is a quote from Stanley, "Galatians 3:10-14," 488, who makes extensive and judicious use of the insights of Kennedy, *Interpretation Through Rhetorical Criticism.*

26. See Mussner, *Galaterbrief,* 25. On Gnostic or syncretistic features in Paul's opposition, see also Lührmann, *Offenbarungsverständnis,* 67–73; Wegenast, *Das Verständnis der Tradition,* 34–40. My understanding of the opponents is similar to that of Beker, *Paul the Apostle,* 42–44; Mussner, *Galaterbrief,* 24–25; and Lüdemann, *Paul,* 44–45; in other words, it is quite traditional.

A primary indication in the letter of the truth of this last assertion is the narrative of the Jerusalem and Antioch incidents, which are usually understood as part of Paul's response to the denigration of his apostolate on the part of his opponents. That view is also accepted here. It is not usually sufficiently emphasized, however, that these incidents have a further and equally important function, *specifically for the Galatian situation,* in Paul's defense of "the truth of the gospel" (2:5, 14). Paul narrates these incidents for his Galatian readers because he sees in them reflections of what is occurring in Galatia.[27] The evidence for this is that the vocabulary employed in these narratives corresponds with vocabulary used specifically of the Galatian crisis (e.g., "compel" in 2:3, 14; 6:12). The Judaizers[28] were "compelling" the Galatians to be circumcised by warning them that if they did not conform to requirements of the Jewish law they had no true part in the covenant of Abraham. Another way of saying this was that the Galatians were not truly "justified" (δικαιοῦσθαι)[29] before God and

27. Pace Cosgrove, *Cross and the Spirit,* 31, who says that "it is far from self-evident how this personal history [1:11–2:21] applies to the Galatians." Cosgrove maintains that modern readers "must join [the letter's] conversation at Galatians 3:1 and nowhere else" (5), but his method is flawed, as I have said, by his refusal to make use of the other letters and Acts. Haenchen, "Petrus-Probleme," 187–97, has demonstrated that the Jerusalem conference was ill-suited to Paul's purpose in vindicating his apostolic authority, since at the time of the conference itself, as opposed to what occurred since, Paul was merely a delegate of Antioch. Paul accordingly gives the conference a significance with regard to his own apostolate other than it actually had (see especially 192–93). Note Haenchen's contextual method here. So also Lührmann, "Abendmahlsgemeinschaft?" 271–86, has argued that the account of the Antioch incident has to be understood in the context of the Galatian crisis (see especially 279).

28. On the meaning of ἰουδαΐζειν ("judaize") see Dunn, "Incident at Antioch," *Jesus,* 149. In itself it is an intransitive verb referring to the adoption by non-Jews of certain Jewish practices. It is appropriate, nevertheless, to speak of the opponents as "Judaizers," since Paul describes his opponents as "compelling gentiles to judaize" (2:14; cf. 2:3; 6:12).

29. Translating δικαιοῦσθαι and its cognates is notoriously difficult, as is noted, for example, by E. P. Sanders, *Paul and Palestinian Judaism,* 470–71; and see idem, *Law and the Jewish People,* 13, n. 18, which adopts

thus could not be true members of God's people with Jewish Christians such as themselves, who obeyed the law. In this respect the Judaizers, in Paul's terms, were destroying the Galatians' "freedom" and denying "the truth of the gospel" (2:3-5, 14).

The climax of these accounts and the transition into the main theological sections of the letter is 2:15-21. This passage bears the main burden of exegesis in this study because it contains a dense summation of the gospel for the Galatians. Its terms and concepts reach back to the initial announcement of the gospel's content (1:4 in 2:19-21) and forward to the themes of bondage under sin (3:10-13, 22), life in Christ as "new creation" (6:15), and the eschatological transforming power of the death of Christ (3:26-28; 5:24). Above all, it provides a forceful statement of the doctrine of justification by faith and *not works of law*. This negative edge is prominent in the letter, and it corresponds, as almost all agree, to the central issue at stake between Paul and the Galatians. Thus the thesis pursued here is that 2:15-21 has primarily Galatia in view, even while Antioch remains as the dramatic backdrop for Paul's assertions.[30] The doctrine of justification in 2:16-17, in the context of the startling division of humanity in 2:15, is formulated by the apostle as the "good news," which the Galatians need to hear, and as the "bad news," which undermines the position of the opponents. In this letter there is a lot of emphasis on the "bad news."

---

a rather drastic solution to the problem. In general I prefer to speak of "righteousness" and "make righteous," but occasionally I use the phrase "justification by faith" and, more rarely, the word "justification" by itself.

30. Eckstein, *Verheißung* 4–5, rightly says that "already from v. 15 Paul's report is formulated with reference to the Galatian situation—and through v. 21 as a speech to Peter." Further, one has to consider in light of 6:12 whether "the accusation of ἀναγκάζειν ἰουδαΐζειν ["compel to judaize"] is already influenced by the present [Galatian] conflict." A very different view is argued by Feld, "Christus Diener," 119–31: "With regard to the Galatians it makes little sense to anticipate a broad presentation of the relationship between the law and Christian faith with a synopsis on the same issue." If Feld were correct, one wonders why Paul would have included 2:15-21 for the Galatians at all.

THE FORM OF PAUL'S RESPONSE TO THE OPPONENTS' ATTACK

That Galatians exhibits the influence of Greco-Roman rhetoric seems to be disputed by no one, but no such unanimity exists with regard to the type of rhetoric found in this letter. Betz's description of Galatians as an "apologetic letter" has not received universal approval.[31] I have already mentioned Lyons' disagreement with this, but even he acknowledges that "the forensic genre of apology" can explain "an aspect of it," though "only an aspect."[32] It does, in fact, seem best to think of Galatians as *primarily* "deliberative" rather than "apologetic," in that it seeks to persuade the Galatians about their *future* decisions more than to provide a defense about *past* actions.[33] A great deal, of course, depends on how one understands the function of chapters 1–2, with their narrative of Paul's history from his "former life in Judaism" to his confrontation with Cephas in Antioch. Lyons, not without good reason, says that the narrative establishes Paul's apostolic "ethos"; the emphasis is less on events than on character, on the fact that Paul's actions have been determined by the will of God,

31. See Betz, *Galatians,* 14; idem, "Composition," 353–79. Betz's major divisions of the letter are *exordium* (1:6-11), *narratio* (1:12–2:14), *propositio* (2:15-21), *probatio* (3:1–4:31), and *exhortatio* (5:1–6:10). These are bounded by the prescript (1:1-5) and postscript (6:11-18). Howard, *Crisis in Galatia,* 48–49, "independently of Betz," compares Galatians to Cicero's *De Inventione* and arrives at a similar structure in order to argue (rightly) that the letter is "a unit and concentrates on one theme" (49). Structure, however, does not determine purpose (see Kennedy, *Interpretation Through Rhetorical Criticism,* 23–25; Lyons, *Pauline Autobiography,* 25–27), and Howard does not seem to see Galatians as apologetic. Brinsmead, *Response to Opponents,* 42–55, and Lüdemann, *Paul,* 46–48, accept Betz's form-critical analysis. I have already noted that Lyons, *Pauline Autobiography,* rejects it; so also do Kennedy, *Interpretation Through Rhetorical Criticism,* 144–52, and (for different reasons) Kieffer, *Antioche,* 27 and n. 26, who particularly objects to separating 2:15-21 from the *narratio* (1:12–2:14).

32. Lyons, *Pauline Autobiography,* 173.

33. For definitions of apologetic ("judicial") versus "deliberative" or "epideictic" rhetoric, see Aune, *Literary Environment,* 198, who in part follows Kennedy, *Interpretation Through Rhetorical Criticism,* 19–20.

and thus that Paul "is a paradigm of the gospel he proclaims."[34] This is all undeniable. It goes along well, in fact, with traditional views on Galatians. But, of course, identifying Galatians as "deliberative" does not determine its situation, only how Paul chose to respond. More important, it does not preclude that the letter also has apologetic purposes, particularly in chapters 1–2.

David Aune in his 1981 review of Betz's commentary on Galatians conceded that "Gal. 1–2 does appear, in a general way, to exhibit the structures of forensic rhetoric in a manner very similar to Plato, Ep. 7," and goes on to say that "deliberative oratory cannot be entirely omitted when considering the form and function of Gal. 3–4." In general, Aune preferred to see Galatians as "an eclectic combination of various rhetorical techniques,"[35] and in a more recent publication has said:

> Attempts to classify one or another of Paul's letters as *either* juridical *or* deliberative *or* epideictic (or one of their subtypes) run the risk of imposing external categories on Paul and thereby obscuring the real purpose and structure of his letters. Paul in particular was both a creative and eclectic letter writer. The epistolary situations he faced were often more complex than the ordinary rhetorical situations faced by most rhetoricians.

Aune is noncommittal as to whether the apostle's denials reveal "the positive accusations of Paul's opponents," but he concedes that "Galatians can be read as a deliberative letter with some apologetic features."[36] George Kennedy views both 1 Thessalonians and 1 Corinthians as primarily "deliberative" and yet identifies apologetic passages in both of them (1 Thess 2:1-18; 1 Cor 1:13-17). In light of this it is somewhat surprising that he is so noncommittal about the possibility of "refutation of charges" in Galatians. That possibility is at least as defensible in the case of Galatians 1 as in either of those passages.[37] In this study I will

34. Lyons, *Pauline Autobiography,* 132–34; last quote is on 134.
35. Aune, *Religious Studies Review* 7, 326.
36. Aune, *Literary Environment,* 203 and 207 respectively.
37. See Kennedy, *Interpretation Through Rhetorical Criticism,* 142–43, in regard to 1 Thessalonians 2; see 25 and 87 for 1 Corinthians 1. Against the

take Galatians 1–2 as, in part, Paul's *defense* of his apostolate and
gospel against claims and accusations of his opponents, though it
will be important to recognize that the apostle is by no means
merely on the defensive.

The Opponents and Judaism

THE ORIGINS OF THE OPPONENTS

The opponents, in my view, have to be seen as Jewish Christians whose teaching was informed by a conservative, separatist
strand of Judaism. They were not unlike the Pharisaic-Christian
group described in Acts 15:5. Because of this similarity, interpreters sometimes speak of them as "Palestinian."[38] While this is
not impossible, it is more likely that they were from the Diaspora.
As such they could still appeal to Jerusalem as the home of sacred
tradition. Furthermore, a missionary endeavor among Gentile
Christians by conservative Jewish Christians is somewhat more
understandable if those missionaries already lived in an essentially Gentile environment.[39] There is no good reason to see the

---

view that 1 Thessalonians 2 is "apologetic," see Lyons, *Pauline Autobiography,* 182–85; Stowers, *Letter-Writing,* 25–26.

38. For example, Bligh, *Galatians in Greek,* 85, thinks they were ill-
disciplined disciples of the Jerusalem apostles. See also Kümmel, *Introduction to the New Testament,* 300–301; Lüdemann, *Paul,* 59; and Mussner,
Galaterbrief, 57, who says it is possible that they came from Jerusalem, but
see also 26 and note 121: that they may have originated from Paul's "mission regions in Asia Minor . . . which belonged to the province of Galatia."
The contrary idea of Brinsmead, *Response to Opponents,* 50 and 58, that the
opponents were opposed to Jerusalem is highly unlikely.

39. That is, they followed Paul into Galatia deliberately to oppose his
teaching. This, of course, is the majority view: for example, Beyer and Althaus, "Der Brief an die Galater," *Die kleineren Briefe des Apostels Paulus,*
1; Betz, *Galatians,* 7; Brinsmead, *Response to Opponents,* 49; Bruce, *Epistle to the Galatians,* 24–25; Mussner, *Galaterbrief,* 25–26; Schlier, *Galater,*
19. To the contrary are Munck, *Paul and the Salvation of Mankind,* 87–88,
who says they were local Gentile Christians; Tyson, "Paul's Opponents in
Galatia," 241–54, says they were local Jewish Christians.

Judaizers as delegates of the Jerusalem apostles. Paul not only confronted Cephas in Antioch, he called his name and that of James in Galatians. If they had been the intentional authority behind the Galatian opposition, there is no reason to doubt that Paul would have named them as such. Further, Acts 15 shows that the apostles did not completely control the Jerusalem congregations; certainly they could not control the views and practices of Jewish Christians in the Diaspora. Our concern, of course, is with the *teaching* of the opponents, not their origins.

THE SEPARATISM OF THE OPPONENTS AND ANCIENT JUDAISM

If Paul indeed knew his opponents' theological perspective, then he knew it, the letter suggests, not only from their teaching in Galatia but also from his own background in Judaism. Their teaching, it seems, was formed in and characterized by a separatist mentality that was not uncommon in Second-Temple Judaism.[40] In Galatians it is most succinctly expressed in the language, so peculiar for Paul, of 2:15: "We [are] Jews by birth and not sinners of the gentiles." Paul's original attachment to this mentality is dramatically displayed in his having persecuted the church and attempted to destroy it (Gal 1:13). The precise reasons for that persecution are, of course, unknown,[41] but his own language in Gal 1:13-14 and especially in Phil 3:5-6 shows beyond question that in Paul's mind it had to do with defense of the law. Particularly the references to Paul's "zeal" in both of those texts

40. See Neusner, *Judaism,* 45–53. Dunn, "New Perspective on Paul," *Jesus,* 183–206, makes considerable use of the insights of Neusner and shows how essential it is to take Jewish "national identity" (e.g., 185) into account in interpreting Paul's critique of the law.

41. Fredriksen, "Judaism," 548–57, says it was because "the enthusiastic proclamation of a Messiah executed very recently by Rome as a political troublemaker—a *crucified* Messiah—combined with a vision of the approaching End *preached also to Gentiles . . .* was dangerous" (556). In other words, such preaching was "politically sensitive." There may be some truth in this, but of course Paul's own words on the matter—notably Phil 3:5-6 —envisage (at least also) a theological motivation inspired by "zeal" for the law and Israel's integrity; see Dunn, *Epistle to the Galatians,* 60–62.

(cf. Acts 22:3-4) indicate that the church offended strict, law-abiding Jews who believed, in the tradition of Ezra and Nehemiah (e.g., Ezra 9–10; Nehemiah 13), that the distinctiveness of Israel must not be compromised. Though many Jews were very open and generous in their attitudes towards Gentiles, James Dunn has rightly emphasized that "this zeal [for Israel's law] led to taking the sword to maintain Israel's distinctiveness as God's covenant people."[42]

Separatism, in a sense, was part of the very foundation of Israel in that it was intimately linked to divine election and the covenant of Sinai (e.g., Exod 19:5-6; Lev 20:22-26; Deut 7:1-11). But it was not only theologically well founded, it was also sociologically necessary in order for Israel to retain its unique identity. Thus, separatists insisted, also in a Christian context, that there *remained* "Jew and Greek" (pace Gal 3:28; cf. Acts 11:1-3) and that, as James thought, the differences must be respected (Gal 2:11-12). To be sure, within the church as within Judaism, there was a way to overcome the differences. In the view of the Galatian opponents the differences must be overcome by the Gentiles' being circumcised and observing other prescriptions of the law. In the absence of such observance, however, the Gentiles are cut off from the covenant (Gen 17:14), from Israel, and from salvation. For the opponents as for Paul (Gal 5:2-4) the issue was that serious.

I wish to emphasize, therefore, that the term "separatism" implies no judgments of Judaism as a whole. Separatism, in some form, is an inevitable and indeed a necessary phenomenon whenever a religion is under threat of assimilation or persecution. During the reforms of Ezra and Nehemiah and even more so during the Maccabean rebellion and straight through to New Testament times, Judaism had to contend with both. Speaking of "exclusive and inclusive Judaism," John Dominic Crossan observes, "Exclusivity, at its extreme, can mean petrification, isolation and irrelevance. Inclusivity, at its extreme, can mean abdication, betrayal

---

42. Dunn, "Pharisees, Sinners, and Jesus," *Jesus,* 68; also "Incident at Antioch," ibid., 137–40. For evidence of openness to Gentiles see Fredriksen, "Judaism," 542–48; E. P. Sanders, *Paul and Palestinian Judaism,* 206–12. For a fuller description of separatism see chapter 4, under 2:15.

and disintegration . . . a people could lose its soul at the extremity of either direction."[43] The theological debate between Paul and his opponents is all the more fruitful if it is recognized that the latter, in fidelity to their tradition, were fighting for the "soul" of Israel, just as the apostle, according to his lights, was fighting for the "soul" of the gospel. Further, just as Paul's radical views did not represent the entire spectrum of mid-first-century "Christianities" (cf. Matt 5:17-19; 23:1-3), neither did Jewish or Jewish-Christian separatism speak for all Jews or Jewish Christians. It is a mistake, therefore, to read Galatians as though the issue was monolithically "Christianity" versus "Judaism," just as it is also a mistake to deny that sharp differences existed between Paul and adherents of the Jewish law. Paul cannot be interpreted as though he were not a negative critic of important aspects of first-century Judaism, specifically in its insistence on the function of the law in God's plan of salvation.

In the context of recent New Testament scholarship such a statement is not without a measure of controversy. Much of that scholarship goes to great lengths to render Paul, one way or another, a non-critic of first-century Judaism.[44] On the issue of the law, however, it does not seem to me that such a view of Paul can be successful. Deuteronomy, for instance, insists throughout that God's laws *must* be obeyed; to fail to obey them incurs the curse (Deuteronomy 27). It goes without saying, then, as even Sanders admits, that "obedience, especially the intention to obey ('confessing')," though to be sure "it does not *earn* it," is "the *conditio*

43. Crossan, *The Historical Jesus,* 418.

44. Gaston, in *Paul and the Torah,* goes to extraordinary lengths in this regard: for example, he takes "works of law" to be a "subjective genitive" (100–106) and renders Genesis 15:6 as "And he [Abraham] put his trust in YHWH, and he [Abraham] counted it to him [YHWH] righteousness" (47). See the telling review by Dillon in *Theological Studies* 50:2 (June 1989) 360–61. Judaism, it seems to me, needs no defense from Christian exegesis; it is strong enough to stand of itself. Judaism, no less than Christianity, is a way of salvation, and Paul's critique of aspects of Judaism is in no sense a rejection of Judaism as such. Further, within the canons of historical criticism Paul's assertions are not beyond all reproach.

sine qua non of salvation."[45] Obedience to the law, within the context of the covenant, as necessary for salvation is what I would call—to use Räisänen's phrase—"soft legalism." "Hard" or "anthropocentric" legalism, says Räisänen, is that "petty formalism . . . smugness and self-righteousness" that Christian exegetes have wrongly taken to be a wholly accurate account of first-century Judaism in its entirety. On the other hand, a "'soft' or 'torah-centric' legalist would be one whose system of salvation consists of the observance of precepts but who is free of any boasting or a self-righteous attitude."[46] Räisänen would not agree (preceding note), but it seems to me that Paul's opponents, and the separatist tradition they represent, have to be described in terms of "soft" legalism. It also seems clear that Paul accuses his opposition of "hard" legalism in Rom 2:17-20 (cf. Phil 3:2-5; Gal 2:15, 19-20) in that he saw their self-estimation, based on law, as inflated and illusory. That having been said, it must be stressed that Judaism no more "*necessarily tends*" towards petty legalism" than does Christianity or any other religion.[47] "Legalism," however, in a neutral "soft" sense, was undeniably an aspect of the Jewish tradition that Paul knew and that, as an apostle, he opposed.

Stephen Westerholm makes judicious use of Räisänen's distinction. For Westerholm νόμος ("law") in Paul refers primarily to "the Sinaitic legislation," and Paul *agrees* with his opposition that

45. E. P. Sanders, *Paul and Palestinian Judaism,* 141. See also note 58, below.

46. Räisänen, "Legalism and Salvation," 63–64; Paul, says Räisänen, "charges his kinsmen for 'soft' legalism only," but such a charge, he believes, "*cannot* be verified by Jewish sources" (72). Räisänen accepts "covenantal nomism" as an accurate description of first-century Judaism (65–67) and yet, as indicated, rejects "soft legalism." But in both, the law has a necessary soteriological function, and it is that function of the law that Paul rejects. His distancing of the law from God and the covenant (Gal 3:15-21) is a rhetorical device by which he undermines the opponents' teaching, but Paul is not giving a "totally distorted picture of the Jewish religion" (72) in arguing against the law as necessary for salvation.

47. E. P. Sanders, *Paul and Palestinian Judaism,* 427, defends Judaism against this "frequent Christian charge." It seems to me that legalism is endemic to all "religions of the book," Judaism, Christianity, and Islam.

the law demands obedience.[48] His exclusion of the law is *not* based on the view that it is a perversion of the law to see it as requiring "works," since manifestly it does.[49] Judaism can properly be called "legalist" (in the "soft" sense) in that the demands of the covenant, enshrined in the "law," make "life" dependent on obedience and threaten the "curse" for disobedience (e.g., Deuteronomy 27–28; Lev 18:5). This is the major point that the Judaizers insisted upon and that Paul contested. It makes nonsense of Paul, not to mention Exodus, Leviticus, and Deuteronomy, to deny that the law requires obedience and makes such obedience, within the context of the covenant, a prerequisite for salvation.[50]

Once that is seen clearly, then it is easier to see why for the Galatian opponents it was inconceivable to separate faith in Christ from obedience to the Law. But what they refused to do, Paul insisted upon. In that regard Westerholm offers the following valuable distinction:

> The methodological error has often been committed in the past of concluding that, since Paul contrasts grace and works and argues for salvation by grace, his opponents (and, ultimately, Judaism) must have worked with the same distinction but argued for salvation by works. Clearly this distorts Judaism, which never thought that divine grace was incompatible with divine requirements. But we become guilty of a similar methodological error if we conclude that, since Paul's opponents did not distinguish between grace and requirements, Paul himself could not have done so either: . . . *The methodological point is crucial.* Paul must not be allowed to be our main witness for Judaism, nor must Judaism, or the position of Paul's opponents, determine the limits within which Paul is to be interpreted.[51]

48. Westerholm, *Israel's Law,* 105–21; notes 1 and 4 on 106. For his use of Räisänen's distinction, see 132–33. Against the usual "legalist" interpretation of the law's demand for obedience to its "works," see 120–21.

49. Ibid., 130–35, also 142–50.

50. See ibid., 144–47, especially 147. For the view that Judaism regarded obedience to the law within the covenant as necessary for "salvation," see E. P. Sanders, *Paul and Palestinian Judaism,* 420; idem, *Law and the Jewish People,* 129, 132; and see note 58, below.

51. Westerholm, *Israel's Law,* 150 (my emphasis).

In Galatians Paul separates what his opponents wish to hold together, covenant and law, faith and works. This disjunction is not absolute (Romans 14!), but it is made to *appear* absolute— here Paul's polemical rhetoric is in full cry—when requirements of law are seen to compromise belief in the sufficiency of the death of Christ fully to "rescue" humankind from the power of "the present evil age" (Gal 1:4). In these circumstances, when the law is seen to threaten the standing, as "heirs of Abraham," of those for whom Christ died, Paul turns *not* primarily on his opponents but on *the law itself.*

This attack on the law is what most characterizes the polemic of Galatians. In that polemic Paul attacks the law's definition of "righteousness" in terms of its own works (e.g., Lev 18:5), and he exposes as an illusion the presumption of superior status which that definition has produced in the law's adherents. The law-dominated ἐγώ ("I"), which must die "to law" (Gal 2:19), suffers from that illusion, and that is a form of "hard" legalism. It is to be noted, however, that the thrust of Paul's attack is not against the opponents, nor against their boasting in the law,[52] but is directed at the law itself. For Paul the law cannot produce what it promises (3:11-12, 21), and thus it deludes those who rely upon it. This is an important aspect of Paul's critique, which I will attempt to detail in the exegesis of 3:10-14 (chap. 4). It was in reaction to the crisis situation in Galatia that Paul developed this harsh polemic against the law. His "rhetorical situation" was difficult, to say the least. Galatians were on the very edge of apostasy (1:6); some may have "deserted" already (5:2-4). In any event, the polemic became ammunition for his opponents. In Romans, I shall argue, Paul has to explain his teaching against the

---

52. Räisänen, "Legalism and Salvation," 69, says that in Galatians there is "no talk of man's boasting and the like"; and Hübner, *Law in Paul's Thought,* 111, maintains that "renunciation" of boasting, which in Romans is constitutive of the believer, is not apparent in Galatians. "Boasting," however, does not have to be mentioned explicitly in order to be a part of Paul's discussion. The mentality of the "we" of 2:15, which derives status from the covenant and law-observance (cf. Phil 3:2-5), is the same as that of the "I" of 2:19, which must "die to law in order to live to God."

law in very different circumstances. The differences between the two letters in this regard are best understood, in my view, not in terms of developments in Paul's thinking but primarily in terms of historical context,[53] an issue I will take up in chapter 5.

The views espoused here in regard to Judaism obviously owe much to the important work of E. P. Sanders, who certainly has provided scholarship with a "new perspective" on *Judaism.*[54] But with regard to Paul's critique of the law, it is equally obvious that the approach developed here is radically different from his.

DISAGREEMENTS WITH E. P. SANDERS

Prior to the publication of *Paul and Palestinian Judaism* (n. 29), it was all too easy for Christian scholars to speak in terms of "Jewish legalism"[55] (the "hard" variety) and to presume that this characterized Judaism in its entirety and in its essence. To do this, however, is not only an injustice to first-century Judaism, it also extinguishes the fire of the real debate between Paul and his opposition. The apostle's ardor was kindled by more than the straw man of "Jewish legalism," understood as a fastidious externalism that, forgetful of election and covenant, insisted on "works-righteousness" as the only way humans could earn eternal salvation. There is no good reason to see these Jewish Christians in such light. They not only believed fervently what they preached, they had solid foundations for it. Scripture was their

53. Developmental theories have been suggested by Hübner, *Law in Paul's Thought,* and Wilckens, "Gesetzesverständnisses," 154–86, and abbreviated in "Statements on the Development of Paul's View of the Law," in *Paul and Paulinism,* ed. Hooker and Wilson, 17–26.

54. See Dunn, "New Perspective on Paul," *Jesus,* 184. Dunn himself, of course, goes on to disagree with substantive aspects of Sanders' view of Paul.

55. This phrase is used by Bultmann, *Primitive Christianity,* 59–71. E. P. Sanders, *Paul and Palestinian Judaism,* 43–47, takes Bultmann seriously to task for his presentation of first-century Judaism. It is interesting to note that Neusner, *Politics to Piety,* 90, speaks of "Pharisaic legalism," but of course he is not thereby describing Pharisees as petty externalists with no recognition of the love of God.

powerful ally, and Paul was often hard pressed to overturn the
natural meaning of the ancient text (e.g., Deut 27:26 in Gal
3:10).[56] It is, therefore, important to distinguish between Paul's
evaluation of the opponents and their motives (e.g., 1:7; 4:17;
6:12) and their own understanding of themselves and their mission. They were *advocates* of "the gospel of Christ" (1:7) so
long as it was understood in the context of the ancient traditions
of Judaism.

Sanders describes ancient Judaism as a system of "covenantal nomism," whose "'pattern' or 'structure'" can be described as
follows:

> (1) God has chosen Israel and (2) given the law. The law implies
> both (3) God's promise to maintain the election and (4) the re-
> quirement to obey. (5) God rewards obedience and punishes trans-
> gression. (6) The law provides for means of atonement, and
> atonement results in (7) maintenance or re-establishment of the
> covenantal relationship. (8) All those who are maintained in the
> covenant by obedience, atonement and God's mercy belong to the
> group which will be saved. An important interpretation of the first
> and last points is that election and ultimately salvation are consid-
> ered to be by God's mercy rather than human achievement.[57]

In general, I have no disagreement with this as a description of
the relationship between covenant and law in the minds of the opponents.[58] And I agree with Sanders that Paul knew well enough

56. On Paul's free and creative allusions to Israel's Scripture, see Hays,
Echoes of Scripture.

57. E. P. Sanders, *Paul and Palestinian Judaism,* 422; see also 75 and
419–20; see also idem, *Law and the Jewish People,* 45.

58. It is important here to maintain historical perspective. As even
Sanders acknowledges (e.g., *Law and the Jewish People,* 156), "some Jews"
must have been obedient to law for superficial reasons; such is the human
experience in religion. Furthermore, the greater a religion's preoccupation
with legal definition, the greater is the danger of such superficiality and
"hard" legalism. Thus Gundry, "Grace, Works," 7, properly says that though
Sanders has demolished a view of Judaism as amassing deeds for salvation,
"he has not succeeded in relating the law to elective grace in a way that ma-
terially scales down preoccupation with legal interpretation, extension, ap-

that election and covenant provided the essential context for observance of the law.[59]

I disagree, however, that Paul's "real attack" is against "the idea of election" and "the idea of the covenant."[60] It is somewhat ironic that one who is intent to have scholarship be more just in its assessment of Judaism should come up with a Paul who denies the very basis of Israel's existence as the people of God. If Sanders were right, then Paul should have answered yes to his own question in Rom 11:1 ("Surely God has not rejected his people, has he?"), a verse Sanders hardly considers. In fact, Paul emphatically avoided this conclusion (11:1-2, 25-36; cf. 11:11), and in spite of denying Israel's privilege in the coming judgment (3:9-23) and the claim to be exclusively God's people (9:6-24), he presupposes Israel's *priority* in God's plan of salvation (1:16; 2:9; 11:13-24).

Sanders' interpretation of Paul leads him to reject "Paul's own" formulation of the apostle's "critique of Judaism"; "this formulation" (viz., "By faith and not by works of law"), claims Sanders, "actually misstates the fundamental point of disagreement."[61] But

---

plication, and observance." See also Westerholm, *Israel's Law,* 149: "The law and human 'works' are clearly given a soteriological function in Judaism which is denied them by Paul." Quarles, "Soteriology," 185–95, argues persuasively that "the traditional view of first-century rabbinic soteriology as based on works-righteousness is not completely based upon pseudo-scholarship as claimed by Sanders" (195). My purpose here is not to show "legalism" out the front door only to let it in by the back but to keep historical balance. Paul's concern to put "law" in its place is a perennial need for all religions with legal codices.

59. As Dunn, "New Perspective on Paul," *Jesus,* note 16, 204, points out, even Neusner agrees with Sanders on this point. But it is Paul himself, and not merely a Reformation reading of him (pace Dunn, 185), who contests the claim that "works of law" are necessary for salvation and intends by that to exclude *any* works that might be posited as conditional for salvation. Certainly Paul's *earliest* interpreters understood him that way: see Marshall, "Salvation, Grace, and Works," 339–58.

60. E. P. Sanders, *Law and the Jewish People,* 46. See also idem, *Paul and Palestinian Judaism,* 551. I will return to this issue in chapter 5.

61. E. P. Sanders, *Paul and Palestinian Judaism,* 551.

this is a lot to claim against a formulation that Paul repeats over and over in so many different ways and with such programmatic statements as Rom 4:4-5, 14; 11:6, and Gal 2:16; 3:11-12. For Paul the divine-human relationship is not founded on human "desiring or striving, but on God who has mercy" (Rom 9:16). For the apostle, that is true "now" because it was first true in relation to Israel (9:6-18).[62] The law is "good" (7:12) but it is not *foundational* to the relationship *either* in its inception *or* in its continuation. Pace Sanders, the law as "a way of relating to God" is precisely what Paul contests.[63] "By faith and not by works of law" is the heart of the matter.

The issue in Galatians, therefore, does not merely have to do with the "conditions on which Gentiles *enter* the people of God." On this point Sanders has been convincingly refuted by R. H. Gundry.[64] Paul regards the Galatians as already "descendants of Abraham" (Gal 3:29), God's "adopted children" (4:4-7). Far from the issue of *entry,* 5:2-4 speaks of the law as disastrous for *living* the life of grace. What Paul denies is that the law can have anything to do with that *established* relationship. Sanders proposes his view of the Galatian situation by setting it over against the old "legalist" interpretation which, like any straw man, is easily demolished: "The question is not about *how many good deeds an individual must present* before God to be declared righteous at the judgment, but, to repeat, whether or not Paul's Gentile converts must accept the Jewish law in order to enter the people of God or to be counted truly members."[65] In my view neither of these is the issue. The issue is: What is the nature of the relationship that has been established in Christ between God and all believers, and what place does the law have in that ongoing relationship? For Paul the relationship in Christ is founded on grace, as it was in the beginning with Abraham (Gal 3:6-9; Rom 4:1-5). And that means

---

62. See Westerholm, *Israel's Law,* 172.

63. E. P. Sanders, *Law and the Jewish People,* 158.

64. Ibid., 18 (my emphasis); Gundry, "Grace, Works," 1–38; especially 8–12.

65. E. P. Sanders, *Law and the Jewish People,* 20.

that "works of law" are not necessary for the relationship and may even be inimical to it.

The Law Versus the Gospel

It is the negative edge of the doctrine of justification ("not by works of law") that gives Galatians its peculiar sting. In this letter Paul is very much in the business of "razing strongholds, destroying arguments, removing every proud obstacle to the knowledge of God, and taking prisoner, in subjection to Christ, every idea" (2 Cor 10:4-5). On nothing else is it more important to keep in mind the contextual character of the letter, its "rhetorical situation," than on this issue of the abrogation of the law. Perhaps the greatest challenge of Paul's theology is that he both denigrates the law (e.g., Gal 3:15-17) and yet also appeals to its authority (passim!) and insists that believers "fulfil it" (Gal 5:14; Rom 8:4; 13:8-10). The discussion of this in the following chapters is quite extensive. I wish here to emphasize, first, that it was in the cauldron of an intense theological debate, in which Paul saw himself as contesting not only for "the truth of the gospel" but also for the salvation of the Galatians (5:2-4), that his statements on the law were forged. His arguments are rhetorical, his intention is to persuade. But second, they are not *merely* rhetorical. Romans, written in a somewhat more reflective mood, will show that the abrogation of the law in Galatians was not momentary. Third, very careful nuance is required in order to make sense of Paul's abrogating a law to which he constantly appeals. Räisänen's solution to the difficulty, that "contradictions and tensions have to be *accepted as constant* features of Paul's theology of the law," in my view, is an injustice to Paul in that it belittles his theological achievement and, if it were taken as *the* solution, would diminish Paul's value for modern theology considerably.[66]

---

66. Räisänen, *Paul and the Law,* 11. Räisänen himself (14–15) is quite aware that his way of viewing Paul would lead to Paul's stature as a "theologian" being diminished considerably (Räisänen is not sure Paul deserves the title). See the response to this by Furnish (n. 7, above); also Westerholm,

Paul, it must be remembered, did not himself *create* the problem of the law, he simply faced it head on, with far more rigor than any other New Testament writer. For him Israel is God's chosen people, who were entrusted with "the oracles of God" (Rom 3:2) and whose privileges include "the covenants and the giving of the law" (9:4). But now in "the fullness of time" God has called "all the nations" in Christ and has determined to make them "righteous by faith" *apart from* the law (Gal 3:8, cf. Rom 3:21). What then of the law? The problem might have been less intractable if all had agreed either that everyone, including Gentiles, must obey the law or that the law, in the time of the Messiah, was set aside. But, of course, there was no such agreement. To the contrary, though Gentiles had come to faith in Christ apart from law observance, some insisted that also "in Christ" the law remained in full effect. Not even Solomon could be expected to "solve" such a dispute; no more could Paul. He did the best he could and in the process produced theological reflections that have to do not only with the vital issue of what is and is not the place of law in the divine-human relationship, but what is the relationship between ancient and sacred tradition, on the one hand, and the "new thing" (Isa 43:18-19; cf. 2 Cor 5:17) God is now doing, on the other. What is this "gospel of God," which preceded Moses and Abraham as well as Jesus (cf. Mark 1:14) and which "now" exposes even God's law as a temporary and insufficient instrument for the life of God's people? In any age these are not small questions, and no one in the ancient church saw them more clearly or struggled with them more forthrightly than Paul.

The basis of his convictions is the gospel. The strategic situation—the opponents having impugned Paul's gospel by sub-

---

Israel's Law, 182–86, answering Räisänen on specific points of Paul's "inconsistency," and 189–92, answering Sanders, who also (note *Law and the Jewish People,* 65–86) sees Paul as less than successful in "the consistency" of his "theological analysis" (80). Westerholm (192) appropriately says that "the picture of a Paul pursuing arbitrary solutions to problems of his own making needs to be replaced with that of an apostle creatively applying basic principles of his inherited religion to the human situation as revealed by Christ's cross" (192).

verting his apostolate—occasions the initial emphasis on Paul's apostolic pedigree, but the letter's main focus is clearly the gospel.[67] The major sections of the letter deal with the threat to the gospel posed by the teaching of the opponents. Thus from a *strategic* viewpoint "the truth of the gospel in Galatia . . . stands or falls with the truth of his apostolate,"[68] but Paul's *theological* point is almost diametrically the opposite. He places himself and all others under the gospel's authority (1:8-9), and Peter's undoubted status as an apostle in no way guaranteed his proper understanding and guardianship of "the truth of the gospel" in Antioch. The criterion of apostles is the gospel, but only with some reservation can one say that the opposite is the case. To be sure, the gospel is not only the "gospel of God" (e.g., Rom 1:1); it is also that which apostles proclaim and for which they provide the proper interpretation (1 Cor 15:1-11). Paul certainly claims to be the authentic interpreter of the gospel for the Galatians. Nevertheless, it is more the gospel that determines the apostle than vice versa, and in "betraying" the gospel the Galatians are not turning their backs on Paul but on God who "called" them.[69] Ultimately neither Paul, Peter, nor any human authority "matters at all; what matters" is the gospel, the work of God (1 Cor 3:5-9).[70]

---

67. Eckert, *Verkündigung,* 201, properly notes, "It is not Gal 1:1 which provides the primary theme for the first two chapters—this pointed claim regarding Paul's apostolate is placed at this prominent point mainly because of the ancient letter-form—rather 1:6f. introduces the problem and the theme, namely, the contest over the true gospel, and 1:11f. can be seen as the title for the following assertions."

68. Beker, *Paul the Apostle,* 46–47; I disagree, therefore, with Beker's view (43) that "the hermeneutic of the apostolate is Paul's primary concern" (see Eckert, preceding note). Similarly, Brinsmead's statement (*Response to Opponents,* 58) that in Galatians "the authority of the office is seen to guarantee the truth of the gospel" is quite mistaken, in my view.

69. In Paul's usage καλεῖν ("call") always denotes the action of God (Rom 4:17; 8:30; 9:12, 24, 25-26; 1 Cor 1:9; 7:15, 17-24; Gal 1:6, 15; 5:8, 13; 1 Thess 2:12; 4:7; 5:24).

70. On the multifaceted nature of Paul's concept of εὐαγγέλιον ("gospel") see Stuhlmacher, *Das paulinische Evangelium,* 1:56-63. Without wishing to downplay "gospel" as human "preaching" (Stuhlmacher, 58), I

Foundational to Paul's argument in this letter is the subordination of *all* authority, whether of apostles or the sacred tradition of the law, to the authority of the gospel.

In Galatians the gospel is the invasive and invincible power of God, which is presently at work in the world to complete God's plan of salvation. It is God's "call" (Gal 1:6, 15; 5:7), to which Paul and every human authority or sacred tradition are subject.[71] The gospel is for the whole world, and it subjects all humans to itself on the same terms. That is why the negative judgment on the law, as on all human wisdom and philosophy (cf. 1 Cor 1:20-25), also lies at the *heart* of the gospel, particularly in the context of Galatians. This negative edge to the gospel is an aspect of the gospel *as grace,* for it is only when humanity is revealed in its utter nakedness before God that God's grace can truly be known as grace. The gospel, so to speak, clears the ground for itself; it sheds the light that simultaneously exposes and dispels the darkness of the human condition. It is this gospel, which is simultaneously judgment *and* grace, that enables Paul so freely to interpret the law and so radically to set it aside.

* * *

Chapter 2 will examine Paul's defense of himself as the divinely appointed messenger of the gospel for the Gentiles. This involves Paul's negative response to the claims and accusations of the opponents but also his positive portrayal of himself as an instrument of God's eschatological plan for the salvation of the world. It is in this context that we can see Paul's assertion of the supreme authority of the gospel. Chapter 3 will turn to an exami-

---

am focusing here on the gospel as God's action, a full investigation of which would involve far more than the εὐαγγελ- root alone. For Paul, as 1 Thess 2:13 shows, the human and the divine actions are inseparable, and yet it cannot be overly emphasized that for Paul it is the divine initiative and action that is determinative of both believers and apostles.

71. Grässer, "Das Eine Evangelium," 306–44; Stuhlmacher, *Das paulinische Evangelium,* 1:56-108; idem, "Das Ende des Gesetzes," 14–39 (with some differences from Grässer: 22–23, n. 20), and Wegenast, *Das Verständnis der Tradition,* 40–49.

nation of the gospel of the opponents in Galatia and of Paul's encounters with it in Jerusalem and Antioch. Against its claims for the essential role of the law, Paul consistently sets the all-sufficient power of the gospel. Chapter 4, by far the most extensive chapter, mainly comprises a detailed exegesis of 2:15-21, Paul's initial exposition of the gospel, which turns out to be both "good news" and "bad news" for the Galatian audience. It is "good news" in its proclamation of what God in Christ has accomplished for all humanity; it is "bad news" in that it undermines the position of the opponents by attacking the law as a power that has deluded its adherents into a false estimate both of its own power and of their own status as its adherents. Such conclusions naturally lead to an examination of what Paul, in 3:13, calls "the curse of the law," and so to exegesis of 3:10-13. Chapter 5 will provide a summation of the book's major arguments but will also attempt to describe the rationale for Paul's dialectical treatment of the law in Galatians. This will lead into a comparison of Galatians with Romans and to an examination of why, though Romans continues to exclude the law as determinative of the divine-human relationship, it attenuates Galatians' attack on the law and turns instead against Israel's disobedience and unbelief.

II

Paul's Defense of His Apostolate

The Opponents' Claims and Accusations:
Paul on the Defensive

PAUL'S EMPHATIC DENIALS

Investigation of the opponents' claims and accusations against Paul must begin with the letter's negative opening: "Paul an apostle—sent *neither* from human authorities *nor* through a human commission, . . ." (1:1a). It is this extended superscript and verses 4–5 that make this prescript so highly unusual among Paul's letters. It is unusual not because it is extended (cf. Romans!) but because it breaks the usual *form* of Paul's prescripts, ending not with a greeting but with a doxology.[1] The superscript in particular is unusual because of its emphatic double negative, dissociating Paul's apostolate from any human origin. The context of the first two chapters, especially 1:11-19 and 2:1-9, both featuring strong denials, suggests that here we encounter Paul's reaction to an issue of the first importance.

The emphatic opening negatives ("neither from . . . nor through") represent more than rhetoric. As Gerhard Ebeling notes: "At the beginning of a letter so highly charged in style and

---

1. Elsewhere Paul's prescripts always end with the greeting. Here the greeting is extended into an initial statement of the gospel's content (1:4), so that the prescript has to be concluded with the doxology. Also notable is the lack of a thanksgiving, again unique to this letter and due undoubtedly to Paul's urgent intent and angry mood. See Doty, *Letters in Primitive Christianity,* 31.

content, in an antithetical explication of his own apostolic authority clearly placed so emphatically at the start, Paul can hardly be employing purely stylistic variation."[2] The rhetoric must reflect the polemical situation of the letter. This is the more likely when we note the similar denials of verses 11–12 and the parallel expressions, "not of human origin nor . . . from a human source." These denials in turn anticipate the postponed but emphatic main clause of verses 15–17: "I did *not* confer with flesh and blood . . . *nor* did I go up to Jerusalem . . ."[3] Such emphatic and repeated denials reflect the fact that Paul's apostolate has been portrayed by the opponents in Galatia as derivative from Jerusalem, perhaps specifically from Cephas, James, or Barnabas.[4] But then the question naturally arises: how could the opponents discredit Paul by asserting his dependence on Jerusalem, particularly if, as I shall maintain, they themselves take their stand as advocates of Jerusalem's traditions?[5] It is necessary to be clear on

2. Ebeling, *Truth of the Gospel,* 12–13.

3. Ibid., 13 and note 7, suggests that in verse 1 "Paul may have intended a chiastic construction," also found in verses 11–12, in which the denials ("not from humans," etc.) are balanced by affirmations ("but through Jesus Christ," etc.). In any event, Paul certainly is not satisfied merely with denials, as is emphasized in this chapter under the heading "Paul's Relationship with the Risen Christ."

4. That 1:1 was composed with the opponents' claims of Paul's dependence on Jerusalem in mind is the view accepted by a majority of interpreters, for example, Bonnard, *Galates,* 12; Dunn, *Epistle to the Galatians,* 25; Lightfoot, *Galatians,* 27–28; Mussner, *Galaterbrief,* 12; Schlier, *Galater,* 21; Stuhlmacher, *Das paulinische Evangelium,* 1:67-68. For a contrary view, see Lyons, *Pauline Autobiography,* quoted in chapter 1, above.

5. This is the objection of Schmithals, *Paul and the Gnostics,* 23, to the common view that the opponents were Judaizers: "It is inconceivable that the Jerusalem apostles in Galatia accuse Paul of being dependent on themselves or, in case they were only representatives of the Jerusalem authorities, that *like themselves* he is dependent on the authorities in Jerusalem. Therewith one can indeed minimize his authority as an apostle, but certainly cannot reject his gospel." The same objection, quoting Schmithals, has been raised more recently by Verseput, "Paul's Gentile Mission," 37. It is mistaken on two counts: first, it presumes a close tie between the opponents and the Jerusalem apostles, a presumption not founded in the text. Second, the

the nature of their polemic against him. Against what specifically does Paul himself defend?

THE ACCUSATION THAT PAUL HAS PERVERTED
THE JERUSALEM TRADITION

Though there is a virtual consensus that behind 1:1 we are to see the opponents' attack on Paul's apostolate, there has been less consensus about the nature of the attack.[6] Two alternative approaches are proposed by Ebeling that are representative of the various proposed solutions.[7] The first possibility has the opponents claiming for themselves an authority they deny to Paul. If this were the situation behind 1:1, the authority invoked might be the "pillar" apostles (2:9) or Jerusalem as the city of sacred tradition. Dieter Lührmann, for example, maintains that for the Galatian opponents Paul lacks "a tradition which could validate the

---

opponents can assert Paul's dependence *and* discredit his gospel, provided they accused Paul of being "a renegade follower of the Twelve" (Burton, *Epistle to the Galatians,* liv). Schmithals tries to head off this difficulty by asserting that "the charge actually concerns *dependence,* not a single word concerns *apostasy*" (25). But again he is on thin ice. As clear as the fact that Paul is defending his apostolate is that he is defending his gospel against an attack on its truth (also against Schlier, *Galater,* 22). This is already clear in 1:6-9; they teach a gospel contrary to what Paul preached. The assertion that "the men of renown added nothing to me" (2:6) but rather "recognized" Paul's apostolate *and* gospel (2:7, 9) suggests that both were under attack. So also 3:3 indicates that the Galatians were being persuaded of a deficiency in Paul's gospel. On this question see Beker, *Paul the Apostle,* 44; Burton, *Epistle to the Galatians,* liv-lv; Eckert, *Verkündigung,* 233.

6. Schmithals, *Paul and the Gnostics,* 29, says that they have denied that Paul has the requisite divine revelation, so that in 1:12 Paul claims that he too (like the opponents!) received a divine commission (so also Wegenast, *Das Verständnis der Tradition,* 40, note 2; Lührmann, *Offenbarungsverständnis,* 71, note 4; Schlier, *Galater,* 22). The weakness of this is clear, it seems to me, from 1:7-9 and 5:7-10, where Paul avers that the opponents have no calling from God whatsoever. He is surely unlikely, therefore, to place them on an equal footing with himself in 1:12 (on the latter, see below). Against Schmithals here, see Kertelge, "Apokalypsis," 271.

7. Ebeling, *Truth of the Gospel,* 13–14.

gospel." For their part "the opponents have in some fashion appealed to Jerusalem" as the validator of their tradition. This does not mean, says Lührmann, that the opponents were emissaries of the Jerusalem apostles but rather were "Jewish–Christian missionaries oriented to Jerusalem."[8] According to this reconstruction of the situation, Paul avers in 1:1, 11–12 that, unlike his opponents, his apostolate does not derive from human authority. Ebeling rejects this first alternative, properly in my view. The second view has the opponents claiming that Paul's apostolate was not of divine origin but was purely human in nature.[9] They have probably said that Paul was a pupil of the original apostles and have gone on to accuse him of having perverted Jerusalem's instruction to suit his own purposes. In response Paul denies that he was dependent on Jerusalem for his teaching and insists on the divine origin of his apostolate and gospel. It is this solution that is favored here.

According to both solutions Jerusalem is held in high regard by the opponents, and this is clear enough in the letter.[10] It follows

8. Lührmann, *Offenbarungsverständnis,* 71 (and n. 4)–73.

9. This is also part of Schmithals' thesis (*Paul and the Gnostics,* 29–30). Indeed, for him, they denied Paul the title of apostle outright. Eckert, *Verkündigung,* 164–65, on the other hand, maintains that they "reduced Paul to an apostolate of inferior rank in comparison with 'the apostles before him' (1:17) and have made him dependent on human agency." I prefer Eckert here, but for Paul the one attack would hardly have been less offensive than the other. Similar to Eckert are Beyer and Althaus, "Galater," *Die kleineren Briefe des Apostels Paulus,* 10, and Schlier, *Galater,* 21.

10. Some interpreters believe that Paul was portrayed as dependent on Antioch: for example, Ebeling, *Truth of the Gospel,* 14, notes this possibility; see also Stuhlmacher, *Das paulinische Evangelium,* 1:67; Roloff, *Apostolat,* 64. Everything in the letter, however, seems to point to Jerusalem (1:16-2:10 and 4:21-31). The word occurs five times (1:17, 18; 2:1; 4:25, 26) as opposed to four times in Romans and once in 1 Corinthians (nowhere else in Paul). On Jerusalem's importance for the opponents, see Davies, *Gospel and the Land,* 195–98; Beyer and Althaus, "Galater," *Die kleineren Briefe des Apostels Paulus,* 15; Eckert, *Verkündigung,* 192, 214–16, also stressing Jerusalem's importance for Paul. Mussner, *Galaterbrief,* 13, 327; and Jewett, "Agitators," 201 and note 1, suggest that in 4:26 is found a slogan of the opponents ("Jerusalem is our mother").

that the opponents do not impugn Paul's connections with Jerusalem as such. They accuse him rather of not having been faithful to what he was taught there, particularly with regard to observance of the law as a part of the gospel's content. In Jerusalem, they maintain—probably correctly—the law is still observed by the church, thus demonstrating that faith in Christ demands obedience to the Torah. In my view, then, it is not Paul's *lack* of the requisite tradition for which the opponents attack him but his supposed *perversion* of it and his inferior status as an apostle in comparison with the Jerusalem apostles.

With regard to Lührmann's solution, Paul's denials represent too much protest if his purpose is to distinguish himself from opponents who have made Jerusalem the source of their own authority and have denied such authorization to Paul himself. After all, according to this solution the opponents would be agreeing with Paul's denials. But if that were true, why should his denials be so emphatic? Further, such a solution does not properly explain the vehemence of Paul's assertion that his apostolate was of purely divine origin (1:1b, 12–16). On the other hand, if the opponents have asserted that Paul was instructed by Cephas (or perhaps James or Barnabas) regarding the law but has perversely departed from that teaching, then his denials make perfect sense, as does his counter-assertion that his apostolate is "through Jesus Christ" (1:1, 12).

PAUL COMPARED UNFAVORABLY WITH THE JERUSALEM APOSTLES

An inevitable corollary of these claims and accusations by the opponents is that Paul has been compared unfavorably with the Jerusalem apostles. This is suggested when Paul is at pains to demonstrate that his apostolate was (1:15-16), and was recognized to be (2:9), of divine origin, no less than that of the original apostles. The first indication in the letter that Paul is responding to such unfavorable comparison is found in the intriguing opening phrase of 1:12, οὐδὲ γὰρ ἐγώ ("For neither did *I* . . ."). The ἐγώ is emphatic by its mere presence. Burton's paraphrase gives the proper emphasis: "For neither did I any more than they receive

it etc."[11] Γάρ with οὐδὲ indicates that verse 12 provides a negative
reason for the assertion of verse 11, and within that reason the
emphatic ἐγώ must figure prominently. Thus if Paul assures the
Galatians in verse 11 that his gospel is not "of human commission," he provides in verse 12 his reason for that claim and says it
has everything to do with the truth about his own apostolate. The
ἐγώ could be emphasized for either of two reasons: first, he distinguishes himself from claims the opponents have made for
themselves and denied to him, that he lacks the requisite tradition.
It is already clear why this is not to be accepted; Paul's emphatic
denials hardly make sense if his opponents also deny his connections with Jerusalem. Second, Paul denies that which they have
claimed about him, that he was instructed by the Jerusalem
apostles, has no apostolate comparable with theirs, and has be-
trayed their instruction. This alternative sheds clear light on
Paul's thought in this context, where he is intent on demonstrating that he, no less than the Jerusalem apostles, was "entrusted
with the gospel" (2:7). He not only denies the claim that he was
instructed by Jerusalem, he also insists that *he stands on an equal
level with them,* for like them he also has the gospel not from humans but "by a revelation of Jesus Christ." This claim to equality
with the "pillar" apostles becomes most apparent in the account
of the Jerusalem conference.

11. Burton, *Epistle to the Galatians,* 38, whose interpretation I essentially accept here. A survey of interpreters indicates how the phrase by its
very wording demands attention: for example, Oepke, *Galater,* 29, but
Oepke denies that Paul has in mind a comparison of himself with the Jerusalem apostles. The emphatic ἐγώ "aims a subtle blow at the antagonists:
they may be dependent on human authorities, the people in Jerusalem, Paul
is not." This, of course, is similar to Lührmann's view (see above). It recognizes that a comparison is in view but has it between Paul and the *opponents,*
whereas the context (1:15-19; 2:1-9) clearly has in view Paul in relation to
the Jerusalem apostles. Bonnard, *Galates,* 28, also recognizes the emphatic
"I," but his interpretation ("je n'ai *même pas reçu* mon évangile d'un
homme," "I have not *even received* my gospel . . .") misplaces the emphasis. Similar to Bonnard is Lagrange, *Saint Paul,* 10. Better, in my view, are
Bligh, *Galatians in Greek,* 89; Mussner, *Galaterbrief,* 68–69; Ridderbos,
Galatia, 58; Schlier, *Galater,* 45.

THE JERUSALEM CONFERENCE AS VINDICATION
OF PAUL'S GOSPEL AND APOSTOLATE

Introduction: Paul's Aim in This Narrative (2:1-10)

The above considerations make it clear that Paul does not in any way deny the status of the Jerusalem apostles. He can hardly claim to be on a par with them and at the same time be denying their importance. This introduces a further dynamic which is at play in the *narratio,* namely, that Paul strikes a delicate balance between recognizing the authority of the Jerusalem apostles on the one hand and, on the other, not conceding to them an authority that could be interpreted as a right of jurisdiction over his gospel or himself as its messenger.[12] The opponents have claimed, implicitly at least, that Paul's gospel and apostolate are subject to the jurisdiction of Jerusalem and to the traditions of Jewish law observed there. For Paul they concede too much authority to Jerusalem. He wishes to correct that without denying Jerusalem's status as "the center of earliest Christianity . . . the primary locus of salvation history."[13] It is this tense dynamic that accounts for the peculiar difficulties of language in Paul's narrative, especially the incomplete sentences of verses 4–5 and 6.

Paul's purpose is in part to show what kind of relationship existed between himself and the Jerusalem triumvirate, James,

---

12. Interpreters properly note Paul's recognition of Jerusalem's importance: for example, Roloff, *Apostolat,* 58 and 64–65; Schlier, *Galater,* 76. It is another matter, however, to see Paul as accepting Jerusalem's authority to affirm or deny the *validity* of his gospel and apostolate. Such a view, with which I disagree, has been put forward by Achtemeier, *Quest for Unity,* 22–24; Brandon, *Fall of Jerusalem,* 19–20; Holmberg, *Paul and Power,* 23–27. Careful distinctions are required: (*a*) Jerusalem exercised authority over other churches; (*b*) Jerusalem and the "pillar" apostles must have had far greater prestige than Paul; (*c*) Paul, however, did not recognize Jerusalem's authority to contradict his gospel and apostolate. Jerusalem's *recognition* was important for Paul, but, at least in his mind, they had no right of *jurisdiction.* Meier, in Brown and Meier, *Antioch and Rome,* 39 and note 95, does not, in my view, sufficiently account for what is being said in (*c*).

13. Eckert, *Verkündigung,* 216.

Cephas, and John.[14] He must demonstrate that no rift exists between himself and them and thus that the gospel he preaches, so
far from being at variance with Jerusalem's teaching, was recognized by the "pillars" as divinely authorized (2:7-9). In doing this,
however, he must not play into the hands of the Galatian opponents and allow it to be said that Jerusalem has jurisdiction over
his gospel and apostolate, a point that would go a long way toward destroying his argument thus far. Paul's independence as an
apostle by divine commission and the even more important principle that *his gospel can be subject to no human or even angelic
authority* (1:8) are the foundations of his entire defense.

The Purpose of the Visit to Jerusalem

Paul reports that he went to Jerusalem κατὰ ἀποκάλυψιν
("obedient to a revelation," 2:2a). Whether this revelation was to
himself directly or to someone else,[15] his mention of it intends to
make clear that his visit was primarily in obedience to God, not to
human authority.[16] This maintains the dialectic between the auspices of "flesh and blood" (1:16b) and divine auspices as the

14. This does not exhaust his purpose; the account also functions to illustrate what is happening in Galatia, and thus it partakes in his strategy to
vindicate "the truth of [Paul's] gospel" (see 2:5 and 14) for the Galatian
situation. See chapter 3, below.

15. Lührmann, *Offenbarungsverständnis,* 39–40 and 73, maintains that
it was a community *charisma.* Bruce, *Epistle to the Galatians,* 108, says
"Paul's language suggests rather a revelation received by himself."
Lührmann's view accords well with the Acts portrait of Paul as a delegate of
Antioch (Acts 15:2), but of course Luke would see no contradiction between
private revelation and public commissioning (Acts 9:3-6 with 13:2-3); neither necessarily would Paul. It is quite possible that Paul was an Antioch
delegate to the conference, as interpreters often believe: for example,
Conzelmann, *History of Primitive Christianity,* 82; Ebeling, *Truth of the
Gospel,* 18; Haenchen, "Petrus-Probleme," 193; Schütz, *Anatomy of Apostolic Authority,* 140; Stuhlmacher, *Das paulinische Evangelium,* 1:67.

16. That this was Paul's emphasis is generally recognized: for example, Giblin, *Hope of God's Glory,* 56; Mussner, *Galaterbrief,* 102;
Schmithals, *Paul and James,* 39; Schütz, *Anatomy of Apostolic Authority,*
139; Stuhlmacher, *Das paulinische Evangelium,* 1:85-86.

source of Paul's gospel. This must be borne in mind in the interpretation of the crucial μή πως ("for fear that . . .") clause in 2:2b
(below). Paul's purpose was to "present" (ἀνεθέμην) his gospel in
Jerusalem.[17] It should be clear from the first part of the letter that
Paul entertained no doubts about the divine origin or truth of his
gospel. Even if one goes back before the letter to the occasion of
the conference itself, it must be remembered that by that time Paul
had been preaching the gospel for somewhere between fourteen
and seventeen years, depending how one counts the years mentioned in 1:18 and 2:1.[18] It is hardly likely, then, that he went to Jerusalem "to ascertain that the Lord he had seen was in fact the
risen Jesus" or "to see whether his apostolic mission was valid."[19]

The verb ἀνατίθεσθαι ("present") means to "ascribe, at-
tribute," or, as here, to "declare, communicate, refer, with the

17. It is difficult to decide if αὐτοῖς ("to them . . .") refers back to Jerusalem or anticipates the following reference to the δοκοῦντες ("men of
renown"). In other words, does Paul have in mind both a public *and* a private meeting and intend to say that in the latter he and the triumvirate headed
off a split between him and them and thus a split among the churches? This
is probably the case, in spite of Acts 15 (see Burton, *Epistle to the Galatians,*
71; Lightfoot, *Galatians,* 103; Stuhlmacher, *Das paulinische Evangelium,*
1:89). Verseput, "Paul's Gentile Mission," 46, note 16, says the "private
meeting . . . completes the encounter" with the community. Perhaps so, but
Verseput errs in denying the central importance of "Paul's encounter with the
authoritative figures." From Paul's perspective in the Galatians' context,
they, not the community as a whole, are clearly the other protagonists. In
fact, but for κατ᾿ ἰδίαν ("in private") and Acts 15 we would never suspect
that there was anything other than a private meeting.

18. Most count the fourteen years (2:1) from the first visit to Jerusalem
(1:18) and thus reckon Paul's ministry to be fifteen to seventeen years old by
the time of the conference: for example, Bonnard, *Galates,* 35–36; Lightfoot, *Galatians,* 102. For a full discussion of the issue and a slightly different view, see Lüdemann, *Paul,* 61–64.

19. Thus Achtemeier, *Quest for Unity,* 22 and 24 respectively. It is also
inaccurate to say that "the outcome of the conference was the agreement that
Paul would 'remember the poor,' and that was all!" (23). The collection certainly became important later in Paul's career (1 Cor 16:1; 2 Corinthians
8–9; Rom 15:25-26), but in the conference the issue was Paul's gospel and
its acceptance by the "pillars."

added idea that the person to whom a thing is referred is asked for his opinion."[20] The verb clearly has this meaning in Acts 25:14, where Festus relates Paul's case to Agrippa and Bernice. Festus, of course, as the Roman procurator, had the greater authority, so there can be no question of ἀνατίθεσθαι denoting the inferior authority of the speaker. With regard to status the verb is neutral. Similarly, in 2 Macc 3:9, Heliodorus, though having greater authority than the high priest, "imparted" to the latter the business at hand. Again there can be no question that the inferior sought the "approval" of the superior.[21] Paul, then, chose a word that safeguards his earlier claim to be God's independent apostle; he portrays the conference as a discussion among equals of the gospel, which he even now preaches among the Gentiles.[22]

This brings us to the problematic clause, μή πως εἰς κενὸν τρέχω ἢ ἔδραμον ("for fear that I may be running or had run in vain") in 2:2b. It is problematic because to some interpreters Paul appears to concede that in presenting his gospel to the "pillars" his purpose was to gain their approval so that his gospel would not be proved false. Such an interpretation completely misreads Paul's statement.[23] It is not his *gospel* for which Paul is concerned

20. Bauer, *Greek-English Lexicon,* 61. See also Liddell and Scott, *Intermediate Greek-English Lexicon,* 63, who suggest "impart" as the New Testament meaning. An excellent study of this and other vocabulary of the passage is provided by Dunn, "Relationship Between Paul and Jerusalem," *Jesus,* 108–28, who explains that there can be no question of ἀνατίθεσθαι denoting "the relative competence or status of the parties involved" (113).

21. Holmberg, *Paul and Power,* 23, maintains such a view, but no ancient texts support this rendering, as Dunn's analysis makes clear (see preceding note). Stuhlmacher, *Das paulinische Evangelium,* 1:87, *contrasts* Antioch's acceptance of Jerusalem's judicial authority with Paul, whose recognition of Jerusalem he sees as "comparable, but *not the same"* (my emphasis). Stuhlmacher properly says (contra Schlier, *Galater,* 68) that it is a misconstrual of the situation "if Paul in Jerusalem is seen as seeking the confirmation of his mission and message from the binding authorities of the 'earlier gospel' and the 'earlier apostolate'" (88).

22. Note the present tense of κηρύσσω ("I am proclaiming") in 2:2a.

23. Modern translations are sometimes misleading here, since they translate the clause as negative purpose ("lest" or the like). Better are *NIV,* "for fear that," and the original French edition of the *JB* ("de peur de"). *NAB*

but his missionary endeavors ("running"; see below). Paul's purpose in the conference was to have Jerusalem hear and *accept* "the gospel [he proclaims] among the gentiles"; it was *not* his purpose to discover whether his gospel was true.[24] What he expresses in the μή πως clause is the *fear* that the "pillars" might harm his evangelizing efforts of both the future and the past by cutting off the Gentile churches from Christianity's center.[25] It was this apprehension that necessitated the private meeting. Both Paul and the "pillars" realized that a rift between them would be harmful to Paul's missionary endeavors, and not only his; unity was important, presumably, for everyone. Paul's anxiety, however, was not occasioned by doubts as to the truth of his gospel, as the letter shows beyond question (1:8-9, 11-16; 2:11-14).[26] His

---

is also misleading in its translation of προσανέθεντο (2:6), "made me add nothing," suggesting possible compulsion, a nuance the verb does not have.

24. See Blass and Debrunner, *Greek Grammar,* 188, section 370; Funk, *Grammar of Hellenistic Greek,* 2:706, section 879; Zerwick, *Biblical Greek,* 118, section 344. Paul uses μή πως a total of nine times (1 Cor 8:9; 9:27; 2 Cor 2:7; 9:4; 11:3; 12:20; Gal 2:2; 4:11; 1 Thess 3:5). Galatians 4:11 and 1 Thess 3:5, both close linguistically to Gal 2:2, show Paul's understanding of the construction. For him it expresses *apprehension* (e.g., "lest the tempter had tempted you and our labor should be in vain" [1 Thess 3:5]), not negative purpose. Bauer, *Greek-English Lexicon,* 521, takes 1 Cor 9:27; 2 Cor 2:7; and 9:4 as negative purpose (but even these are perhaps better seen as expressing simple apprehension); and Gal 2:2 as "an indirect question."

25. Dunn, "Relationship Between Paul and Jerusalem," *Jesus,* 115, expresses the matter this way: "It was this *effectiveness* of his gospel which Paul was concerned for. . . . Jerusalem's refusal to acknowledge the validity of this proclamation would render it ineffective (not false), . . . ; an adverse decision by the Jerusalem apostles would make it impossible for the Gentile churches to be seen in their true continuity with the religion of Israel, of the prophets, of Jesus' first disciples."

26. That Paul's concern was for his churches, not the validity of his gospel, is the view of many interpreters: for example, Barrett, *Freedom and Obligation,* 11; Bornkamm, *Paul,* 38; Bruce, *Epistle to the Galatians,* 109; Ebeling, *Truth of the Gospel,* 88; Hay, "Paul's Indifference to Authority," 36–44; Mussner, *Galaterbrief,* 102–3; Schütz, *Anatomy of Apostolic Authority,* 139; Stuhlmacher, *Das paulinische Evangelium,* 1:85-88; Giblin, *Hope of God's Glory,* 57. It is necessary to register disagreement, however,

anxiety was for his churches, which would certainly be jeopard-
ized if Jerusalem rejected the gospel in which they had become
believers, namely, the gospel of freedom from the law. Such a rejection would also cause a schism between Paul and the Jerusalem apostles, and every congregation would ultimately be placed
in the position of having to choose between one gospel or the
other, a decision that would undoubtedly split individual
churches—particularly along Gentile versus Jewish lines. Paul's
fear, therefore, had a serious basis. The issue at stake for Paul
was, will the Jerusalem leaders *accept*—not, will they *approve*—
the gospel of freedom from the law? Paul recognized Jerusalem's
ability to destroy unity (κοινωνία 2:9) but not their right to invalidate his gospel.

   This interpretation is confirmed by examining the metaphor
of "running" (τρέχειν), which Paul uses on a number of occasions to speak of the efforts he exerts in his missionary labors (1
Cor 9:24-25; Phil 2:16; cf. 2 Thess 3:1). It is sometimes coupled
with κόπος or κοπιάω ("labor"), his more regular word for the
apostolic work of himself or others (Rom 16:6, 12; 1 Cor 15:10;
1 Thess 1:3; 3:5; 5:12). Indeed, in Gal 4:11 Paul expresses the
fear (μή πως) that his "labor" for the Galatians may have been in
vain. Similarly in Phil 2:16 he expresses the hope that the church
will remain faithful so that on "the day of Christ" it will be apparent that Paul neither "ran" nor "labored in vain." A similar
thought is expressed in 1 Thess 3:5. In these instances Paul's fear
is not at all for the truth of his gospel—as though that could be
called into question by human infidelity—but for the welfare of
his churches and the fruitfulness of his apostolic efforts.[27] So also

---

with the latter's suggestion that Paul *did allow* Titus to be circumcised "on
counsel from 'those of repute.'" The latter view is also accepted by Brandon,
Fall of Jerusalem, 136, but is rejected by the vast majority of interpreters.

   27. Holtz, "Die Bedeutung des Apostelkonzils für Paulus," 110–48,
recognizes the importance of Gal 2:2 and that Paul's apprehension was for
his churches (121–22). Holtz, however, is in pursuit of the thesis that *previous* to the conference and the Antioch incident the unity of the church was
"irrevocably essential" (123), "a necessary constituent of the gospel" (126),
whereas *afterwards,* due to the [supposed] defeat at Antioch, where strict

at the conference, if his gospel had been rejected, he would no more have concluded that it was false than he would have done in Philippi, Thessalonica, or Galatia if any of them succumbed to temptation and rejected the gospel. For Paul the gospel is not subject to human judgment; it is God's eschatological deed, sovereign in its power, unquestionable in its authority.[28] Paul, then, was not seeking Jerusalem's authorization for his gospel but was struggling for the welfare of his churches, which lived by the gospel of freedom from the law.

Paul Claims That He Is Equal to the "Pillars" in Authority

Paul adopts the attitude in this account of one who stands on an equal level of authority with the other apostles as regards the gospel, and yet as one who recognizes that he does not stand alone; κοινωνία with them is important (2:7-9). It is particularly in verse 6 that Paul's balancing act—claiming but also conceding authority—comes to clearest expression. The verse's opening

---

separation for meals persisted (124), Paul reversed himself and subsumed the unity of the church to the truth of the gospel (126). It is the latter, says Holtz, that is reflected in Gal 1:6-9, but the proof for the fact that this was not always Paul's thinking is Gal 2:2 (120). Accordingly, at the Jerusalem conference, where church unity was still paramount in Paul's thought, his fear was not whether or not the authorities would recognize his churches, but "he fears by his preaching to have established and to be establishing no communities" that are truly "communities of Jesus Christ" (126). Hence, Paul's question at the conference was, "Is this in fact the gospel, or is this preaching non-gospel?" (127). If the latter, then Paul would have to admit that though his churches were communities that shared a common faith, they were not "communities of Jesus Christ." That, according to Holtz, is how 2:2 is to be interpreted. He makes Paul's text, it seems to me, subject to dubious historical reconstruction, and he makes 2:2 say what *linguistically,* even on his own admission, it simply does not say.

28. As Grässer, "Das Eine Evangelium" (1969) 321, expresses it: "The gospel is not a system of statements and doctrines *about* God; it is rather an event in which God makes himself known in a very definitive manner and for a very definite purpose. His call has the character of power. For with it God himself steps into the arena as the one who rules and prevails." Compare Käsemann, "Righteousness of God," *New Testament Questions,* 174.

ends in yet another anacoluthon (cf. v. 4). Into the middle of the verse Paul inserts a lengthy parenthesis emphasizing that the status of the "pillars" is a matter of indifference to him.[29] The main clause asserts that the triumvirate "added nothing to me," which in the context means that contrary to the claims of the opponents, they had no quarrel with the gospel preached by Paul. The verb προσανατίθεσθαι is very rare.[30] No more than ἀνατίθεσθαι does it suggest that Paul recognized Jerusalem's authority over himself. Holmberg attempts such an interpretation, translating it, "to impose something on someone."[31] But no such meaning is attested. Like ἀνεθέμην in 2:2, this verb also is neutral regarding authority. It is precisely in order to guard himself against the view that the triumvirate had authority over him that Paul adds the lengthy parenthesis, "What they once were makes no difference to me; God shows no partiality."

What "they once were" is undoubtedly a reference to the triumvirate's past personal relationship with Jesus,[32] which, in the eyes of the opponents, continues to grant them a place of preeminence in the church. Paul concedes that they are important au-

29. Hay, "Paul's Indifference to Authority," is most helpful on 2:6. He goes too far, however, when he speaks of the apostles, in Paul's view, as "divinely appointed guarantors of his revelation" (38) and as "infallible" (39, 42). Paul knew only too well the fallibility of apostles (2 Cor 11:13; 12:11), including of Cephas (Gal 2:11-14), and at least its possibility in himself (1 Cor 9:27).

30. The only two occurrences of the word in the Greek Bible are to be found in Gal 1:16, where it means "consult," and 2:6. Bauer, *Greek-English Lexicon,* 718, for 2:6 has "to add" or "to contribute." Liddell and Scott, *Intermediate Greek-English Lexicon,* 686, suggest "contribute." See also Burton, *Epistle to the Galatians,* 89–91, and Dunn, "Relationship Between Paul and Jerusalem," *Jesus,* 116–18.

31. Holmberg, *Paul and Power,* 24 and note 63.

32. See Betz, *Galatians,* 92–95, for lengthy discussion of the phrase, "what they once were." Betz, however, seems to think that it was their "past status at the conference" of which Paul speaks (95; so also Verseput, "Paul's Gentile Mission," 48); but Bruce, *Epistle to the Galatians,* 117–18, and Lightfoot, *Galatians,* 108, rightly say that if that were the case then Paul would have written τότε ("then") not πότε ("once"). On the interpretation espoused here, see Burton, *Epistle to the Galatians,* 87, and Schlier, *Galater,* 75.

thorities, but authority over himself on the basis of external criteria—the very thing he precludes in the second half of the verse—
he will not allow; "it makes no difference to me." The second half
of the parenthesis seems to be a paraphrase of Deut 10:17 (cf. Sir
35:12-13 LXX).[33] The point is that God has no regard, as might a
human judge (Deut 1:17), for the status of those present for judgment. This has to be borne in mind in interpreting δοκοῦντες
("men of renown"). It is unnecessary to press the connotation that
δοκεῖν can convey, "to have the appearance," in the sense of an
appearance that belies the reality.[34] That they had authority among
the churches is not for him in dispute. But for the opponents their
authority is normative, such that Paul ought to be subject to it. For
Paul, however, their apostolic status, like his own, is to be determined by "the truth of the gospel" (2:5, 14).[35]

This is a crucial point. Paul's denial that he either did or
should derive his authority from Jerusalem is ultimately based on
his conviction that the gospel he preaches, and thus his apostolate,
derives from God's revealing "his Son" to him, that he "might
preach him among the gentiles" (1:16; cf. 4:4-5). Paul himself,

---

33. The notion of "lifting up" or "fearing the face" is quite common in
biblical texts (2 Chr 19:7; Acts 10:34; Rom 2:11; Eph 6:9; James 2:1; 1 Pet
1:17). In Deut 10:17 LXX God "does not wonder at the face." This refers to
God's just judgments remaining unswayed by external criteria. Thus God
gives judgment for the orphan and widow who have no advantage with
which to sway the judge. On the phrase, see Betz, *Galatians,* 95, and Hay,
"Paul's Indifference to Authority," 39–42.

34. Pace Hay, "Paul's Indifference to Authority," 40. There may be sarcasm here, but it would be aimed at the obsequious attitude of the opponents
rather than at the "men of renown" themselves. See Lüdemann, *Opposition
to Paul,* 100, for a very balanced discussion of this phrase.

35. Kertelge, "Das Apostelamt des Paulus," 173–74, remarks, "The criterion of their apostleship in his eyes is no different than his, namely, the
gospel and the service of the gospel." And Grässer, "Das Eine Evangelium,"
343, states with appropriate forcefulness, "The gospel is not true because it
is the gospel of Paul or indeed of any apostle. But it is true since and insofar
as it is manifest as gospel. . . . And the truth of the gospel is this, that Christ
brings himself to expression in it (Rom 15:18f.; 2 Cor 5:20). Hence the message carries the messenger, and not the messenger the message." See also
Schütz, *Anatomy of Apostolic Authority,* 145.

the opponents, the Jerusalem apostles, and the churches themselves live under the power of the gospel and are accountable to it. This will also be crucial, of course, when we come to consider the gospel and the law directly.

The "Pillars'" Recognition of Paul: Κοινωνία

Paul was not seeking from the Jerusalem leaders an imprimatur for his gospel. He sought from them that which he received, "recognition" (ἰδόντες, v. 7; γνόντες, v. 9) and "fellowship" (κοινωνία, v. 9). Verses 7–9 are crucial for Paul's establishing, against the opponents, his equality and unity with James, Cephas, and John. The emphatic adversative opening (ἀλλὰ τοὐναντίον, "but on the contrary") indicates that they, far from having found anything deficient in Paul's gospel, "recognized" that he had been "entrusted with the gospel to the uncircumcised, as Peter had to the circumcised." To be sure, Paul places here a greater focus on himself than was probably the case at the conference itself, where the recognition was accorded to Paul "and Barnabas."[36] It is also probable that the equality he has with the "pillars" in his own eyes may not have been recognized by them nor by all others. But to understand Paul it is essential to be clear on his convictions, especially since these are the convictions that also drive him later in his confrontation with Peter at Antioch and in his arguments with regard to the law.

The use of the word εὐαγγέλιον ("gospel") in 2:7 recalls its earlier use in 1:7, 11; 2:2, 5 and the cognate verb εὐαγγελίζεσθαι in 1:8-9, 11, 16. Paul is speaking of the "gospel of Christ," whose truth is being "perverted" by the opponents (1:7) but which in fact must not be compromised, for it was revealed by God for the salvation of the world, Jews and Gentiles alike. The recognition of the "pillars" that Paul had been entrusted with this gospel for the Gentiles as surely as Peter had for the Jews[37] is a major part of

36. This point has been well made by Haenchen, "Petrus-Probleme," 192f.

37. Haenchen, *Acts of the Apostles,* 466–67, maintains what is the general consensus, that the division of missionary enterprises in verses 7–9 is not a geographical division and has no firmly drawn lines. He goes on to say

Paul's argument and a cogent reason why he does not denigrate their status. As Wegenast remarks, "With their doctrine the heretical Galatians are taking a stand in opposition not only to him [Paul], but also to the whole church."[38]

The fact of this recognition is accentuated in verses 8–9 with the focus now falling on the recognition of Paul's apostolate.[39] The parallelism of phrases here is striking: they recognized that "I have been entrusted [by God] with the gospel to gentiles, as has Peter to the Jews, for the one who empowered Peter for the apostolate to the Jews *also empowered me* to the gentiles." First, gospel and apostolate stand here in such close identity that they can barely be distinguished; to recognize the gospel is to recognize

---

that verses 7–9 is not the official wording of the agreement itself but "was coined from the viewpoint which governs the whole of Gal. 2 . . . to demonstrate that the gospel he preached to the Gentiles met with approval." The possibility that Paul makes some reference to the language of the agreement cannot be denied outright, but I essentially agree with Haenchen here (see Betz's careful statement, *Galatians,* 97). On this see also M. Smith, "Pauline Problems," especially 123–24, and Stuhlmacher, *Das paulinische Evangelium,* 1:93-94. A detailed attempt has been made by Lüdemann, *Paul,* 69–75, to show that verses 7–8 derive from a tradition about Paul from *before* the conference (i.e., the visit of 1:18), while verse 9 derives from the protocol of the conference itself, but this is not convincing.

38. Wegenast, *Das Verständnis der Tradition,* 47.

39. The phrase, "the grace given to me," always in Paul refers to the grace of his apostolate (Rom 1:5 where "and" is epexegetic; see 12:3; 15:15; 1 Cor 3:10; 15:10; cf. Col 1:25). On this see Käsemann, *Commentary on Romans,* 14; Roloff, *Apostolat,* 68. Betz, *Galatians,* 98–99, and notes 394, 395, misses the significance of this usage and concludes that the Jerusalem apostles did not recognize Paul's apostolate even though they "recognized his gospel as equal with theirs." From the fact that "apostolate" is not used directly of Paul in 2:8, Betz concludes that "by the time of the Jerusalem conference Paul was not called and did not call himself 'apostle,' but apparently (1:1) claimed this title only later." This is utterly refuted by Paul's language, as already noted. Others may indeed not have recognized Paul as an apostle, but Paul's claim in 2:8-9 is that the "pillars" did so. Similar to Betz is Lüdemann, *Paul,* 76, and idem, *Opposition to Paul,* 37 and 100, against whom see McLean, " Paul's Apostolic Status," 67–76.

the apostle.[40] This recognition leads to κοινωνία ("fellowship").[41]
It was for the latter that Paul had been apprehensive at the outset
of the conference (2:2). Thus the result of the meeting corresponds for him to its purpose. Second, what was true for the "pillars" as apostles empowered by Christ was true also for Paul and
Barnabas. The painstaking parallelism, in that respect not unlike
the repeated denials of chapter 1, bespeaks Paul's concern to refute definitively the opponents' suggestion that his apostolate was
subordinate to the jurisdiction of Jerusalem. The qualification of
δεξιά ("right hand") by κοινωνίας precludes the thought that
those who "gave the right hand" thereby demonstrated their superior position.[42]

This agreement, however, was almost certainly not easily
achieved. Paul's disjointed language, especially in verses 4–6,
suggests that he felt the pressure of explaining a conference at
which κοινωνία for some time hung in the balance, a point to
which I shall return.[43] Nevertheless, the essential facts are clear
for Paul: his relations with the Jerusalem authorities are basically
harmonious because they recognized the preeminent fact that his

40. See Eckert, *Verkündigung,* 205–6; Haenchen, "Petrus-Probleme,"
192. This, of course, is a further reason for disagreeing with Betz and Lüdemann that Paul's apostolate was not recognized at the conference (see preceding note).

41. This is an important word in Paul's vocabulary (e.g., 1 Cor 1:9;
10:16; 2 Cor 8:4; 9:13; Phil 1:5; 2:1; 3:10; Philemon 6) and here represents
his interpretation of the conference for the Galatians. For Paul, this agreement leads to the conclusion of unity among all as expressed in Gal 3:28 and
6:15; that this was not everyone's interpretation is apparent from 2:11-14!

42. See Burton, *Epistle to the Galatians,* 95; and Lightfoot, *Galatians,*
110, who provide extensive background on the meaning of this gesture in ancient times. In light of the close parallelism even Betz, *Galatians,* 100 (cf. n.
39, above), is constrained to recognize that "the agreement was made between equal partners." But he then relativizes what "equal" means. Κοινωνία, he maintains, "can include various forms of relationship, anything
from unity to separation"!

43. See "The Account Geared to Galatia: Paul's Tendentious Language" in chapter 3, below. Of course, Paul's portrait of "fellowship" between himself and the triumvirate suits his present purpose well. On this, see
Schmithals, *Paul and James,* 38–43.

gospel and apostolate had been conferred by God, including his right to exempt the Gentiles from the demands of the law. The opponents' claim that Paul was dependent on Jerusalem and their accusation that he had departed from its teaching are to be rejected as baseless. His mention of the agreement on behalf of the poor in Jerusalem (2:10) is Paul's final blow against the opponents' claim that he and the Jerusalem apostles were at odds.[44]

CONCLUSIONS

1. The opponents have claimed that Paul was originally instructed by the Jerusalem apostles and has no apostolate comparable with theirs.

2. They have accused Paul of having departed from the gospel as taught to him in Jerusalem; specifically, his gospel is inadequate since it lacks instruction in the law.

3. At least by implication, they have denied the divine origin of Paul's gospel and apostolate.

4. In response Paul denies any dependence on human authorities and claims that in fact his gospel and apostolate were

44. In discussing the relationship between Paul and the "pillar" apostles the question inevitably arises whether there were grades of apostleship in the early church. There is no evidence, it seems to me, of any official ranking among apostles, but both individuals and communities clearly had their preferences. In some circles, even beyond Matthew, Peter was "first" (Matt 10:2; cf. the lists in Mark and Luke); presumably Paul would get first ranking in his churches, but some in Corinth apparently preferred Cephas (Peter) or Apollos (1 Cor 1:11-12). Paul says that "Andronicus and Junia" (a married couple?) were "prominent among the apostles" (Rom 16:7), and perhaps the same could have been said of Prisca and Aquila (Rom 16:3-4; 1 Cor 16:19; Acts 18:2, 26; 2 Tim 4:19), but we know so little of these and other possible "apostles"; indeed the very definition of "apostle" is disputed, as Acts 1:21-22, in comparison with, say, 1 Cor 9:1-2, makes clear. Paul himself says that in the estimation of some he was "not an apostle" (1 Cor 9:2), and that probably included opponents in Corinth and Galatia and perhaps also in Philippi, Rome, and Jerusalem. See Dunn, *Unity and Diversity,* 254–57, and Lüdemann, *Opposition to Paul,* 112–15, who both believe that Jerusalem *refused* the collection. Even Luke does not seem to include Paul and Barnabas among the apostles (in spite of Acts 14:4, 14). See note 9, above.

recognized by the "pillar" apostles as divinely conferred. No rift exists, he says, between Jerusalem and himself.

5. In his portrait of the relationship between himself and the "pillars" Paul maintains a fine balance. On the one hand, he will not allow that they have any jurisdiction over the gospel he preaches or over himself as an apostle. On the other, he avoids denigrating their status in any way, since he recognizes the authority they have among the churches and because their affirmation of him is an important aspect of his argument against the claims and accusations of the opponents.

Paul's Relationship with the Risen Christ: Paul on the Offensive

GOD'S CALL AS "CREATION OUT OF NOTHING"

So far our concern has been Paul's denial of the opponents' false claims and his setting straight the record of his relationship with Jerusalem. In this section the focus shifts abruptly. The concern with Paul's response to the claims of the opponents remains, but now Paul appears not in a defensive but in a self-assertive posture. Not denials are in focus now but bold affirmations regarding the God who raises the dead and transforms humanity by grace. It will also become apparent here that Paul understood his apostolic authority to be second to none; the authority he claims and exercises is unsurpassed.

After the denials of 1:1a Paul extends the superscript even further, describing the origin of his apostolate as being "through Jesus Christ and God the Father who raised him from the dead." This connects Paul's summons to be an apostle with Christ's resurrection, a connection that has importance for Paul (Rom 1:1-5; 1 Cor 9:1; 15:1-10).[45] In the present context Paul's point is that God, who accomplished salvation for all in the death and resurrection of Christ, also called Paul to be the bearer of the gospel of Christ. The Christ-event and Paul's call to apostleship are two

45. This point is well made by Stuhlmacher, *Das paulinische Evangelium*, 1:81-82.

moments on the continuum of God's plan of salvation, especially as that is to be worked out for the Gentiles (Gal 1:15-16; cf. Acts 13:47).[46]

In Galatians this (1:1) is Paul's only reference to the resurrection. For the rest he focuses on the cross as God's wholly sufficient act of salvation (1:4; 2:20-21; 3:1, 13; 5:24; 6:14). Nevertheless, this reference to God as the raiser of the dead is an important part of Paul's persuasive rhetoric. This becomes clear from the use of καλεῖν ("to call," 1:6, 15; 5:8, 13), which Paul sometimes places in parallel with strictly resurrection vocabulary (notably Rom 4:17).[47] The primary terms of this vocabulary are ἐγείρειν ("raise," Rom 8:11; 2 Cor 4:14; Gal 1:1) and ζωοποιεῖν ("give life," Rom 4:17; 8:11; 1 Cor 15:22). Καλεῖν has a wider reference than these, denoting the call that initiated faith (e.g., Gal 1:6; 5:13) as well as the call that is ongoing (e.g., 5:8). Grässer has pointed out that ὁ ἐγείρας (1:1) and ὁ καλέσας (1:6, 15) function as "names" for God, which, at the beginning of Galatians, are brought into close coordination.[48] Paul, in fact, consistently uses καλεῖν as well as its cognates, κλῆσις and κλητός (noun and adjective), to speak of God's calling believers to a new existence: thus for instance, "into the fellowship of His Son" (1 Cor 1:9), into "peace" (7:15) and "freedom" (Gal 5:13; cf. Rom 8:30; 9:12, 24–26; 1 Thess 2:12; 4:7; 5:24). For Paul God's call is ongoing creative power, as is most apparent when the present participle is

46. Stuhlmacher, "Problem von Gegenwart und Zukunft," 430, says: "In Paul's understanding, what God's Christ is doing in the heavens, Paul is occupied with on the earth; both prepare the way for the dominion of God, and Paul's existence *corresponds to an ongoing manifestation of Christ in history*" (my emphasis).

47. For Paul, God's raising of Christ from the dead is the basis of Christian hope (1 Thess 1:10; 4:14). Christ is the "first fruits" (1 Cor 15:20), "the first born" in a vast family of those "called" (Rom 8:28-30) and, thus, the pledge that in him "all shall be made alive" (1 Cor 15:22). Faith knows that "the One who raised Jesus the Lord will raise us also with Jesus" (2 Cor 4:14; cf. 1 Cor 6:14; Rom 6:4; 8:11). Thus Christian hope follows Abraham's in finding its focus in "the God who *gives life* to the dead and *calls* into being what has no being" (Rom 4:17).

48. Grässer, "Das Eine Evangelium," 327.

used (Rom 4:17; 9:12; Gal 5:8). Like the word in Genesis 1 and Isaiah 55, God's call accomplishes its purpose.

What emerges in Galatians 1 is the unity of God's action in raising Christ (1:1), calling Paul to apostleship (1:1, 15–16), and, we may now add, in calling the Galatians to faith (1:6). Each event (note the aorists) proceeds from God's initiative of "grace" (1:6, 15) and effects transformation: of Christ from the dead, of Paul from persecutor to apostle, of the Galatians from slavery to freedom (4:8-9; 5:1). Each represents, in other words, "creation from nothing." They belong solely to the realm of the Creator's sovereign power and owe nothing to human effort. Paul refutes the opponents' claims, then, not only with denials but by appeal to God's eschatological action in Christ and in himself.

PAUL AS A PARADIGM OF THE GOSPEL FOR THE GALATIANS

That Paul's call to apostleship can be accounted for only on the basis of grace (χάρις) is illustrated graphically in 1:13-16. He begins by reminding the Galatians at length of his "former life in Judaism," stressing the period when he "persecuted the church of God and tried to destroy it."[49] Stress also falls on the *reason why* he "tried to destroy the church," namely, his surpassing zeal for the ancestral traditions of Judaism. That the latter was Paul's motivation for the persecution is even clearer in Phil 3:5-6: "As to the law, a Pharisee, as to zeal, a persecutor of the church."[50] These au-

49. The imperfect tense of the verbs ("persecuted" and "excelled") and the present participle ("being exceedingly zealous") indicate the duration of this activity over a period of time as well as its violence ("tried to destroy," conative imperfect). The point, of course, is the contrast between that activity and what God has since made of him.

50. On "zeal for the law" as accounting for factionalism within Judaism and for Paul's persecution of the church, see Dunn, "Pharisees, Sinners, and Jews," *Jesus,* 67–69, and note 41, chapter 1. The issue of precisely what was offensive in the church's behavior is not easy to decide, especially since some Jewish synagogues were very open and accommodating to Gentiles (see Fredriksen, "Judaism," 540–43). As Dunn indicates, Paul's persecution probably represents the reaction of strict Pharisaic Judaism to the church's compromising the boundaries between Israel and the Gentile world.

tobiographical texts and self-descriptions like ἔκτρωμα ("miscarriage") in 1 Cor 15:8 all have the same function of bringing into sharp focus the miracle accomplished by grace: "By the grace of God I am what I am" (1 Cor 15:10). His zeal for the law, which even drove him to attempt to "destroy the church," excludes the possibility that his apostolate, dedicated to preaching to the Gentiles the gospel of freedom from the law, could be "by [mere] human authority." His history has become for Paul the foil against which the power of grace can be seen all the more clearly in his own existence.[51]

What Paul wants the Galatians to recognize is that the same grace that was at work in his life was, and is, at work in their own. "Grace" is a crucial term for Paul. It characterizes God's disposition toward humankind, to "give freely" (κεχάρισται) the blessings of Abraham to all nations (Gal 3:18), indeed to bless them with "all things," including the sacrifice of "his own son" (Rom 8:32) and the gifts of the Spirit (1 Cor 2:12). "Grace" is a near summary of Paul's entire gospel, since it has to do with God's initiative for the liberation of humans from sin and law (Gal 2:21; 5:4; Rom 3:24; 4:16). It was that this gospel of grace might be proclaimed to the Gentiles that God called Paul. "Grace" is both the source of that call (1:15) and the gospel's content (2:21). So is Paul able to present himself as a paradigm of the gospel, "the living exemplification of the truth of the kerygma."[52]

The transformation in Paul's life corresponds to what the Galatians should know was true also for them when they accepted the gospel with faith (3:2-5).[53] In 1:6 Paul employs of their call the

51. On the significance of ἔκτρωμα in 1 Cor 15:8, see Conzelmann, *First Epistle to the Corinthians,* 259, and note 95; Kertelge, "Das Apostelamt des Paulus," 166 and note 19; Schütz, *Anatomy of Apostolic Authority,* 104–5. On Gal 1:13-14 as "bringing out the miracle of this call," see Roloff, *Apostolat,* 42. Stuhlmacher, "Ontologischen Charakter," 27, speaks of the call as "existence shattering."

52. Schütz, *Anatomy of Apostolic Authority,* 106; see also Lyons, *Pauline Autobiography,* 134.

53. It was "the power of the divine καλεῖν" (Grässer, "Das Eine Evangelium," 327) that began the Galatians' experience of the Spirit and the

same vocabulary (καλεῖν ἐν χάριτι) he employs of his own in 1:15 (καλεῖν διὰ τῆς χάριτος). In their case, however, the Galatians are in danger of "deserting the Caller" and of denying this grace (1:6; 2:21; 5:4). The true meaning of their near turning to the law is thereby brought into view. They are not, as they suppose, bringing God's action to completion (3:3) but betraying it. The apostle, for his part, having abandoned "the ancestral traditions" (1:14), will not look back; no more should they (4:8-9). In thus weaving together the Galatians' experience with his own, Paul endeavors to demonstrate the true meaning of their initial faith and the true character of his apostolate. Both represent the eschatological intervention of the Creator who has wrought "new creation" in the lives of both the Galatians and the apostle.

PAUL AS GOD'S ESCHATOLOGICAL MESSENGER: "REVELATION" IN GALATIANS 1–2

It is not enough, for Paul, to say that his apostolate is independent of human authority; the full truth of the matter is that it derives from a unique and direct intervention of God. What the opponents reject is what is crucial for Paul, that his gospel and apostolate derive from a divine ἀποκάλυψις ("revelation"). This is apparent from the parallel phrases that bind together the adversative clauses of 1:1 ("but through Jesus Christ . . .") and 1:12 ("but by a revelation of Jesus Christ") with the account of the call in 1:16 ("called me . . . to reveal his son in me").[54] The central

---

transformation spoken of here. This has been rightly argued in detail by Lull, *Spirit in Galatia,* 54–57. I disagree, then, with Stuhlmacher, "Ontologischen Charakter," 28, who sees καλεῖν and its cognates as belonging to baptismal vocabulary and asserts that "baptism according to the early church and Paul bestows the Spirit." Though the latter statement cannot be denied outright (see Acts 2:38), Paul's language in Galatians (3:1-2) focuses "the word of the cross" (1 Cor 1:18) as the center of Paul's preaching and the occasion of their receiving the Spirit. The divine "call," then, comes primarily with preaching (see 1 Cor 1:14-17). Acts 10:44-47 indicates that also for Luke the Spirit's reception might be independent of baptism.

54. On this parallelism see Kertelge, "Apokalypsis," 268. Paul's choice of this term in Galatians 1–2 is to demonstrate his equal standing with the

idea holding these verses together is "revelation"; that evidently is what Paul has in mind already in 1:1. "Revelation" is expressive of the eschatological framework of Paul's thought, which is apparent at other important points of the letter (1:4b; 3:23-25; 4:4; 5:5; 6:4-10).[55] Elsewhere in Paul ἀποκάλυψις refers to Christ's future coming and its accompanying events (e.g., Rom 2:5; 8:19; 1 Cor 1:7), and to a χάρισμα ("gift") experienced in the community (e.g., 1 Cor 14:6, 26, 30). The latter is related to the "visions and revelations" that Paul himself experienced (2 Cor 12:1, 7; Gal 2:2).[56] The verb has a wider scope. In Rom 8:18 (cf. 1 Cor 3:13) it looks to the eschatological revelation of the παρουσία ([Christ's] "coming"), and in Phil 3:15 it seems to have in mind the "revealing" that God will do in the community. Most

other apostles (270; with reference to Schlier, *Galater,* 45–46), but more importantly, says Kertelge (281), "the reference to the origin of his gospel in the *'apokalypsis Jesu Christi'* removes his preaching from the clutches of his critics and defends its unique eschatological character."

55. Martyn, "Apocalyptic Antinomies," 410–24, properly maintains that Galatians, though sometimes regarded as an anomaly among Paul's letters because it does not dwell on Christ's imminent return, is in fact "fully as apocalyptic as are the other Paulines" (420). I would agree, though I would stress that "realized eschatology" is more pronounced in this letter than elsewhere in Paul for reasons related to the letter situation.

56. As Kertelge, "Apokalypsis," 273, 275, makes clear, ecstatic experience and vision are not primary in Paul's concept of ἀποκάλυψις, but neither are they excluded. Lührmann, *Offenbarungsverständnis,* 40–41 and 73, goes too far when he insists that "vision" has nothing to do with Paul's concept. On the further question of the relationship between the present and the future orientations of revelation, this is best understood by keeping in mind that the sole author of revelation in Paul is God; there is no instance where the risen Christ can clearly be said to be the source (thus "revelation of Jesus Christ" in 1:12 is best taken as objective genitive). Paul does not speak of revelations out of the past, for example, from the Old Testament (Lührmann, 82–84, 154–55). Revelation is primarily God's present action in the preaching of the gospel. It does, however, have a future orientation in that God will soon bring redemption to completion (note the parallel phrases in Rom 8:19 and 23: "await the revelation" and "await the adoption, the redemption of our bodies"). On the revelation in Galatians 1, see especially Kertelge, "Apokalypsis," 275.

often, however, it designates God's revealing the significance of the Christ-event (e.g., 1 Cor 2:10; Gal 1:16). As Lührmann insists—particularly with reference to Gal 4:4 over against 1:16—it does not designate the sending of the Son so much as the "*interpretation* of this event" for humans.[57] With regard to the revelation described in 1:12 and 16 it clearly has a place of fundamental importance for Paul, surpassing by far the revelations of 2 Corinthians 12 or Gal 2:2, which had primarily personal significance. The revelation of Galatians 1 has to do with God's plan for the salvation of the Gentiles. Thus Lührmann is quite correct to say that "Paul attributes [this] revelation to a new divine decision (1:15) parallel to the decision of sending [the Son] (4:4)."[58]

It should also be noted that there is a specific content to this revelation, as is already suggested in the sequence of 1:13-16 and in the title, "the Son." The exegesis of 2:20 will show that the title "the Son of God" and the designation of believers as "sons of God" are more than usually in evidence in Galatians. For present purposes it is noteworthy that "the Son of God," as Lührmann shows, is the title that corresponds in Paul's thought to Christ's redeeming humans from the law.[59] This again is apparent from the correspondence between 1:16 and 4:5, particularly the purpose clauses: God revealed "his Son" to Paul *"in order that"* he "might proclaim him among the gentiles," just as God had "sent his Son, born of a woman, born under law, *in order that* he might redeem those under law." This indicates that in 1:16 Paul is already looking to the content of the gospel as liberation from the law. It is with regard to this content of the gospel more than simply for the sake of his apostolate that Paul exercises his authority as God's eschatological messenger, for to turn from the gospel Paul

57. Lührmann, *Offenbarungsverständnis,* 78–79 (my emphasis). Lührmann, however, downplays the aspect of the former "hiddenness" of the revelation (13 and 133–40 in relation to 1 Cor 2:6-9), a point which does not seem convincing.

58. Ibid., 79; see also Kertelge, "Apokalypsis," 275.

59. Lührmann, *Offenbarungsverständnis,* 77–78. When used of Jesus υἱός in Paul is always preceded by the definite article ("*the* Son"); this is not so when it is used of believers.

preaches is to turn not from Paul but from the God who calls (1:6). That brings us to the issue of Paul's exercise of apostolic authority.

PAUL'S APOSTOLIC AUTHORITY

In the description of his call Paul uses language reminiscent of Isa 49:1, 6 (cf. Jer 1:5). Particularly striking is Paul's claim that God set him apart (1:15, cf. Rom 1:1, Acts 13:2) from his "mother's womb," a deliberate espousal of the prophet's role.[60] The goal of God's setting Paul apart and calling him was "to reveal His Son in me (ἐν ἐμοί), that I might proclaim him among the gentiles" (1:16). In other words, Paul is God's eschatological instrument for the salvation of the Gentiles (see Rom 15:15-16; 11:13). This is confirmed by the correspondence between the purpose clauses of 1:16 and 4:5, which has been noted. God's revelation of the Son to Paul was, in Paul's view, both extraordinary in itself and conferred on Paul an extraordinary authority. Thus ἐν ἐμοί ("in me") in 1:16 is equivalent to more than a simple dative;[61] it expresses rather how that revelation invaded Paul's existence and

---

60. LXX Isa 49:1, 6 reads: "From my mother's womb he called my name (ἐκ κοιλίας μητρός μου ἐκάλεσεν τὸ ὄνομά μου). . . . 'I have established you as a *light to the nations* (φῶς ἐθνῶν), that my salvation may reach to the end of the earth'" (cf. Acts 13:47). Paul's language is closer to Second Isaiah than to Jeremiah, but "Isaiah" is probably following Jeremiah's lead (note LXX Jer 1:5, "I have made you a prophet *to the nations*" [εἰς ἔθνη]). Paul's consciousness of continuity with the prophetic tradition is apparent also in his self-designation, δοῦλος ("servant," e.g., Rom 1:1, Gal 1:10), which in the LXX translates the Hebrew עֶבֶד, an important term for the prophets in the Hebrew Scriptures (e.g., Amos 3:7; Jer 7:25; Isa 49:3, 5). On this see Betz, *Galatians,* 69 and note 129; Grässer, "Das Eine Evangelium," 123; Hill, *New Testament Prophecy,* 110–18; Mussner, *Galaterbrief,* 81–82 and note 24.

61. Blass and Debrunner, *Greek Grammar,* 118, takes it as equivalent to simple dative, as do Lührmann, *Offenbarungsverständnis,* 79, note 1; Oepke, *Galater,* 33; Stuhlmacher, *Das paulinische Evangelium,* 1:82, note 1; and others. Schlier, *Galater,* 55, however, makes a case for seeing in ἐν ἐμοί "the intensity of the revelation of the Son who came to occupy the very center of Paul's existence," as also do Betz, *Galatians,* 71; Bruce, *Epistle to the*

shattered his previous perceptions and loyalties (1:13-14). Contrary to Luke's view (Acts 23:6), Paul's experience was that subsequent to God's call he *ceased* to be a Pharisee, indeed he came to regard that part of his history as "rubbish" (Phil 3:5-8). Henceforward the center of Paul's existence was Christ as the one who liberates from the law (2:19-21).

Because of this experience of being changed from Pharisee to God's eschatological messenger, the authority Paul claims and exercises goes beyond the authority of an Isaiah or Jeremiah.[62] His gospel bears a definitive, once-for-all character; it is the gospel of God's Son, who in the fullness of time, with the power of both judgment and grace, set aside human expectations and the sacred traditions on which they were based and established for all humanity a new reality by his death on the cross. It is God who is the guarantor of Paul's gospel and apostolate.[63] Hence, in 1:8-9 Paul exercises authority in absolute terms. Stuhlmacher maintains that 1:8 has the form of the anathema from the Lord's supper liturgy, which has been identified by Bornkamm, and says further that Paul "experiences his gospel and its authority as the basis of a holy law. Gospel and apostolate are united [here] in a sacral law relationship."[64] This means that in pronouncing the anathema Paul speaks in the name of the church's Lord and coming judge. The indefinite conditional clause of 1:8, however, leaves open the question whether the curse is actually to come into effect, but in 1:9 all doubt is dispelled; εἰ ("if") with present indicative points

---

Galatians, 93; Dunn, *Epistle to the Galatians,* 64; and Lietzmann, *An die Galater,* 8.

62. Roloff, *Apostolat,* 42–44, properly points out the contrast between Paul and the Old Testament prophets: "He [Paul] is distinguished from them because of his place in salvation history as by the content of his mandate" (44).

63. See Kertelge, "Apokalypsis," 268; idem, "Das Apostelamt des Paulus," 169ff.; Grässer, "Das Eine Evangelium," 317ff.

64. Bornkamm, *Early Christian Experiences,* 169–76; Stuhlmacher's reference (*Das paulinische Evangelium,* 1:69) is from 171. See also Käsemann, "Sentences of Holy Law," *New Testament Questions,* 66–81, especially 70 on 1:9.

to the present fulfillment of the condition by the opponents. Paul solemnly pronounces the curse and takes personal responsibility for it (λέγω, "I say").[65] More authority is wielded here, therefore, than is described by Bornkamm with regard to the anathema of the Lord's supper liturgy. It is not here a matter of forewarning unworthy participants in worship but of excommunicating those who "pervert the gospel of Christ" (1:7), for in Paul's view his gospel alone is "the true criterion" of the opponents, himself, or even the Jerusalem apostles.[66]

THE SUPREME AUTHORITY OF THE GOSPEL

Paul wields the gospel's authority, but it must be noted immediately that Paul also stands under the gospel's authority. With the words, "If even we or an angel . . ." (1:8a), Paul subordinates all authorities, natural or supernal (cf. the "angels" in 3:19), to the authority of the gospel. The apostolate is grounded in the gospel, but the reverse is never true.[67] The rationale for this is already apparent in 1:6, when Paul affirms that the Galatians' "desertion" is a turning from God (not from the apostle). Neither the call nor the gospel originate with the apostle. The gospel is the supreme authority, and with it has come the age of grace and faith, which disqualifies "the former things," the time of the law's tutelage (Gal

---

65. The prefix of προειρήκαμεν ("we have said *before*") in 1:9 indicates the forewarning not of verse 8 but of Paul and his companions first preaching the gospel in Galatia. This is generally acknowledged: Betz, *Galatians,* 53–54; Beyer and Althaus, "Galater," *Die kleineren Briefe des Apostels Paulus,* 7; Burton, *Epistle to the Galatians,* 28–29; Lightfoot, *Galatians,* 78; Mussner, *Galaterbrief,* 61. Schlier, *Galater,* 40, prefers the reference to verse 8.

66. Stuhlmacher, *Das paulinische Evangelium,* 1:68, properly says: "As God's true revelation, only his [Paul's] gospel can be the valid norm of his behavior and of the legitimacy or illegitimacy of his opponents, and indeed even of the Jerusalem apostles. In other words, *Paul urges his gospel as the only true criterion of all the events of Gal 1 and 2, since it is the proclamation of God's new age*" (="neuen Welt-Zeit Gottes").

67. See Grässer, "Das Eine Evangelium," 343; Kertelge, "Das Apostelamt des Paulus," 169–75; Schütz, *Anatomy of Apostolic Authority,* 121–23.

3:23-25; 4:5; cf. Isa 43:18-19 with 2 Cor 5:17). The gospel is the "new thing," God's eschatological deed, which no authority in heaven or earth can contradict. And thus the opponents' claims, *whether on behalf of the law or of Jerusalem as the home of sacred tradition,* are disqualified when they are raised in judgment over the gospel or as its necessary companion. It will be important to keep this in mind when we turn in the next chapter to consider the gospel's content over against the "gospel" of the opponents and to broach the central issue of the relationship between the gospel and the law.

CONCLUSIONS

1. Paul connects his apostolate closely with Christ's resurrection. Not only is his apostolate conferred by the Raiser of the dead, but both events—resurrection and apostolic call—belong on the one continuum of God's plan for the salvation of humankind. The purpose of Paul's call (1:16) corresponds to the purpose of the sending of the Son (4:4-5).

2. The power of God as the "Creator out of nothing" that underlies the gospel also underlies Paul's apostolate. Thus in his own life Paul is the paradigm of the redemptive power of the gospel.

3. Just as the gospel is God's definitive eschatological deed, so also Paul, as the recipient of God's revelation of the gospel, is God's authoritative messenger who proclaims the demise of the law and the salvation of the Gentiles.

4. The content of the revelation to Paul is "the Son of God" as the one who establishes humankind in a new relationship with God as adopted children who are free from the law.

5. The authority that Paul claims and exercises is unsurpassed; it goes beyond prophetic authority because Paul is the eschatological messenger who, as such, can pronounce the divine verdict against those who have perverted the gospel.

6. Paul is aware that he himself stands under the gospel's claim, for the gospel is God's action; it is not at the disposal of Paul or of any human authority, not even Jerusalem, but subjects them all to itself.

7. These assertions are directed both against the Galatians, who have come to doubt the authenticity of Paul's gospel and apostolate, and also against the opponents, who have impugned Paul's apostolate as being of human origin and his gospel as lacking an essential aspect, the law.

III

The Gospel Versus the Other Gospel in Galatia, Jerusalem, and Antioch

The Other Gospel in Galatia

INTRODUCTION

Thus far attention has been devoted exclusively to Paul's personal defense, his counter-assertions to the opponents' claims impugning the divine origin of his apostolate, and the truth of his gospel. Attention has not yet been given either to the content of the gospel as Paul articulates it for Galatia or to the "gospel" of the opponents, which Paul dismisses as being no gospel at all (1:6-7). The apostle does not begin a detailed treatment of his gospel until 2:16. He does, however, provide a significant, preliminary statement in the letter's prescript (1:4). This preliminary statement is crucial because its developments in the letter indicate the thrust of Paul's polemic against the opponents' teaching. It is, as I shall argue, his initial response to that teaching.

THE OPPONENTS' GOSPEL

The Continuity of the Law

The opponents, also referred to here as Judaizers, seem to be intruders into the Galatian churches[1] who have denied the adequacy

---

1. Martyn, "Law-Observant Mission," 312, prefers the designation "The Teachers" and rejects the terms "Judaizers" and "opponents" (312) because they suggest that the "teachers" were merely reacting to Paul's

of Paul's gospel. It is inadequate because it excludes the law in general and circumcision in particular as necessary for salvation.[2] The opponents have sought to remedy the deficiencies in Paul's gospel by teaching the Galatians the demands of the law. Their teaching must have included reference to Gen 17:14: "Any uncircumcised male . . . shall be cut off from his people, he has broken my covenant."[3] Unless the Galatians heed the demands of the law they cannot be included in the inheritance of Abraham (3:18, 29). From the Jewish viewpoint of Jewish Christians—and that Jewish perspective is crucial for the opponents—this is an understandable position.[4] Their teaching has nothing to do with "hard" legalism;[5] the seriousness of their theological views cannot be so easily dismissed. They were relying on an understanding of the law that the law itself fosters in all of those texts that insist that the law's demands are to be obeyed (e.g., Deuteronomy, passim!) and that attach "curse" or "blessing" to the law's performance (e.g., Deut 27:26–28:6; cf. Gal 3:10).

If Paul characterizes their teaching as "compulsion" (6:12), this is because it presents an impressive show of authority in its

---

preaching whereas Martyn's thesis is that they "are in the full sense of the term evangelists, finding their basic identity not as persons who struggle against Paul, but rather as those who preach God's good news" (314). A diametrically opposed view, and more correct in my view, is Lüdemann, *Opposition to Paul,* 113.

2. Lull, *Spirit in Galatia,* 31 (see also 103), believes that the opponents' claim was that "circumcision would finish what the Galatians had begun with the Spirit, that is, it would bring it to perfection. . . .[T]he Galatians had been persuaded their conversion would be complete only with accepting circumcision." For a similar view and my disagreements with it, see the references to Cosgrove, *Cross and the Spirit,* in chapter 1, above.

3. They could also have quoted Gen 34:15-16; Exod 12:3, 44-48; Lev 12:3; Josh 5:2-7; not to mention the sacrifices of the Maccabean martyrs (1 and 2 Maccabees; see especially 1 Macc 1:60-63); also Ezek 44:9 or Isa 56:6-8 (see E. P. Sanders, *Law and the Jewish People,* 18), though circumcision as such is not mentioned here.

4. See Beker, *Paul the Apostle,* 52; Hübner, *Law in Paul's Thought,* 16; E. P. Sanders, *Law and the Jewish People,* 18, 20.

5. The distinction between "hard" and "soft" legalism (Räisänen, "Legalism and Salvation") was discussed in chapter 1, above.

appeal to Jerusalem and, above all, in the endless opportunity to quote Scripture and Israel's sacred traditions: "If the Old Testament is the common ground of Paul, his opponents and the Galatian communities, then in fact the opponents had an easy time of it: they needed only refer to Genesis 17 and to say, 'thus it stands written—in the scriptures which Paul himself quotes'!"[6] To the Galatians such authority could only have been impressive. Christ, after all, is the fulfillment of the promises to Israel, as even Paul admitted (3:16-19; cf. Rom 4:13-16);[7] far from annulling the law he brings it to completion (Matt 5:17-19; contrast Gal 2:18!). For the opponents the law and Christ *together* are the way to salvation. To substantiate their claims for the law was not difficult, but for Paul to overturn those claims was another matter. Deut 27:26 (3:10) fits their argument far better than Paul's, as also does Lev 18:5 (3:12). To substantiate his assertion of the law's demise Paul has to reject the natural meaning of those texts and several others (e.g., Gen 13:15 in 3:16). To a large extent the debate centers on the law's continuity (the opponents) or its discontinuity (Paul).[8] On the face of it the opponents have everything in their favor.

Exclusion from the Inheritance of Abraham

An inevitable corollary of the opponents' teaching was the establishing in Galatia of two classes of believers. The one group comprised the Judaizers, who, as "Jews by birth" (2:15) and adherents of the law, were true "seed of Abraham." The other group was the Galatians themselves, whose faith in Christ was inadequate by itself for such status. The Galatians were thereby excluded

6. Hübner, *Law in Paul's Thought,* 16; see also Kertelge, *Rechtfertigung,* 201.

7. Paul, to be sure, does not use the language of fulfillment in the manner of, say, Matt 3:14; 7:17. Nevertheless, Christ is the goal of the "promises to Abraham and his seed" (Gal 3:16); indeed, Christ *is* "the seed to whom the promise was made" (3:19).

8. See Keck, "Paul as Thinker," 31-32; Kertelge, "Gesetz," 387; Lührmann, *Offenbarungsverständnis,* 78; Wegenast, *Das Verständnis der Tradition,* 38.

from the inheritance of Israel,[9] and the separatism of "Jews by birth" from "sinners of the Gentiles" intruded itself into the churches of Galatia.

That separatism was an important issue is apparent from several texts in the letter. First, in the Jerusalem conference, the "false brethren" (2:4) insisted that Gentile Christians must be circumcised (also Acts 15:1) and tried to "compel" the circumcision of Titus (2:3; cf. 6:12). Second, in the Antioch incident, Peter, under pressure from James, "separated himself" (2:12), an action Paul describes as "compelling the gentiles to judaize" (2:14). Third, it is separatism that Paul takes up thematically in 2:15 and shows to be illegitimate under the gospel in 2:16-18. Fourth, the climax of Paul's exposition of the gospel of faith alone and not the law is, "There is no longer Jew nor Greek, slave nor free, male and female, for you are all one in Christ Jesus" (3:28; cf. 5:6; 6:15). In other words, with the demise of the law go also the divisions in humanity that the law fosters.

A likely further reference to the opponents' separatism is 4:17, ἐκκλεῖσαι ὑμᾶς θέλουσιν ("they want to shut you out"). This is a difficult verse,[10] and not all would agree with interpreting it against the background of separatism that I am suggesting.[11]

---

9. Byrne, *Sons of God,* 158ff., 189, stresses that "inheritance" (κληρονομία) rather than "adoption" (υἱοθεσία) "overarches the whole discussion from 3:15 . . . to 5:1" (189). This is evident, for instance, at 3:29, where belonging to Christ leads to the climactic point of belonging to Abraham (see also 4:7b). On this, see also Hübner, *Law in Paul's Thought,* 15-20.

10. On 4:12-20 see Betz, *Galatians,* 221-37, who takes the section as an "appeal to friendship" (221) and sheds much light on its interpretation (I do not agree, however, with his interpretation of 4:17; see n. 13, below); see also C. Smith, "᾽Εκκλεῖσαι in Galatians 4:17," 480-99.

11. Richardson, *Israel in the Apostolic Church,* 91 and note 4, translates ἐκκλεῖσαι as "hinder, prevent" (i.e., from seeing the truth of the gospel about circumcision), but that is not the most natural sense of the verb (see Liddell and Scott, *Intermediate Greek-English Lexicon,* 239). Schmithals, *Paul and the Gnostics,* 50, has "They want to separate you from me." This presupposes Schmithals' Gnostic interpretation in which Paul's illness (4:14) brings on him the charge of being a mere "sarkic," so that the Galatians should reject him, but this reads too much into the text. In my view

The natural meaning of ἐκκλεῖσαι, however, characterizes the opponents' teaching as divisive. Furthermore, θέλουσιν ("they desire") aligns this verse with the letter's other direct references to the opponents, which also employ θέλειν: 1:7 ("they *desire* to pervert the gospel") and 6:12-13 ("they who *desire* to make a good showing in the flesh . . . *desire* you to be circumcised").[12] The near parallelism of these verses indicates that ἐκκλεῖσαι has to do with the impact, including the theological impact, that the opponents are effecting in Galatia;[13] their gospel denies that the Galatians are "seed of Abraham." This is the more likely if the opponents, as seems probable, quoted Gen 17:14 in their preaching. In the opponents' thinking Gentiles *as Gentiles* are necessarily excluded from God's elect.

ἐκκλεῖσαι should be given its natural meaning, "shut out, exclude"; the teaching of circumcision "excludes" the uncircumcised Galatians. On this, see Beyer and Althaus, "Galater," *Die kleineren Briefe des Apostels Paulus,* 37; Burton, *Epistle to the Galatians,* 246; Giblin, *Hope of God's Glory,* 79; Lightfoot, *Galatians,* 177; Schlier, *Galater,* 212; Mussner, *Galaterbrief,* 310-11, who also provides a summary of various interpretations. What they are being excluded from must coincide, in my view, with Paul's emphasis on the "inheritance" of Abraham, and this probably extends to exclusion of the Galatians from table fellowship with the Judaizers, as is suggested by 2:11-14 (see Acts 11:1-3).

12. The explicit and direct references to the opponents in the letter are 1:7-9; 4:17; 5:7-12; 6:12-13; θέλειν ("desire," with reference to the opponents) appears in 1:7; 4:17; 6:12, 13. This, of course, is Paul's description of the Judaizers' motivation, but only in 6:13 can we assume that it truly represents their wishes. With ζηλοῦν in 4:17 (see Betz, *Galatians,* 229, and Burton, *Epistle to the Galatians,* 247, on its use in 4:18) Paul tries to expose their strenuous efforts as perverse: "they are not zealous for you in a good way . . . [rather] they want you to be zealous for (or "envious of") them." See especially C. Smith, "Galatians 4:17."

13. Betz, *Galatians,* 231, rejects "a theological interpretation [of ἐκκλεῖσαι] as Schlier offers" (Schlier, *Galater,* 212). For Betz, Paul's language intends to "discredit his opponents emotionally rather than 'theologically,'" but there is no either-or here, and "exclude" in this context has to be a theologically loaded term.

PAUL'S INITIAL RESPONSE (1:4) AND ITS DEVELOPMENTS
IN THE LETTER

Introduction

This is an obtrusive verse simply by reason of its presence. In his other letters, even in the extended prescript of Romans, Paul always concludes the prescript with the greeting. But here he extends the greeting, taking up the name "Jesus Christ" into a participial clause in order to introduce, at the very head of the letter, this confessional statement on the salvific power of the death of Christ. This suggests that 1:4 has a special function in the letter analogous to the similarly unusual denials of 1:1, namely, to serve the letter's polemical intent. This can be corroborated from the content of the verse, which comprises a statement of the gospel message in terms that have clear echoes in the body of the letter.

The developments of 1:4 answer the questions that have been raised among the Galatians by the teaching of the opponents. The Galatians have come to doubt Paul's gospel and believe they must compensate for its deficiencies.[14] Christ has come to be understood in terms of the strict Jewish traditions of the opponents. The division between Jews and Gentiles is not transcended by faith alone; even the issue of the Galatians' deliverance from sin has been put into question. God's "fullness of time" (4:4) is a mere continuation of the time before faith, and the rescue from "the present evil age" (1:4b) has turned out to be nothing of the kind. It is in order to expose and destroy these notions that Paul uses the traditional formula of 1:4 and develops what it confesses in the body of the letter. There are three main

14. Note the present tenses in 1:6-7; 4:17, 21; 5:10, 12; 6:12. In other words, even as Paul writes the letter he is aware that the opponents' influence and the Galatians' threatened apostasy continue. Martyn, "Law-Observant Mission," 313, says, "Paul knows that the Galatians will listen to his letter with the Teachers' sermons still ringing in their ears, and probably with the Teachers themselves at their elbows." See also Mussner, *Galaterbrief,* 54. It is in this context that θαυμάζω ("I am amazed," 1:6) should be understood. On this see White, "Introductory Formulae," 96; Betz, *Galatians,* 47 and note 39; Stowers, *Letter-Writing,* 87, 39.

lines of development: (*a*) the death of Christ and its salvific effect (1:4a; note the ὑπέρ formula ["for us/me"] in 2:20; 3:13; cf. 2:19, 21; 3:1; 5:24; 6:14); (*b*) all humans have sinned (note "sins," 1:4a; cf. 3:22, and "sinners," 2:15, 17); and (*c*) believers are rescued from the age of sin and law (1:4b; cf. "redeem" 3:13; 4:5; and 2:19-21; 3:22-25). Though these developments have yet to be confirmed by exegesis, it ought to be observed that each has its place in the *propositio* (2:15-21) as well as in the *probatio* (3:1–4:31).

The Death of Christ

That the formula of 1:4a predates Paul as a confession of the churches is confirmed by 1 Cor 15:3.[15] Probably the formula developed from an application to the death of Jesus of the Servant texts of Second Isaiah, notably Isa 53:6, 12.[16] It declares that "Christ gave himself for our sins," though it can be abbreviated to a simple "for us" (e.g., Rom 5:8; Gal 3:13) or even "for me" (Gal 2:20; cf. 1 Cor 8:11). It describes the salvific purpose of Christ's death as an atoning sacrifice "for our sins," though whether the sacrifice is seen as expiatory (as in Rom 3:25) or as vicarious is not always clear, nor is it crucial for our purposes. In Galatians the formula is explicitly taken up in 2:20 and 3:13. In this letter it is the death of Christ that provides the main springboard for Paul's arguments against the Judaizers.

Though it was inherited from the tradition, Paul saw in the formula the essence of the gospel message,[17] since it points always

15. This is universally acknowledged. It is also possible that 1:4b is from the tradition, since its vocabulary is unusual for Paul: see Betz, *Galatians*, 41-42 and notes 49, 55, 58, 59, 61; Mussner, *Galaterbrief*, 50 and note 38, but this is by no means certain.

16. Most favor this connection: for example, Beker, *Paul the Apostle*, 203-4; Bruce, *Epistle to the Galatians*, 75; Käsemann, "Death of Jesus," *Perspectives on Paul*, 39; Mussner, *Galaterbrief*, 51. Betz, *Galatians*, 42 and note 55, declares such influence "uncertain"; even more dubious is Bultmann, *Theology of the New Testament*, 1:82–83.

17. In full or in part the formula is apparent in the following texts: Rom 4:25; 5:6-10; 8:32, 34; 14:15 (cf. 1 Cor 8:11); 1 Cor 1:3; 11:24; 15:3; 2 Cor

either to God's initiative of love for humankind (Rom 8:31-39) or, more often, to Christ's loving self-sacrifice (Rom 5:6-10; 1 Cor 1:13), though the one emphasis always presupposes the other (Rom 5:6-8). In the present verse both emphases are brought forward ("Christ gave himself . . . in accordance with God's will"). The death of Christ is God's seizing of the initiative for humanity's salvation in a manner that sets aside the relationship presupposed and fostered by the law (2:19-21; 3:10-13). By their insistence on the law the opponents have dulled this most fundamental aspect of the gospel, introducing prescriptions of law in a manner that destroys the divine-human relationship as created by God in the death of Christ. In the name of Israel's tradition—for Paul the sacredness of the tradition is of no consequence (1:8-9)—they have made God's initiative conditional upon the demands of the law. Just as for them Paul's abrogation of the law is intolerable, so for Paul their teaching is a blasphemous compromise of the power of the death of Christ, as though God's eschatological deed in the Son is insufficient of itself to fulfill its purpose: "If righteousness is through law, then Christ died for nothing" (2:21). That is the fundamental issue, and therefore Paul returns repeatedly to Christ's death and its salvific effect (2:19-21; 3:1, 13; 5:24; 6:14).

All Humans Have Sinned

If Christ died "for our sins," then it follows that "we" are "sinners." Paul insists on the radical meaning of 1:4a by asserting that the sins for which Christ died are the sins of Jews and Gentiles alike (2:15-17; 3:22): "there is no difference" (Rom 3:22). In the letter's polemic this is an important aspect of Paul's undermining the separatism of the opponents. The latter undoubtedly

---

5:14-15, 21; Gal 1:4; 2:20; 3:13; 1 Thess 5:10; see also 2 Cor 5:19; Phil 2:8; Col 2:13; see also Käsemann, "Death of Jesus," *Perspectives on Paul,* 39-40. In Gal 1:4 the manuscript tradition is divided over the preposition, some favoring περί over ὑπέρ; Lightfoot, *Galatians,* 73, even sees a difference between the two, but this is doubtful; see Betz, *Galatians,* 42, note 55; Bauer, *Greek-English Lexicon,* 650f.

accepted the formula of 1:4a. In their understanding, however, the sins of "sinners of the gentiles" were a different matter than the sins of "Jews by birth" (2:15) who were obedient to the law: "While chastening us [for sin] you scourge our enemies ten thousand times more" (Wis 12:22). Both the book of Wisdom and Second Maccabees, primarily in light of the cruel persecutions of Antiochus IV (160s B.C.E.), meditate on the difference between God's punishments upon Israel's sin as opposed to the much greater punishments on Israel's enemies (see 2 Macc 6:12-16; Wis 12:19-22; 15:14–16:10). For "them" there is "no healing," but God's "children" are "not conquered . . . for your mercy came to their help and healed them" (Wis 16:9-10).[18]

For Paul, however, the light of the gospel exposes all human history as sinful (Rom 3:9-23). This is the assertion he makes in the protasis of Gal 2:17, pointedly taking up "we Jews by birth" from 2:15 and asserting that "we too" in coming to Christ "were found to be sinners" no less than the Gentiles.[19] This is the conclusion from the principle enunciated in 2:16: since there is no justification for *anyone* "by works of law," then Jews are in no different a situation before God than are Gentiles. Both are to be saved only by the death of Christ.

The same line of argument is followed in 3:21-22. The protasis of 3:21 asserts that the law was not given "to confer life," and thus from law there is no "righteousness." Rather (ἀλλά) God's purpose in the "scripture"[20] was that "all" (τὰ πάντα) should be subject "under sin" (see Rom 3:20; 11:32). Paul thus

18. See Betz, *Galatians,* 115, note 27. Betz unfortunately sees 2 Macc 6:12-17 as "*the* Jewish position" (my emphasis) in regard to this distinction, whereas of course it represents simply one part of the spectrum of Jewish views of Gentiles: for example, see Fredriksen, "Judaism," 533–45. Romans 1–2, especially the caricature in 2:17-20, provides far stronger evidence than does Galatians for the separatist viewpoint on Gentile sins.

19. This point will be argued in detail in the exegesis of 2:17 in chapter 4, below.

20. The switch from νόμος ("law") to γραφή ("scripture") here (cf. 3:8) signals a *positive* view of law as God's revealed will (cf. Rom 15:3-4), which is extremely important for understanding Paul's dialectical view of the law.

radicalizes the formula of 1:4a beyond the understanding of the opponents. The "sins" for which Christ died are the sins of the Jews no less than the Gentiles. The law provides no advantage.

Rescue from "the present evil age"

The purpose clause (ὅπως, 1:4b) provides an immediate interpretation of the traditional formula. It introduces new emphases that, as they are developed in the letter, strike a telling blow against the teaching of the opponents. The effect of Christ's death is described more fully with a decidedly apocalyptic emphasis, evoking the notion, which predated Paul both as a Jewish and a Christian concept, of two radically separate "ages."[21] Human history, according to the general terms of this concept, works itself out in "the present evil age." This age or "world" is always presumed to be inherently evil even when that is not explicitly stated (see Rom 12:2; 1 Cor 1:20; 2:6-8; 3:19; 7:31). This age is evil because it is bound under the enslaving power of sin, and for Paul in this Galatian context that means also under the oppressive power of the law (3:23–4:7).[22] The "rescue" of believers from the evil age, on the other hand, means that they belong to the eon of grace and faith, which leaves behind the age of the law's oppressive tutelage. But Paul must contend with the fact of the Galatians' threatened apostasy and the reality of sin, even among those who have received the Spirit (6:1). Accordingly he describes the evil age as ἐνεστώς; it remains a "present" and indeed a prevailing and "threatening" reality,[23] as is apparent when the

21. On this see Schoeps, *Paul,* 88–97; Betz, *Galatians,* 42 and notes 58, 60; Keck, "Paul as Thinker," 30–36; Mussner, *Galaterbrief,* 51 and notes 43, 44.

22. This is clear when we note that ἁμαρτία occurs only three times in Galatians over against forty-seven times in Romans. This corresponds with the fact that whereas in Romans the ultimate culprit for humankind's plight is "sin" (e.g., Rom 7:7-13), in Galatians it is νόμος. Obviously the situation of each letter dictates these differing emphases.

23. Ἐνεστώς is the perfect participle of ἐνίστημι; in the middle (intransitive) voice, as here, it can connote "present" in the sense of "threatening." See Liddell and Scott, *Intermediate Greek–English Lexicon,* 263; see also Mussner, *Galaterbrief,* 51; Schlier, *Galater,* 33.

Galatians are ready to "turn back" to its allurements (4:9). This links up with the fact that πονηρός ("evil") is in an emphatic position.[24] Believers live with the paradox of having been rescued from the world and yet still living in range of its evil influence, particularly the entanglement of the law.

It is, of course, the influence of the opponents that has exacerbated the paradox for the Galatians of "living in the *flesh* by *faith*" (2:20). Portraying Paul's gospel as inadequate, they have denied that the Galatians were truly rescued from "the evil age." Hence Paul is struggling with believers who are being lured back into the old age unconvinced of their standing in the age of faith (3:23) as "heirs of Abraham" (3:29). Accordingly 1:4b prepares for positive assertions that describe the reality and characteristics of the new age. While the formula of 1:4a ("for our sins") looks primarily to the *past* of believers, the purpose clause ("that he might rescue") extends the effective range of Christ's death forward into the *present* and *future* of believers' lives. This rescue is in large part what Paul means by δικαιοῦσθαι ("to be made righteous"); far more than the mere removal of sins, it envisages believers "living to God" (2:20) as those who are truly "righteous before God" (3:11). Indeed, it looks to the reality of "new creation" (6:15) that stands in stark antithesis to "the present evil age."[25]

In the body of the letter this emphasis on the present reality of salvation is developed by a whole series of Paul's central theological terms. Corresponding to the unique occurrence of ἐξαιρεῖσθαι ("rescue") in 1:4 are the only occurrences in Paul of ἐξαγοράζειν ("redeem"), in 3:13 and 4:5.[26] The unusually numerous occurrences

24. Lightfoot, *Galatians,* 71, paraphrases "the present age with all its evil" (see also 73); note Burton, *Epistle to the Galatians,* 13, on the emphatic position of πονηρός. Beker, *Paul the Apostle,* 217, expresses the tension of believers in the present time by describing sin in Paul's understanding, as "an impossible possibility." See also Betz, "Geist," 90.

25. On this see Stuhlmacher, "Ontologischen Charakter," 8; on δικαιοῦσθαι as "new creation" see Mussner, *Galaterbrief,* 260.

26. There are two middle-voice instances in Eph 5:16 and Col 4:5, but their meaning, of course, is quite different from the active voice instances in Galatians. See Bauer, *Greek-English Lexicon,* 271.

of ἐλευθερία ("freedom") and its cognates (verb and adjective)[27] with the antithetical term δουλεία ("slavery") and its cognates (verb and noun, "slave") attest to Paul's preoccupation with the freedom of believers in the present as opposed to the slavery from which they were redeemed (4:8-9; 5:1). Similarly, time-notices such as πρό ("previously") over against οὐκέτι ("no longer") in 3:23-25 (n. 2:20; 4:7); χρόνος . . . ἄχηρι ("time . . . until") in 4:1-4; τότε ("then") over against νῦν ("now") in 4:8-9; and 1:23 (cf. 1:13-15) in regard to Paul himself point unmistakably to the transition from the dominion of the old age to the freedom of the age of faith. And finally, in this connection it is no accident that, unique to this letter, the Spirit is envisaged not as "first fruits" or "down payment" of eschatological salvation, as in Romans (8:23) and 2 Corinthians (1:22; 5:5), but as the *fulfillment* of the promise (Gal 3:14; cf. 3:2-5) and the guarantee of an adoption *already* received (4:5-7).[28] In Galatians as nowhere else Paul makes the point that what God promised to Abraham is *now present* for believers (3:22, 29; 4:28).

All of this means that in Galatians there is far more stress than is usual for Paul on "the eschatological present."[29] Future ex-

27. "Freedom": noun (2:4; 5:1, 13); verb (5:1); adjective (3:28; and five times in the Hagar allegory, 4:22-31). Elsewhere the verb is found four times in Romans, the noun once each in Romans and 1 and 2 Corinthians, the adjective twice in Romans, six times in 1 Corinthians (once in Colossians). On the importance of "freedom" for understanding Paul's gospel in Galatia see Betz, "Geist," especially 89. Note "slavery" (4:24; 5:1); "slave" (3:28; 4:1, 7—leaving aside 1:10); "be a slave" (4:3, 8, 9, 25; 5:13). The antithesis of δοῦλος ("slave") is not only "free" but also and perhaps more importantly υἱός (literally, "son"), as 4:7 shows. Elsewhere, as a metaphor of unredeemed existence "slave[ry]" occurs twice in Romans (6:16-20) but nowhere else, though see 1 Cor 7:22; 12:13.

28. The genitive πνεύματος ("[the promise] of the Spirit," 3:14) is epexegetic ("the promise which the Spirit *is*"), and the phrase itself is unique in Paul (cf. Acts 1:4; 2:33; Luke 24:49).

29. Beker, *Paul the Apostle,* 58: "The eschatological present dominates the letter"; Brinsmead, *Response to Opponents,* 60, not without justification says, "It is Paul [as opposed to the opponents] who would appear to border on eschatological enthusiasm." Schlier, *Galater,* 34, says, "The action of Jesus Christ, as a sacrifice which took our sins on itself, enables the future

pectation recedes almost completely into the background. It emerges fleetingly, though without emphasis, in 2:16c-17 and only truly makes a belated impression in the letter's final section (5:5; 6:4-10). In the context of the Galatians' fear for their status as "children of Abraham," the two-age schema serves Paul well. Its antithetical language—freedom versus slavery, "then" versus "now"—exposes their idea, that "hearing with faith" requires "completion" by "works of law" (3:2-5), as a denial of God's deed in Christ. It presents a radical either-or that the Galatians could not possibly miss.

The development of 1:4b in the *propositio* is important and must be noted briefly. In 2:19-20 Paul succinctly but unmistakably indicates what "rescue from the present evil age" means. The ἐγώ, which was in bondage under the law, "died to the law at the hands of the law." The result is a life "to God," a life that Christ lives "in me" to the exclusion of the law. Life, of course, is still lived "in the flesh"; the evil age and its influence are within range. Nevertheless, the new life is lived "by faith in the Son of God who loved me and surrendered himself for me." That event of Christ's death and the believer's participation in it ("I have been crucified with Christ," 2:19) have a transforming effect; God's action has left nothing undone. Paul knows, of course, that salvation is not yet complete (5:5), but the power of grace enables that future to cast its light in the present. The event of faith means the shattering of the old eon of the law (2:18, "I destroyed [the law]"; 2:19, "I died to the law") and the ushering in of the new eon of living "to God."

BUILDING THE CONTEXT OF 2:15-21

The context for study of 2:15-21 is now a step nearer completion. The initial polemical announcement of the gospel's content in 1:4 is developed in line with the contingencies of the Galatian crisis. And in this development 2:15-21 has a significant

---

age to break through for us." Betz, *Galatians,* 42, note 60, takes Schlier to task for this. Schlier's emphasis seems correct to me. None of this, however, contradicts Martyn, "Apocalyptic Antinomies," 420, that Galatians is "fully as apocalyptic as are the other Paulines."

place. This suggests that this passage constitutes for Paul the initial theological development of the gospel's content *for the Galatian situation.* The formula of 1:4a is explicitly recapitulated in 2:20-21; Christ's death "for our sins" is the cornerstone of his case against the opponents' theology. Everything stands or falls, for Paul, with the significance that is attached to Christ crucified. If we are to pursue Paul's statement of the gospel in this letter we must turn to the *propositio;* it focuses the ideas Paul wishes to pursue as he answers the assertions of the Judaizers. Briefly recapitulated, those ideas are: (1) the all-sufficient power of the death of Christ; (2) humanity's common bondage under sin, denying any superior status to Christians who are obedient to the law; and (3) the present reality of the rescue "from the evil age."

The context for the study of our passage, however, is not yet complete. The "other gospel" made itself felt, Paul tells his readers, also in Jerusalem (2:1-10) and Antioch (2:11-14). There also Paul contended for "the truth of the gospel" (2:5, 14) against the separatism introduced by insistence on circumcision (2:3-4) and the food laws (2:12). With regard to these accounts the thesis pursued here is that Paul narrates them because he finds them illustrative of the Galatian crisis. More than that, he tailors these accounts precisely with a view to his Galatian readers; they and their situation are uppermost in his mind. This, of course, can only be substantiated by exegesis of the texts themselves, but even now the thought can be ventured that if indeed Galatia can be shown to be in the forefront of Paul's mind in 2:1-14, then we may all the more be persuaded that that is the case in 2:15-21.

CONCLUSIONS

1. The opponents came into the churches of Galatia and taught that Paul's gospel was seriously defective in that it did not include proper instruction on the necessity of obedience to the law; in the strict mentality of the Judaizers, beyond the law there is no salvation.

2. In particular, the opponents were insisting upon circumcision and were quoting Scripture, the authority of which was very much their natural ally, to "compel" the Galatians to conform.

3. The corollary of the opponents' teaching was the establishing of two classes of believers, the Judaizers and those who followed their lead, and the Galatians who were not circumcised and who were therefore excluded from the inheritance of Abraham.

4. Paul's initial response is 1:4. Its developments in the letter confirm its purpose as an initial polemical response to the opponents' teaching.

5. Its developments are threefold: *(a)* that Christ's death is the sufficient sacrifice "for our sins"; *(b)* that the sins for which Christ died are the sins of Gentiles and Jews equally; all are in the same situation before God; and *(c)* that the rescue of believers from the "evil age" is a present reality on which the Galatians can rely; the blessings of the eschaton are already real for believers.

6. The death of Christ is the central pillar of Paul's case against the opponents; by that death believers are rescued from the power of the law.

7. The development of these major themes takes place in the *propositio* as well as elsewhere in the letter. This passage represents the initial theological development of the gospel for Galatia as Paul wishes to articulate it in these circumstances. Context for study of the *propositio* has to include study of the Jerusalem and Antioch incidents.

The Other Gospel in Jerusalem (2:1-10)

THE ACCOUNT GEARED TO GALATIA: PAUL'S TENDENTIOUS LANGUAGE

What is immediately apparent about these verses is their tortured syntax. Thoughts left incomplete (vv. 4, 6a) and lengthy parenthetical explanations (vv. 6, 8) give the impression that Paul is narrating an event that does not wholly conform to his present purposes in Galatia. A close reading reveals that Paul's vocabulary either serves to support the apostle's claims regarding his apostolate, as has been noted, or is reflective of the vocabulary used against the opponents (notably vv. 3–5). Betz observes: "The purpose of his report was not to give an objective eyewitness account, but to use it as proof in his defense. This must have led to a certain selectivity and tendency in his account, but does not necessarily render the facts reported unreliable."[30] Paul, in other words, has carefully tailored the narrative to suit his purposes.

To assess this accurately it is necessary to attend to clues indicating where Paul is being evasive or creative with regard to some aspect of the meeting. We can presume that the dynamics at play in his composition were the dynamics of the Galatian crisis. No ammunition must be provided his opponents for their claims that he was dependent on Jerusalem but had defected from the gospel as taught and practiced there. Paul can be expected to gloss over anything that might indicate that the "pillars" opposed him on the essential issue of the circumcision of Titus (vv. 3–4). At the same time, the success of the conference must speak as loudly as possible on his behalf. Paul zigzags his way between these concerns, leaving unsaid in verse 4, by means of anacoluthon, what might be interpreted as disagreement between himself and the "pillars" and emphasizing in verse 9, with the choice of κοινωνία ("fellowship"), the significance of the agreement. That the conference was indeed difficult for Paul is even suggested by Luke, who in spite of his idyllic picture of the early church allows us to see how vexatious the issue was (Acts 15:2a, 5).

THE OPPOSITION OF THE "PILLARS"

Verse 3 is straightforward and shows that the occasion of the conference was a demand for the circumcision of Gentiles, as in Acts 15:1-5. This convergence is impressive, and there is no good reason to set it aside.[31] The words ἠναγκάσθη περιτμηθῆναι

30. Betz, *Galatians,* 81, and see 83; also Bornkamm, *Paul,* 32; Haenchen, "Petrus-Probleme," 192–95; Lyons, *Pauline Autobiography,* 132–33; J. T. Sanders, "Paul's Autobiographical Statements," 343, who says that "Paul does not give an *historical* but rather an *historic,* i.e., significant account of his early life as a Christian."

31. Schmithals, *Paul and James,* argues that the meeting was "mainly in the interests of Jerusalem" (52; see 39ff.) and that its essential agreement was that Paul should not preach to Jews (59–60). To do so, Schmithals has to discount Acts from the evidence (see 38–42; 57ff.). On the view adopted here, see Bornkamm, *Paul,* 32; Conzelmann, *History of Primitive Christian-*

("was [not] compelled to be circumcised") are striking in that
they correspond exactly to the vocabulary Paul uses of the Galatian crisis, ἀναγκάζουσιν ὑμᾶς περιτέμνεσθαι (6:12, "they are
compelling you to be circumcised"). This immediately gives reason to believe that the exigencies of Galatia impinge upon Paul's
description of the conference.

With verse 4 we come upon the passage's first anacoluthon
(also v. 6a). What is to be supplied to complete the thought begun
by: "But because of the false brothers . . ."? The context makes
it clear that some did demand that Titus be circumcised. In the
first instance, that must have been those Paul calls "the false brothers." According to Luke they were "Pharisees who had become
believers" (Acts 15:5). But if they were the only ones to make
such a demand, Paul could have written the less-problematic
phrase ὑπὸ δὲ τῶν . . . ψευδαδέλφων ("by the false brothers")
and then have completed his thought. The "because" (διά) and the
anacoluthon, suggesting evasiveness while not wishing to deceive,
hint that the demand was also urged by "James, Cephas, and
John," who are not named because of the potential harm to Paul's
case. As Lightfoot says, "The counsels of the apostles of the circumcision are the hidden rock on which the grammar of the sentence is wrecked."[32] What Paul passes over is the heated debate,

---

ity, 83–84; Eckert, *Verkündigung,* 184. Bruce, *Epistle to the Galatians,*
108–17, has challenged the almost universal consensus that Galatians 2 and
Acts 15 refer to the same event and maintains that Galatians 2 is equivalent
to the visit of Acts 11:30. To do this, Bruce has to dismember Gal 2:3-5,
separating it from its context in 2:1-10 and seeing verses 4–5 "as a parenthesis within the digression [of] vv. 3–5" (116). Thus he makes verse 3 refer
to the meeting of Acts 11:30 (though Luke, of course, never mentions Titus!)
and verses 4–5 to Antioch when "the question of circumcising the Gentile
converts was first raised" (116). But first, it is dubious method to attempt to
harmonize Galatians and Acts, and second, Bruce gives the visit of Acts
11–12 a significance about which Luke seems to know nothing.

32. Lightfoot, *Galatians,* 106. See also Betz, *Galatians,* 82; Bornkamm,
Paul, 34 and 38; Burton, *Epistle to the Galatians,* 77; Giblin, *Hope of God's
Glory,* 57 (who goes further and says that Paul *gave in* to them); Lüdemann,
Opposition to Paul, 36. Mussner, *Galaterbrief,* 107, understands verse 4 to
be saying, "'Because of the false brothers' Paul holds out for an official

which at first featured the "pillars" in opposition to Paul, urging him to concede. Paul glosses over this initial embarrassing opposition and moves on to a rather telling description of the "false brothers."

THE "FALSE BROTHERS"

Paul's description of these Jewish Christians is a clear instance of the Galatian crisis influencing Paul's narrative. First, παρείσακτος ("smuggled in") and παρεισῆλθον ("sneaked in")[33] along with the designation *"false* brothers" suggest that these people did not belong in the assembly at all. Schmithals' interpretation along these lines, however, misses the point. A purely Jewish incursion into the Christian community is not attested and would not give rise to a discussion about the *gospel,* such as evidently occurred.[34] These opponents of Paul were believers in Christ, were almost certainly baptized, and were, we should presume, quite sincere in their beliefs and in their concerns for the Gentiles. As "Pharisees" who remained strict in their views on the law, however, they were immersed in that separatist mentality that

---

agreement between the leaders of the earliest church and himself." But this hardly explains the difficult anacoluthon. Schlier, *Galater,* 70, understands the δέ ("but") in verse 4a to be non-adversative and to introduce an explanation that is completed in verse 5 with the repeated reference to the false brothers. This unnaturally separates verse 4 from verse 3 and avoids all question of dispute between Paul and the "pillars."

33. Translation of these cognates is notoriously difficult. Paul focuses their (to him) duplicitous motives by emphasizing their "sneaky" action, but others (including the "pillars") may have regarded them with far more respect. Burton, *Epistle to the Galatians,* 78, persuasively shows that there is no emphatic "passive sense" in the adjective, and the verb, of course, is middle voice.

34. Schmithals, *Paul and James,* 107–8 and note 14; he believes that the "false brothers" were non-Christian Jewish supervisors of the church (109ff.). Against Schmithals, see Betz, *Galatians,* 90, note 302; see also Burton, *Epistle to the Galatians,* 78; Wegenast, *Das Verständnis der Tradition,* 47, note 1. Schmithals (42) does recognize that the gospel was discussed at the conference, but he does not explain why the church would debate the gospel in response to an external threat.

made intimate association at meals with uncircumcised Gentiles impossible.[35] Their viewpoint, in other words, corresponded very closely with that of Paul's opponents in Galatia; Lüdemann, in fact, believes they were "identical."[36] In any event, Paul uses the resemblance to the hilt, as is apparent with the vocabulary of "freedom" and "enslavement." The importance of this vocabulary in the letter has already been noted. The opponents in Jerusalem, says Paul, attempted "stealthily to destroy"[37] "the freedom which we have in Christ Jesus, that they might enslave us." This, in Paul's view, is precisely what is happening in Galatia (4:9; 5:1). A more objective assessment of their action and intent would be radically different than Paul's description, but Paul of course paints them with the colors of the Galatian crisis.

Further support for this view is found in the purpose clause (ἵνα) of 2:5. The phrase "the truth of the gospel" is unique to Galatians and appears at a crucial point also in the Antioch incident (2:14). With this Paul portrays himself as the champion of the gospel against the opponents' wish "to pervert the gospel of Christ" (1:7; cf. 5:7). Similarly in 4:16, in contrast to the opponents who "court the favor" of the Galatians but "not for good" (4:17), Paul "tells the truth," which corresponds to his claim that it was "for you" (the Galatians) that he defended "the truth of the gospel" in Jerusalem. Πρὸς ὑμᾶς ("for you") here is a striking example of Paul making the Jerusalem meeting relevant to the Galatians. Even if by the time of the conference Paul had already been in Galatia, which is by no means certain,[38] it was still certainly

---

35. Schmithals' (*Paul and James,* 47) attempt to show that "if the Jewish Christians [of Jerusalem] clung to the law, they must have done so for entirely practical reasons" shatters on the consensus of Paul and Acts that the law was a crucial *theological* datum for a considerable body of Jewish Christians.

36. Lüdemann, *Opposition to Paul,* 101.

37. Burton, *Epistle to the Galatians,* 83, on the meaning of κατα-σκοπῆσαι ("spy out") in 2:4.

38. Acts 16:6 and 18:23 suggest that Paul did not evangelize Galatia until after the conference. If the provincial theory were accepted (see n. 1 in chap. 1, above) and if the first missionary journey of Acts 13 is historical— Bornkamm (*Paul,* 43) puts this journey after the assembly—then Paul could

known to the Galatians that the conference had been occasioned otherwise than by their concerns. Paul's aim, however, is to personalize the conference for them, to draw them into the picture on his side ("*our* freedom . . . to enslave *us*") so that they will identify with him against the Jerusalem opposition who have become a transparent image of the opponents in Galatia.

These observations, in my view, confirm the propriety of Haenchen's method of interpreting this passage: Paul's account is far from objective. For Haenchen this is clear when Paul has to admit, "in obedience to the truth," that Barnabas also was given "the right hand of fellowship," indicating that the triumvirate recognized the Antioch mission, not Paul's individual mission to far-flung regions. At the time of the conference, Haenchen believes, Paul was a delegate of Antioch, not the independent missionary he later became.[39] Be that as it may, it is certainly apparent that with respect to the Jerusalem triumvirate's support, Paul strives to give the conference a significance not completely in evidence at the time. This is why he carefully arranges syntax and vocabulary, leaving unsaid what was damaging to his cause (v. 4) and emphasizing what was supportive (vv. 5, 6–9). A final instance of these dynamics will bring us to the Antioch incident.

---

have been in Galatia before the assembly, as Bruce, *Epistle to the Galatians,* 55, and Lüdemann, *Paul,* 71 and 92, believe. There is also διαμείνη in 2:5, which is properly translated "continue" (Burton, *Epistle to the Galatians,* 85) rather than "be preserved" *(RSV),* and thus might suggest that the Galatians knew the gospel previous to the conference, but this is doubtful, as Mussner, *Galaterbrief,* 111, explains. Neither Bruce nor Lüdemann appeals to διαμείνη.

39. Haenchen, "Petrus-Probleme," 192 and 194. Different is Bornkamm, *Paul,* 38: "At the assembly he was obviously the principal speaker and the really controversial figure." In my view Bornkamm perhaps overstates the case, just as Haenchen understates it. Nevertheless, I agree with Haenchen that Paul's placing himself on a par with Peter is part of his Galatian defense strategy. It is also apparent that, at least by the time of the Galatians letter (1:8-9), Paul truly believed he had such status. Whether the "pillars" would agree is doubtful, and of course it is certain that others denied him any authoritative status. See Lüdemann, *Opposition to Paul,* 35–113.

Κοινωνία ("FELLOWSHIP")

Into his wording of the agreement emphasizing the recognition of his apostolate and gospel, Paul introduces the word κοινωνία (v. 9). This noun and its cognates play an important part in Paul's vocabulary.[40] The noun is used of the collection for the poor in Jerusalem (Rom 15:26; 2 Cor 8:4; 9:13); in 1 Cor 10:16 it is used of the Eucharist, and on other occasions it refers to either the communion of believers with one another (Phil 1:5; Philemon 6) or with the Lord (1 Cor 1:9; Phil 3:10). With this vocabulary Paul thinks of that "sharing" that both expresses and brings about unity (Rom 15:26-27; Gal 6:6; cf. Acts 2:42-46; 4:32). In the present context it is a reasonable assumption that κοινωνία is Paul's word, representing his interpretation of the agreement. To be sure, it serves first to exclude any notion of Paul's subjection to the authority of the triumvirate, but in a letter that has as a major theme the unity of Jews and Gentiles in Christ, and in the context of describing a division of missionary responsibilities to these, κοινωνία must also look to the letter's concern for the unity of all believers under the one gospel.

But if κοινωνία is Paul's word and represents his interpretation of the agreement, it must also be said that his interpretation was not unanimous. The decision, "we to the uncircumcised, they to the circumcised," is hardly equivalent to Paul's assertions that "neither circumcision nor uncircumcision counts for anything" (5:6; 6:15) and that in Christ "there is no longer Jew nor Greek" (3:28). On the contrary, the agreement describes a style of missionary endeavor that is to respect fully "the state in which God has called" both Jews and Gentiles (1 Cor 7:17). The latter will not be called upon to submit to the law, nor the former

40. The noun occurs thirteen times in Paul's letters, though the authenticity of 2 Cor 6:14 is sometimes doubted, and for good reason (see Betz, "An Anti-Pauline Fragment?" 88–108). The other twelve instances are Rom 15:26; 1 Cor 1:9; 10:16 (x2); 2 Cor 8:4; 9:13; 13:13; Gal 2:9; Phil 1:5; 2:1; 3:10; Philemon 6. The verb κοινωνέω occurs in Rom 12:13; 15:27; Gal 6:6; Phil 4:15, and adjective κοινωνός in 1 Cor 10:18, 20; 2 Cor 1:7; 8:23; Philemon 17.

presumably to abandon it. The very difficulty of the debate, however, prevented settlement of such details as what was to happen when Jewish and Gentile believers were "sharers" in the same congregation.

The difference between Paul and others seems to be that not everyone penetrated to the fundamental principles of the issue in the manner that he consistently did.[41] Paul sees the agreement as a relativizing of the law for salvation in a manner that would in no way compromise the possibility for Jewish and Gentile believers to be in fellowship. It was for him an affirmation of the shared baptismal principle that "all are one in Christ."[42] James, however, saw no such affirmation. Not unreasonably, he understood the agreement to represent a holding pattern, where the law would continue to have its full force among Jewish Christians but was not to be fully imposed on Gentile Christians. The corollary of this, however, was that these two groups could not mix freely in complete disregard of the law's demands, and for James the compromise would have to be on the side of the Gentiles (2:11-12). Κοινωνία is Paul's carefully chosen word expressing his understanding of the agreement as he wished to present it to the Galatians. Throughout he has had that situation in view. The appearance in the account of harmony between Paul and the "pillars" probably belies the fact that there was a heated debate between them. Certainly this appearance of harmony does not prepare us for the confrontation in Antioch.

---

41. Eckert, *Verkündigung,* 24, notes this and observes further, "It must therefore be taken into account that Paul sees and describes the position of the opponents far more fundamentally than it was understood or advocated by its authors." This can also be applied to those like James and Peter who were not radical opponents of Paul but whose view of the issue at hand was not as based in fundamental principles as was his.

42. It should be noted that Gal 3:28 represents Paul's quotation of a traditional baptismal formula, which is also apparent in 1 Cor 12:13 and Col 3:11 (cf. 1 Cor 11:11-12). On the formula as traditional, see Betz, "Geist," 80-83, and Byrne, *Paul and the Christian Woman,* 4–10.

CONCLUSIONS

1. Only with some difficulty is Paul able to bend the Jerusalem conference to his purpose; the event itself did not go wholly Paul's way. Although he was able to secure the essential agreement that Gentiles were not to be compelled to be circumcised, the "pillars" had provided some initial opposition to him on this issue, particularly with regard to Titus.

2. Accordingly Paul writes a tendentious account for the Galatians. His language, most notably in verses 3–5, indicates that he narrates the event in such a way as to make it illustrative of the Galatian crisis and so as to disarm its difficulties for his cause.

3. What Paul represents as the κοινωνία of the conference was not an easily attained universal agreement, nor was the agreement universally interpreted according to Paul's understanding. The Antioch confrontation is evidence that the conference was less than completely peaceful and that its resolution was differently understood by James than by Paul.[43]

---

43. It might be useful at this point to describe, as I see it, the spectrum of views on the law that was probably evident among the participants at the conference, though acknowledging that there must have been considerable fluidity, not to say uncertainty, on the question: *(a)* Paul abrogated the law for himself and for all (Jews and Gentiles alike), making faith in Christ alone necessary for salvation; *(b)* James, by conviction (and Peter and Barnabas by his persuasion), maintained the necessity of the law for Jewish Christians, making full communion at meals with Gentile Christians impossible unless the latter accepted certain prescriptions of the law, such as those in the apostolic decree (Acts 15:20); *(c)* the Galatian opponents like the Christian Pharisees of Jerusalem (Acts 15:5) insisted on the law as necessary for all believers; that is, unless Gentiles accepted the law they could not be saved, much less could they enjoy full communion with Jewish Christians. I differ, then, with Brown, "Types of Jewish/Gentile Christianity," 74–79, with respect to where Paul belongs on the spectrum. In my view he was more radical than Brown allows, although he does concede that "the Paul of Galatians is more radical" (78, n. 14). Finally, it should be noted that the spectrum of views on the law within Christianity was preceded and matched by an analogous spectrum within Judaism, on which see Segal, *Paul the Convert,* 201–7.

The Other Gospel in Antioch

INTRODUCTION

Both the Jerusalem conference and the Antioch confrontation bring to the fore the primary issue in Galatians, namely, the relationship of the gospel and the law. Both debates represented for Paul a challenge to "the truth of the gospel" (2:5, 14). Both are illustrative, therefore, of what this important phrase means for Paul and of how the gospel relates to the law. It is true, to be sure, that the Antioch incident has a climactic role to play for Paul in vindicating the independence of his gospel and apostolate, but the latter end is served to a large degree because this pericope partakes in the leitmotif of the letter—the subordination of all authorities, Peter and Barnabas not excepted, to "the truth of the gospel." In the investigation of these verses, then, attention must be paid to this motif as well as to the manner in which the passage reflects the Galatian crisis. The latter concern, on the other hand, remains a major issue. As with 2:1-10, so here Paul has his sights on how the narrative can mirror to the Galatians the situation in which they are embroiled.

PETER'S INITIAL TABLE FELLOWSHIP WITH GENTILE CHRISTIANS

Sometime after the Jerusalem conference "Cephas came to Antioch."[44] In these verses as elsewhere (1:1; 3:10) Paul begins with the conclusion to be argued. He leaves his readers in no doubt as to what the judgment on Peter should be: he "stood condemned" *(RSV)*. Verse 12 begins the explanation. There are several exegetical problems in this verse, but we can begin with the undeniable observation that συνήσθιεν ("he used to eat") in the imperfect tense is expressive of the situation that had prevailed

44. Munck, *Paul and the Salvation of Mankind,* 74–75, avoids the difficult sequence of agreement in Jerusalem and conflict in Antioch by reversing the order of events. A far more thorough proposal of this idea employing extensively Betz's form-critical analysis has been made by Lüdemann, *Paul,* 57–59, 75–77; Betz, *Galatians,* 105, note 436, cites others who also favor this reversal, but he himself rejects the notion, as do most interpreters.

for some time in Antioch, and that ὑπέστελλεν ("withdrew") and ἀφώριζεν ("separated"), also imperfects, denote Peter's gradual, perhaps tentative, "retreat."[45] Peter's participation in the communal meals necessarily involved him in compromising the food laws, which, to many Jews and Jewish Christians, were an important aspect of religious observance and identity.[46] Peter's own ambivalence on the matter surfaced after the arrival of "the people from James."

Τινας ἀπὸ Ἰακώβου (THE PEOPLE FROM JAMES)

With the phrase τινας ἀπὸ Ἰακώβου we come upon one of this verse's major problems. What was the relationship of these people to James? More important, what does their coming indicate about the understanding of the Jerusalem agreement and the problem of the gospel's relation to the law? Their relationship to James is disputed, although most interpreters properly recognize that they are his representatives. The difficulty is in deciding

45. Burton, *Epistle to the Galatians,* 107, and Lightfoot, *Galatians,* 112, both note the "military" sense of ὑποστέλλειν. On the force of the imperfects see also Kieffer, *Antioche,* 19.

46. That such sensitivities were widespread in Paul's time is attested by a large number of sources, not least his own letters (Romans 14; 1 Corinthians 8; see also Mark 7:1-23; Acts 10:10-16 with 11:3). Burton, *Epistle to the Galatians,* 104; Betz, *Galatians,* 107–8 and notes 448, 464; Mussner, *Galaterbrief,* 140, cite numerous Old Testament and intertestamental texts on this. Dunn, "Incident at Antioch," *Jesus,* 137–48, provides detailed documentation. See also Neusner, *Judaism,* 49–50, who believes that "the Mishnah as we know it originated in its Division of Purities," which is particularly concerned with "cleanness of meals, food and drink, pots and pans." These laws, says Neusner, "represent positions and principles adopted before 70." Neusner's discussion is instructive for understanding the theological seriousness of the Jewish and Jewish-Christian viewpoint on such matters. Finally, see also Redditt, "*Nomos* in Fourth Maccabees," 249–70, who shows the sensitivity regarding foods of even a highly Hellenized Jewish author (e.g., 4 Macc 5:14-38). What makes 4 Maccabees so interesting for our purposes is that its probable date ("between 20 and 54 [C.E.]," 267) and place of origin (Antioch is "a good guess," 268) place it very close to Paul and his contemporaries.

whether τινας ("some persons") is connected more closely with the preceding "came" or the following "from James." Lietzmann clearly favors the former when he says, "It is simply a matter of a few people friendly with James who came from Jerusalem to Antioch with no purpose that is exactly defined and who refuse to become involved in this custom."[47] Eckert mentions this possibility without especially favoring it, and he properly points out that to interpret "from James" as a designation of the *place* from which these persons came (so Lietzmann and others) is unacceptable.[48] They are best seen—at any rate this is Paul's view—as a delegation sent by James for the purpose they accomplished, to have Peter "and the rest of the Jews" withdraw from a scandalous intimacy that in James' view must have compromised the Jerusalem agreement and perhaps also the relations of Jews in both Antioch and Jerusalem with their local populations.[49]

This confirms what seems already to be presupposed in the Jerusalem debate, namely, that the law was still observed as a matter of course in the Jerusalem church. For that church the problem of the gospel and the law had not surfaced as an acute problem except insofar as it affected the demands to be made on Gentile Christians.[50] Jewish Christians in Jerusalem and else-

47. Lietzmann, *An die Galater,* 84. Of a similar mind are Oepke, *Galater,* 57; Schlier, *Galater,* 83. Bonnard, *Galates,* 50 and note 2, is somewhat undecided but leans towards Lietzmann's position. On the other hand, Burton, *Epistle to the Galatians,* 107; Lagrange, *Galates,* 42; and Ridderbos, *Galatia,* 96, note 7, connect τινας ("some") with ἀπο ᾽Ιακώβου ("from James"). On these people as a delegation from James see Betz, *Galatians,* 108; Bruce, *Epistle to the Galatians,* 130; Burton, *Epistle to the Galatians,* 107; Mussner, *Galaterbrief,* 139. Lightfoot, *Galatians,* 112, takes the middle ground: "It is not improbable, however, that they came invested with some powers from James which they abused."

48. Eckert, *Verkündigung,* 195–96.

49. This danger is specified by Bruce, *Epistle to the Galatians,* 130; Fredriksen, "Judaism," 556. See following note.

50. Fredriksen, "Judaism," 559–61, maintains that from the beginning Jewish Christians, like ordinary Jews, especially in the Diaspora (540–43), accepted Gentiles into the church *without requiring circumcision and observance of the law,* and that the demand for the latter only arose in the late 40s

where, especially those who derived from strict traditions like Paul's (Gal 1:13-14; Phil 3:5-6), were not only observing the law but were presuming that as believers in Christ they *must* do so. For James the conference's agreement did not mean the elimination of the law for Jewish Christians, and thus neither did it mean the elimination of distinctions between Jews and Gentiles. In this respect James and, under his influence, Peter and Barnabas are seen to be almost diametrically opposed to Paul. The conference had settled the issue that Gentiles should not be required to accept circumcision. It had not, however, settled the far more sensitive and fundamental issue of the relationship between the gospel (viz., Christ's death as salvation for all) and the law, as understood from the perspective of strict Pharisaic Judaism. Thus, whereas for Paul mixed communities of Jews and Gentiles were no problem, for James they certainly were. For the latter it was unthinkable that Jews should "destroy" the law by their faith in Christ, but for Paul, though he was no Marcion, such language and thinking were appropriate (Gal 2:18-19).[51]

Τοὺς ἐκ περιτομῆς (THE CIRCUMCISION PARTY)

In modern exegesis this phrase has occasioned varying interpretations, but inquiry into Paul's motivation for this choice of words is lacking. Lagrange and Lietzmann take the phrase to be a reference to Jewish Christians in general and thus avoid identifying the "circumcision party" with the "people from James." Bonnard thinks of them as Jewish Christians who had remained obedient "to Jewish ritual prescriptions," but he does—correctly,

---

as a response to various new factors: *(a)* the non-arrival of the parousia, *(b)* increasing numbers of Gentiles in the church, and *(c)* the corresponding lack of conversion of most Jews. In response, the "false brethren" devised "something both awkward and new: a Jewish *mission* to the Gentiles" (561). If this is correct it would help explain the intensity of the debate following the conference of 48/49.

51. Just how serious this issue would be for the James group and how sharply they differed from Paul is well brought out by Böttger, "Paulus," 87–90.

in my view—see the two groups as identical.[52] Schmithals and Bruce take the phrase to refer to non-Christian Jews who applied pressure on Jewish Christianity to convince the latter to remain separate from Gentile Christianity.[53]

To be sure, the only other occurrence of the phrase in Paul (Rom 4:12) denotes "Jews" in the ethnic sense. Elsewhere in the New Testament, including in the deutero-Pauline tradition (Acts 10:45; 11:2; Col 4:11; Titus 1:10), it denotes Jewish Christians. In Paul περιτομή always denotes either "the Jews" (e.g., Rom 3:30; Gal 2:7; cf. Eph 2:11), the state of circumcision or—and this is crucial here—it bears a strong figurative sense (e.g., Rom 2:25-29; Phil 3:3; Col 2:11). Especially Rom 2:25-29 and Phil 3:3 (see also Rom 4:9-12) show that for Paul the term carried a heavy symbolic meaning that he was willing to turn to his advantage against his Judaizing opponents. Galatians, of course, is the letter beyond all others in which Paul struggles with the issue of circumcision. The choice of the word, then, in this context is almost certainly deliberate and polemical, and the object of his attack has to be James' delegation as a mirror image of the Galatian opponents.

To confirm the identification of the James delegation with "the circumcision party," it is useful to begin with the simple observation that verse 13 begins with καί ("and"), which brings τοὺς ἐκ περιτομῆς into close connection with οἱ λοιποὶ Ἰουδαῖοι ("the rest of the Jews"). Stuhlmacher, with reference to Schmithals' interpretation of "the circumcision party" as meaning simply "Jews" in this context, says forthrightly: "I consider this impossible. Since verses 12b and 13 belong indissolubly together and οἱ λοιποὶ Ἰουδαῖοι in verse 13 clearly designates Jewish Christians, then οἱ ἐκ περιτομῆς emerges as a stylistic variation of that second phrase and, just like it, designates Jewish Christians." This strikes a telling blow against Schmithals' position, especially since he himself admits that "the rest of the Jews" must mean

---

52. Lagrange, *Galates,* 43; Lietzmann, *An die Galater,* 14–15; Bonnard, *Galates,* 50. Those not favoring this identification are Bruce, *Epistle to the Galatians,* 131; Schmithals, *Paul and James,* 67; Tyson, "Paul's Opponents in Galatia," 248, note 1. This seems to be the minority view.

53. Schmithals, *Paul and James,* 67; Bruce, *Epistle to the Galatians,* 131.

Jewish Christians.[54] The "circumcision party" is then, in all probability, to be seen as identical with "the people from James." A priori this is the more likely. If the two phrases do not refer to the same people then the introduction of τοὺς ἐκ περιτομῆς is abrupt in the extreme. It is, of course, not impossible that Paul is making a reference his readers would easily recognize and we do not, but in the present context a more simple explanation lies at hand, and thus most interpreters accept this identification as the best solution (see preceding note). It was, in Paul's description, due to Peter's fear of the men from James that he withdrew from table fellowship with the Gentile Christians of Antioch.

The motivation for Paul's description of the James group as "the circumcision party" is, like the vocabulary already noted in 2:3-5, the polemical situation in Antioch. James, in fact, was demanding circumcision of no one, but the Galatian Judaizers were. Of this description Stuhlmacher says: "Paul even dares to deny the title of brother to the Jewish Christians attached to James. He speaks neither of οἱ ἐκ περιτομῆς πιστοί ["believers of . . ."] nor of ἀδελφοί ["brothers"], but contemptuously of οἱ ἐκ περιτομῆς or alternatively simply of οἱ Ιουδαῖοι (v. 13). In consequence this can only mean that the curse of 1:8f. emerges as a threatening possibility also between Paul and the Jewish Christians who follow Peter or James, that therefore the community of the church threatens to break apart."[55] This seems to me essentially correct, except that it must be remembered that Paul engages here in strident polemical rhetoric. To repeat, James and

54. Stuhlmacher, *Das paulinische Evangelium,* 1:106, note 1, against Schmithals, *Paul and James,* 71. Also contra Schmithals, see Eckert, *Verkündigung,* 196, note 8. That "circumcision party" must designate Jewish Christians is the majority view, for example, Betz, *Galatians,* 109–10 and notes 467, 473; Burton, *Epistle to the Galatians,* 107; Lüdemann, *Paul,* 123f., note 102; Mussner, *Galaterbrief,* 141. Most also identify them with the "people from James," for example, Lüdemann, *Paul,* 124; Kieffer, *Antioche,* 19; Lührmann, "Abendmahlsgemeinschaft?" 278. "The rest of the Jews" probably denotes the Jewish Christians of Antioch as opposed to the "circumcision party" who were from James in Jerusalem.

55. Stuhlmacher, *Das paulinische Evangelium,* 1:106.

Peter were not demanding circumcision. Paul nevertheless caricatures them in this way in order to draw the battle lines clearly and to illustrate that the same fundamental principles as were at stake in Jerusalem and Antioch are now the issue in Galatia. Περιτομή here prepares for defining the battle lines in terms of "flesh" and "spirit" (3:2-5). It looks also to the accusatory question of 2:14 and to the antithesis of "Jews by birth" versus "sinners of the gentiles" in 2:15. It is the Galatian crisis that determines Paul's choice of words here.[56] This is also apparent with the words "fear" and "hypocrisy."

PETER'S "FEAR" AND "HYPOCRISY"

With regard to Peter's "fearing" it is important to remember that this is Paul's description of Peter's motivation. In part it may indeed be accurate, but Paul passes over the fact that there were cogent reasons why Peter should "withdraw," not least of which was the Jerusalem agreement as understood from the viewpoint of James and other Jewish Christians. Peter undoubtedly scandalized the latter by his "eating" (cf. Acts 11:2-3) even as he scandalized Gentile Christians and Paul by his "withdrawal." For Peter the problem was considerable. Should he sacrifice the law and "ancestral traditions" (1:13) for the sake of unity in Christ or unity for the sake of the traditions? While in Jerusalem Peter was comparatively sheltered from this issue, but once faced with a mixed congregation the issue came to the fore sharply. At this point Peter's well-documented reputation for impetuosity and fickleness seems to be justified.[57] He had some-

56. With regard to Paul's harsh language in 2:11-14, Lührmann, "Abendmahlsgemeinschaft?" 279, says, "The reason for this polemic is again to be sought in the Galatian situation, since now as previously in Jerusalem and Antioch 'the truth of the gospel' is at stake." Dunn, "Echoes of Intra-Jewish Polemic," 459–77, shows that the passage's polemical terms had to do with debates among Jewish Christians and may, in part, reflect the vocabulary of James' people (e.g., 464).

57. I am thinking, of course, of Peter in such texts as Mark 8:29-32; 14:29-31, 66-72; Matt 14:28-30; Luke 5:4-8; John 21:7. This is also noted by Mussner, *Galaterbrief,* 142, but Eckert, *Verkündigung,* 197, feels the

what blindly projected himself into a difficult situation. What the James delegation exposed in him was a lack of conviction on the relationship between the gospel and the law. The fact that "the rest of the Jews and even Barnabas" followed Peter is an indication of just how difficult the issue was. Paul's less than generous estimate of Peter's motivation is symptomatic of how he lets his emotions regarding Galatia impinge on his description of Antioch.

Like "fear," "hypocrisy" is not a wholly inappropriate term for Peter's behavior; it is not my purpose to exonerate Peter and company.[58] Nevertheless it is Paul who passes judgment and Peter who is on the horns of a dilemma. Bornkamm rightly says: "It must in all fairness be said that, from the others' standpoint, Paul's view of the matter was unwarranted. For this was the first appearance of the problem which had not as yet come to the surface . . . , the question of the unity of Jewish and Gentile Christians in a mixed church. Thus neither Cephas nor James can be accused of acting in an underhand way."[59] And yet accuse Paul does. His charge, however, echoes the description of the opponents' duplicitous motives in 4:17 and especially in 6:12-13: "They want to make a good showing in the flesh . . . only in order that they may not be persecuted. . . . [They] do not themselves keep the law, but they desire to have you circumcised that they may glory in your flesh" *(RSV)*. Paul's evaluation even of the opponents is a manifestation of his intense concern for the gospel and the threat to it in the Galatian context. Peter, whose conduct in Antioch was reprehensible in its own right, has become for

---

comparison is inappropriate, as does Böttger, "Paulus," 88. I agree with the latter that the issues, "for Peter & Co.," opened up "horrifying possibilities" ("Abgründe auftaten"); Peter's impetuosity is apparent in his not having thought this through before the consequences of his action were already upon him.

58. On this vocabulary as properly descriptive of Peter's behavior, see Burton, *Epistle to the Galatians,* 108–9; Bruce, *Epistle to the Galatians,* 131; Schlier, *Galater,* 85.

59. Bornkamm, *Paul,* 46; see also E. P. Sanders, *Paul and Palestinian Judaism,* 519: "Paul's charge in Gal 2:14 . . . was not quite accurate."

Paul a convenient reflection of the Galatian Judaizers. This is most apparent in 2:14.

"THEY WERE NOT WALKING IN ACCORDANCE WITH THE TRUTH OF THE GOSPEL"

What is meant by this phrase (ἡ ἀλήθεια τοῦ εὐαγγελίου), which has already appeared in 2:5? Burton takes the genitive in both instances to be possessive: "The truth is the truth contained in and so belonging to the gospel." Stuhlmacher, on the other hand, seems to take the genitive to be subjective, in that "the truth of the gospel" has to do with "the validity of the salvation now already bestowed on the world by God . . . ; it is the eschatological and sovereign power of God, now available in the gospel."[60] One might also think in terms of epexegetic genitive ("the truth" which "the gospel" *is*). Stuhlmacher's emphasis is instructive. As God's "call," the gospel pronounces divine truth over the world. "Within it" is the revelation of "God's righteousness" (Rom 1:17), and thus within its adherents it produces a "conviction" (εἰδότες, Gal 2:16) regarding God's act of justifying ("making righteous") humankind. The "truth" it announces and enacts has to do with freedom from the law. This becomes clear in the immediately following context (2:15-21), where the reader expects Paul to expound the content of this truth. Within the present context the subordination of Peter, Barnabas, Paul, and the rest to the gospel is unmistakable.

With regard, however, to its truth Paul says that they οὐκ ὀρθοποδοῦσιν.[61] Ὀρθοποδεῖν is rare. Mussner, following Kilpatrick, translates: "They do not take the direct route toward the truth of the gospel." He accompanies this translation with the ob-

---

60. Burton, *Epistle to the Galatians,* 86 (cf. Lightfoot, *Galatians,* 107); Stuhlmacher, *Das paulinische Evangelium,* 1:90.

61. This is the only occurrence of this word in the New Testament. See the study of Kilpatrick, "ὀρθοποδοῦσιν," 269–74, also the literature cited by Betz, *Galatians,* 111, notes 483, 484; Bruce, *Epistle to the Galatians,* 132.

servation that "the route is determined by the goal."[62] But this interpretation pushes the metaphor too far and reduces Paul's criticism to a simple theological statement, whereas it is an *ad hominem* rebuke intended to expose Peter's behavior as perverse. Lagrange's observation that "the preposition πρός could as well be κατά" is quite to the point.[63] Such a use of πρός, while unusual, is not unprecedented in Paul or the New Testament in general (2 Cor 5:10; Eph 3:4; Luke 12:47). Furthermore, if πρός is translated "in accordance with," then ὀρθοποδοῦσιν has the sense that is "most widely attested," namely, that which treats it "as the opposite of χωλεύειν," which designates the "limping" of the physically disabled.[64]

Such a meaning makes sense in parallel with the charge of hypocrisy, for it brings out that Peter acted contrary to the truth, which according to verse 16a, he as a believer "knew." Thus Kilpatrick's remark about "revelation progressively comprehended" (see preceding note) is irrelevant to this context, where Paul's charge is that Peter denied that which he knew well enough. The polemic against Peter's behavior is not too dissimilar to the charge of "perversion" leveled against the opponents in 1:7. Peter twists the gospel and obscures its truth. In the name of the law he is compromising the status in the church of those for whom Christ died, and thus he confounds the gospel and the law. But again, all of this says more about Paul's understanding of the Galatian crisis than about Peter himself.

62. Mussner, *Galaterbrief,* 144.

63. Lagrange, *Galates,* 44; this is also noted by Mussner, *Galaterbrief,* 144, note 47, but his reliance on Kilpatrick so sways his interpretation that Lagrange's insight is essentially ignored. On πρός as meaning "according to" in this context, see Burton, *Epistle to the Galatians,* 111. He suggests the paraphrase, "to deal honestly and consistently with [the gospel], not juggling or warping or misrepresenting it"; see also Bauer, *Greek-English Lexicon,* 717; Bonnard, *Galates,* 51; Lightfoot, *Galatians,* 113.

64. Kilpatrick, "ὀρθοποδοῦσιν," 274. Kilpatrick himself, however, prefers the meaning, "being on the right road," and he takes πρός in the sense of "toward."

"COMPELLING GENTILES TO JUDAIZE"

Paul's tendentious vocabulary is perhaps most clear in his final accusation against Peter, "You are compelling gentiles to become Jews."[65] Peter, of course, had no such purpose; the issue for him was the opposite, Jews being "compelled" into unacceptable Gentile behavior. His concern was the scandal he was undoubtedly causing the Jerusalem church. He was trying to appease those who interpreted the Jerusalem agreement in a conservative fashion, which stressed the necessary separation of Jews and Gentiles, as opposed to Paul's view, which saw the relativizing of the law for salvation as the signal for Jews and Gentiles to be "one person in Christ" (Gal 3:28). It was not in Peter's mind to "compel gentiles to become Jews," but the Judaizers had precisely that aim in mind (6:12). Only if we believe that Peter was supportive of the Galatian opponents can we take Paul's accusation with full seriousness as stated. But if the accusation is not to be taken literally, then it is apparent that Paul has caricatured Peter, drawing the lines of his behavior more heavily than it deserves. Peter's wavering on the matter of meals with Gentiles demonstrates both the lack of explicit instruction from Jesus on the question[66] and Peter's lack of conviction on the issue of the gospel's relation to the law. The only defense for Peter is that for him and others "the refinement of doctrine on Christian freedom had not yet reached the point where every trace of doubt could be removed."[67]

---

65. A number of interpreters note that these words especially reflect the Galatian crisis, for example, Betz, *Galatians,* 62 and note 111; Mussner, *Galaterbrief,* 145, note 52. Lührmann, "Abendmahlsgemeinschaft?" 280, includes 2:14 with 2:15-21 as being "aimed pointedly at the Galatian readers," and thus it is "not a verbatim report" of the Antioch speech.

66. It goes without saying, as Acts 11:1-3 shows, that the issues faced by Peter and Paul in Antioch were not settled during the ministry of Jesus; see Dunn, "Bridge Between Jesus and Paul," *Jesus,* 10–31.

67. Bonnard, *Galates,* 50; on this point, see also Mussner, *Galaterbrief,* 159, and Ebeling, *Truth of the Gospel,* 114–15, who says that Peter in withdrawing "embraced Paul's own chosen principle," referring to 1 Cor

The Antioch incident is a convenient cameo for Paul, in which the clash between the gospel and the law is displayed paradigmatically. Not only does it enable Paul to show his independence of Peter, but it also highlights the threat that the law is to the gospel when the law is allowed to be determinative of believers' existence. The gospel reveals grace as the determining power of that existence; the law, though itself truly grace, requires "deeds," and thus it divides humanity according to fulfillment, or otherwise, of its demands. Peter's action denied the power of Christ's death "for our sins," so to "justify" the Gentiles that they could be one people in Christ with Jewish believers. For Paul the central issue was, does the law continue to be determinative for believers in Christ? His response to that, of course, is a resounding no, as he asserts in 2:15-21. Before turning to that passage directly, the nature of the Antioch meals requires some attention. Specifically, why is it that Paul makes nothing either of the eucharistic nature of the Antioch meals or of the Eucharist in general? Discussion of this sheds light on what it is that Paul wishes to say about the gospel and on just what the gospel is for him.

THE ANTIOCH MEALS

In his article "Abendmahlsgemeinschaft?" Lührmann has made much of the eucharistic nature of the table fellowship in which Peter participated at Antioch. Many interpreters share his view that the meals must have been eucharistic.[68] It is not my

---

9:19-23 and 10:32: "Give no offense to Jews or Greeks or to the community of God."

68. Lührmann, "Abendmahlsgemeinschaft?" 274–75, note 20, provides a listing of scholarly opinions in favor of the eucharistic interpretation as well as opinions of some who are undecided. Others in favor include Beyer and Althaus, "Galater," *Die kleineren Briefe des Apostels Paulus,* 19; Bruce, *Epistle to the Galatians,* 129; Haenchen, "Petrus-Probleme," 196. Also undecided are, among others, Betz, *Galatians,* 107; Mussner, *Galaterbrief,* 138. Lagrange, *Galates,* 42, and Burton, *Epistle to the Galatians,* 104, completely reject the eucharistic interpretation. Most persuasive, in my view, is Stuhlmacher, *Das paulinische Evangelium,* 1:105, who says that the meals were "community *agape* celebrations and not only . . . isolated

purpose, however, either to deny or to affirm the eucharistic interpretation as a historical fact. The evidence is too scanty for a decision either way.[69] What is important is that for Paul it clearly made no difference whether or not the meals were eucharistic. Neither in 2:11-14 nor in the rest of the letter does Paul make any allusion to the Eucharist, even though it could undoubtedly have served as a powerful lesson on unity among believers (cf. 1 Cor 10:17; 11:17-34). The reason for this was that in the Galatian situation the issue was far more fundamental than eucharistic fellowship as such. The latter, after all, presupposes that which the gospel creates and is impossible without it, namely, the unity of all in Christ regardless of status with respect to the law (Gal 3:28). And it was the gospel in this fundamental aspect that was being undermined by the opponents' teaching.

More fundamental than a fracturing of eucharistic fellowship is the denial that Christ's death is sufficient to "justify" all humans equally before God so that believers can indeed be "one in Christ." The separatism of the opponents did not merely destroy eucharistic fellowship, it challenged the very existence of the reality that Paul claimed the gospel had created: "There is no

---

eucharistic celebrations" (see also Lightfoot, *Galatians,* 112; Ridderbos, *Galatia,* 96). Oepke, *Galater,* 57, properly says that the Lord's supper was "probably" included, "since according to all that we know, Lord's supper and community meals were still at that time inseparable from one another"; see 1 Cor 11:20-22; Acts 2:46; 20:11.

69. Both the compound συνεσθίειν ("eat with") and the simple ἐσθίειν are neutral terms that can be used of ordinary meals as well as eucharistic meals. The former occurs elsewhere in Paul only at 1 Cor 5:11, which is as ambiguous as Gal 2:12. In Acts 10:41 it *may* refer to the Eucharist, but it has no such connotation consistently in Luke (e.g., Luke 15:2; Acts 11:3, both somewhat reminiscent of Gal 2:12 in that food laws were the issue).ʼΕσθίειν is equally ambiguous. It is used of the Eucharist in 1 Cor 11:20-34, but Rom 14:2-6 and 1 Cor 8:10-13 preclude seeing it as a eucharistic term as such. On this, see Bonnard, *Galates,* 49–50, but Bonnard thinks that the following verbs, which describe Peter's withdrawal ("retreated . . . separated himself") "give the distinct impression" that Eucharist is envisaged. In fact, however, neither of these verbs is connected with the Eucharist anywhere in the New Testament.

longer Jew and Greek." The separatism of the opponents made the law and its definition of righteousness constitutive of the Christian community, so that Galatians were at a disadvantage over against those who belonged "by nature" to the covenant of Abraham. But this meant that "nature" determined "grace" (2:15-21), that "flesh" determined "Spirit" (3:2-5). Such an attack on the gospel's power and fundamental reality required more than a defense in terms of eucharistic fellowship; it required a radical statement on the gospel as God's definitive eschatological deed, which asserted both what the gospel *destroyed,* the claims of the law, and what it *created,* new life "to God" in Christ. Such is 2:15-21.

As Paul writes this crucial passage he hews to this motif of conflict between law and gospel. He does so in typically Pauline uncompromising fashion, so that law and gospel emerge as exclusive alternatives, either faith or works, either grace or law. This radical language raises difficulties of its own, but the language must not therefore be tempered or evaded. What Paul *means,* the theology beyond the rhetoric, ultimately emerges clearly enough. The rhetoric is appropriate because the attack on the gospel is so radical. And Paul is indeed quite serious that in the realm of the gospel the law has no determinative role. But the *positive* role of the law as "scripture" (Gal 3:8, 22) and, to use a word from Romans, as "instruction" (διδασκαλία, Rom 15:4; see also νουθεσία, 1 Cor 10:11) also ultimately emerges. Thus the radical abrogation of the law on the one hand and Paul's creative appeal to it on the other are not, in my view, the result of "contradictions and tensions" that "have to be *accepted* as *constant* features of Paul's theology of the law."[70] Rather, it is a matter of taking into account the situation within which Paul was writing. His choice of words in the Jerusalem and Antioch narratives is witness enough of that.

Those narratives also indicate that Galatians is not pure theological reflection. The letter as a whole and the *propositio* in particular are completely rooted in the exigencies of the Galatian crisis. The crisis, to Paul, is severe indeed; the Galatians are in

---

70. Räisänen, *Paul and the Law,* 11.

danger of "falling from grace" (5:4). It is not enough to reassure the Galatians of their place in the inheritance of Abraham, he must also "raze [the] strongholds and destroy [the] arguments" of his opponents (2 Cor 10:4). Therefore the sharp negative edge of the gospel, its power to expose illusion and human rebellion (cf. Rom 1:18–2:29; 1 Cor 1:18-25), comes forcefully into play. And, indeed, it is turned above all against the law itself. Nevertheless, the gospel also shines through positively as God's power of new creation, so that while much of the *propositio,* for the advocates of law and tradition, might have the impact of "bad news," for the Galatians it is also intended as "good news," assuring them that what God accomplished in Christ was in no sense incomplete. On the other hand, the exigencies of the crisis do not take over so completely that the coherent center of Paul's thought is lost, drifting off into "opportunistic impulses."[71] The Jerusalem and Antioch incidents set the stage for the *propositio* because they demonstrate, on the one hand, how the contingencies of the present situation impinge on his language and, on the other, how the central issue, the gospel's relation to the law, is his constant theme. The entire crisis is for Paul a question of the supreme power of the gospel, which cannot be compromised in the name of even the most sacred authorities.

To conclude, I would slightly amend Lührmann's valuable insights on the Antioch narrative. He states:

> The Eucharist, and this is Paul's essential argument against Peter . . . , as a *community meal of sinners who have been made righteous,* can permit no divisions. Eucharistic fellowship is, therefore, . . . the mode of existence which conforms to the Christology of justification by faith alone. . . . Eucharistic fellowship is ultimately an eschatological celebration in that here there is realized "new creation," in which the differences and polarizations so necessary for the world no longer hold true, since, before the one God

---

71. See Beker, *Paul the Apostle,* 235: ". . . unless Paul's various argumentative moves are simply intuitive, opportunistic impulses, they must be shown to cohere in an intelligible pattern consistent with the organizing center of his thought."

and the one Lord, all are simply sinners who have been made righteous.[72]

This statement is essentially unassailable. But in Galatians Paul does not say this of the Eucharist but of the *gospel.* It is the gospel that creates the reality Lührmann describes, and it is the "other gospel" that now threatens to destroy that reality. The threat to the gospel is the law, and thus in the *propositio,* anticipating the bulk of the letter, the law becomes Paul's target.

CONCLUSIONS

1. The Antioch confrontation exposed in Peter a lack of conviction on the relationship of the gospel and the law. James, on the other hand, had firm convictions on this matter and, through his delegates, swayed Peter in his direction.

2. Paul writes the Antioch narrative in large measure as an illustration of the Galatian crisis. This is apparent in Paul's overly severe critique of Peter and particularly in the phrases "circumcision party" and "compel to Judaize," which have far more to do with the opponents of Galatia than with those of Antioch.

3. In Paul's view the central issue in both Jerusalem and Antioch is the same as that which has occasioned the Galatian crisis, the relationship of the gospel to the law. For Paul the gospel is neither dependent on nor inclusive of the law as determinative for belonging to the inheritance of Abraham. In this context that is "the truth of the gospel."

4. It also emerges from both narratives that in Jerusalem the law was observed by (at least a significant body of) Jewish Christians, including as it influenced table fellowship with Gentiles. Unlike the Galatian opponents, however, the Jerusalem church as a whole did not demand that Gentiles must be circumcised in order to be saved.

5. Finally, it is important to note that though the Antioch meals may have been inclusive of Eucharist, it is not that aspect of the confrontation on which Paul centers. The reason for this is

72. Lührmann, "Abendmahlsgemeinschaft?" 285.

that Paul is concerned with the more fundamental issue of the gospel itself: was the death of Christ "for our sins" sufficient in itself or not? Did it truly effect "new creation," or are the law's demands also necessary? Does the divine-human relationship "in Christ" also enable a new relationship between Jews and Gentiles, or, again, are the law's prescriptions also required?

IV.

Paul's Response to Jewish-Christian Separatism and the Threat of Galatian Apostasy

2:15-21 Directed Primarily at the Galatian Situation

It is appropriate first to look more fully at the question whether the *propositio* is essentially a report of the Antioch speech or whether there is not, as many interpreters believe, a rather more definite break between verses 14 and 15, so that in this transition passage the Antioch issue, while by no means disappearing, recedes into the background and the Galatian crisis comes to the fore. The view held here is that whatever Paul said to Cephas at Antioch, Galatians 2:15-21, as well as verse 14, *primarily* was written with the Galatian situation in mind. Paul's caricature of Peter as "compelling gentiles to Judaize" may not in fact represent Paul's words in Antioch but rather his description of Peter's fault for the Galatians. Lührmann, it seems to me, sums up the situation well: "The speech of Paul in 2:14-21 is not, as is well known, a verbatim report of his original indictment against Peter before the Antioch community, rather it is directed pointedly at the Galatian readers as a fundamental presentation of the one gospel for Jews and gentiles."[1]

---

1. Lührmann, "Abendmahlsgemeinschaft?" 280. The following also see the Galatian context as primary: Betz, *Galatians,* 113–14 and note 14; Brinsmead, *Response to Opponents,* 51; Lietzmann, *An die Galater,* 15; Ridderbos, *Galatia,* 98; Schlier, *Galater,* 87–88; Wilckens, "Aus Werken,"

This, of course, is not to deny the obvious importance of the Antioch incident as illustrative background for the Galatian situation and thus for our passage. The "we" of verses 15–17 is clearly inclusive of Peter, Paul, Barnabas, and "the rest of the Jews" in Antioch; the connection with verses 11–14 is thus secured. It remains an important question, however, whether 2:15-21 is, as I believe, Paul's theological development of the meaning of the Jerusalem and Antioch incidents for the Galatian situation. Maintaining this Galatian focus is important, for instance, in interpreting verses 17–18, as will become clear in my disagreements on these verses with Kieffer, Mussner, and others. Furthermore, with regard to the doctrine of justification in verse 16, this highly polemical formulation, directed radically against the law itself, can best be understood as the message Paul wishes the Galatians to hear. Peter, after all, even though implicitly denying the full scope of justification by faith, was not seeking justification "by works of law." It was the Galatians who were doing so.

Form-critical observations suggest that this passage, however it is named, is a "new section," which "sums up the legal content" of the *narratio* and prepares for the coming debate in the *probatio*.[2] To these considerations of form, there are also the in-

---

Rechtfertigung, 86–87; Winger, *By What Law?* 126–28. Mussner, *Galaterbrief,* 145–46 and 167, note 2, recognizes Galatia as primary but interprets 2:17-18 primarily in terms of Antioch (176–79). That 2:15-21 is essentially a continuation of the Antioch speech is maintained by Beyer and Althaus, "Galater," *Die kleineren Briefe des Apostels Paulus,* 19; Byrne, *Sons of God,* 143; Feld, "Christus Diener," 120–21; Lagrange, *Galates,* 46. Kieffer, *Antioche,* 53ff. wants to use both contexts, but in fact Antioch dominates. Adopting a more or less neutral position, at least at the outset, are Bonnard, *Galates,* 52; Burton, *Epistle to the Galatians,* 117; Bruce, *Epistle to the Galatians,* 136–37; Lightfoot, *Galatians,* 113–14. Oepke, *Galater,* 56, appropriately says that though in *form* it remains a speech to Peter, its *content* is aimed at the readers; see also Eckstein, *Verheißung,* 4–5.

2. Brinsmead, *Response to Opponents,* 51 (see also 69), and Betz, *Galatians,* 114, respectively. See also Betz, "Composition," 367–68. Kennedy, *Interpretation Through Rhetorical Criticism,* 148–49, who sees the letter as "deliberative," rejects *propositio* as a proper title for this section; he calls it "an epicheireme" (148), but he also sees it as distinct from the *nar-*

dications in the letter's content that have been noted, namely, that the Jerusalem and Antioch narratives are composed in terms that closely resemble Paul's description of the Galatian crisis. We have seen that Paul describes the contest with the Jerusalem "false brothers" and the threat they posed (2:3-5) with the same vocabulary he uses to refer to the opponents' activity (6:12) and to the issues of slavery, freedom (4:1-9, 21-31; 5:1); and truth (2:5, 14; 4:16; 5:7) involved in that activity. In the Antioch narrative the words "compel" and "the truth of the gospel" are again taken up, and "circumcision" is caustically introduced into the description of James' delegates. Peter also is described in terms more suited to the Judaizers than to himself. If these narratives already have Galatia so much in view, we can reasonably expect that this is even more true of 2:15-21.

The passage leads to the rebuke "O stupid Galatians!" (3:1). But this is by no means the first time the letter directly involves the addressees in its content (1:6; 2:5). In fact the reason for the rebuke, that "Christ was displayed" before the Galatians as "crucified," directly connects with what precedes, where Paul has argued for the power of Christ's salvific death against the claims of the law (2:19-21). Thus 3:1 looks back to the *propositio* as well as forward to the *probatio* and indicates that in 2:15-21 it is the "bewitching" of the Galatians by the law that has been in the forefront of Paul's mind. The immediate context, therefore, also suggests that 2:15-21 has the Galatians in the foreground. They, after all, are the addressees of the letter, and as Lightfoot remarks, this letter "is especially distinguished among St. Paul's letters for its unity of purpose."[3] That purpose is the repudiation of the opponents' claims for the law and their concomitant critiques of Paul's gospel and apostolate. Their teaching was evidently seen by Paul as an attack on the very heart of the gospel as he knew it. His response in terms of fundamental principles produced a letter that to this day has often been seen as offensive in its direct attack on

---

ratio (1:13–2:14). Lyons, *Pauline Autobiography,* 134–35, distinguishes 2:11-14 and 2:15-21 as two different types of "comparison" (σύγκρισις); 2:15-21 compares Paul's "ethos" with "that of other exemplary individuals."

    3. Lightfoot, *Galatians,* 63.

the Jewish law. In what follows we must be careful neither to dull
the sharp edge of Paul's views on the law nor to forget the context within which they were crafted. The latter has a great deal to
do with the former. Context, therefore, in both its broad historical
and its immediate epistolary dimensions, is primary.

2:15 The Antithesis of "Jews" Versus "Gentile Sinners"

"We, though Jews by birth and not sinners of the gentiles, . . . "

This is a remarkable opening to the *propositio.*[4] That very
separatism that is the gospel's antithesis, and that Paul has just told
his readers he contested in both Jerusalem and Antioch, is nowhere
expressed more succinctly and pointedly than here. "We" includes
Peter, James, Paul, and all Jewish Christians. In the context of 2:11-
14, "We Jews by birth" is not without a measure of sarcasm. Paul
has just distanced himself from Peter and "the rest of the Jews," but
now he appears to align himself with them as though, together as
"Jews," they stood over against the "heathen gentiles." In this respect "Jews by birth" is reminiscent of the caustic use of "circumcision" in verse 12. In antithesis, as it is, to "sinners of the gentiles,"
it brings to mind a division in humanity that has a place in Judaism
(e.g., Deut 7:1-6; see below) and in Paul's own past (Phil 3:2-5). Indeed, startling though this language is in this context, it is not without precedent in Paul, as we will see. It presupposes that the
"gentiles" as a whole are "sinners," and they are such because "by
nature" (cf. Rom 2:14) they are excluded from God's chosen

4. Verses 15–16 comprise one sentence, the "we" of verse 15, emphatically repeated in verse 16, being the subject of the main verb, ἐπιστεύσαμεν. The contrary view of Bultmann, "Zur Auslegung," 394, and more
recently Eckstein, *Verheißung,* 5–7, that verse 15 is an independent sentence
is most unlikely both because verse 15 has no verb and because the next sentence (v. 16) would have to begin with a participle (εἰδότες, "knowing"),
which would be separated too much from its governing pronoun. On the
more common view adopted here see Bruce, *Epistle to the Galatians,*
136–37; Mussner, *Galaterbrief,* 167 and note 2; Kümmel, "Individualgeschichte," 158–59; Wilckens, "Aus Werken," *Rechtfertigung,* 88 and
note 23.

people.[5] In the separatist context "sinners" has in mind the immorality of Gentiles by virtue of their "lawlessness," and Paul knew this connotation well (e.g., 1 Cor 5:1; 12:2); but in the present context "sinners" is not primarily an ethical term.[6] It denotes, rather, those who, because they do not belong to the covenant of Israel, which teaches God's will and the means of atonement for sin, stand in an essentially inferior relationship to God compared with God's chosen people. That Paul should employ such an antithesis at all leads his readers, not least his Gentile readers, to suspect a particular motivation for its use. To understand this verse and its sequel accurately it is essential to understand this motivation.

What is remarkable is not so much that he describes the Gentiles as "sinners" but that he seemingly excludes Jews from that description and thus divides humanity according to the criteria of "ancestral traditions" he has supposedly abandoned (1:13-15). This stands in stark contrast to Paul's well-known view that "there is no difference; all sinned and come short of the glory of God" (Rom 3:22-23). One must conclude either that Paul has done a complete *volte-face* or that he is making a sarcastic tongue-in-cheek concession to his opponents. The former is excluded not only by 3:22 but also by 2:17 ("if we also were found to be sinners"), which on the basis of linguistic criteria can only be interpreted as *conditio realis*.[7] In other words, it is not Paul's intention to espouse this antithesis but to destroy it.[8]

5. Among many others, see Bonnard, *Galates,* 52; Bruce, *Epistle to the Galatians,* 137; Dunn, "Echoes of Intra-Jewish Polemic," 464; idem, "Pharisees, Sinners, and Jesus," *Jesus,* 73–77. E. P. Sanders, *Judaism,* 233–35 and 265–70, is especially helpful, since he places the discussion of "exclusivism" in the context of the "doctrine of election" (265), and he balances the negative views with the positive. "Although Jews maintained various kinds of relations with Gentiles," he says, "exclusivism was part and parcel of Judaism" (266). See also Fredriksen, "Judaism," 534–35.

6. Properly noted by Betz, *Galatians,* 115; Burton, *Epistle to the Galatians,* 119; Kümmel, "Individualgeschichte," 160; Schlier, *Galater,* 89.

7. The content of the supposition ("we are sinners") is taken by Paul to be factual (see below).

8. Pace E. P. Sanders, *Law and the Jewish People,* 69, Gal 2:15 does *not* show that Paul "knows full well that observant Jews are not in fact sinners

The theology behind it is one that he would have accepted fully in the time of his persecuting the church (Phil 3:5). It is a theology that derived from Israel's self-awareness as God's chosen, fostered in recent generations—especially since the Maccabean rebellion—to enable Israel to maintain its identity despite the encroachments and persecutions of Hellenism.[9] This mentality is succinctly mentioned at this point because it sums up the opposition in Jerusalem and Antioch as well as Galatia. Sarcasm aside, this antithesis of "Jews" versus "gentile sinners" captures the most negative aspect of the views of the Galatian opponents. Of course, both for the opponents and for Paul, more fundamental than this "separatism" was the theology that lay behind it, namely, the opponents' claims for the law. Thus the law as such becomes the object of Paul's attack. But again and again Paul's arguments against the law bring him back to the issue that is the inevitable corollary of the opponents' teaching, that Gentile believers in the absence of the law cannot attain to the status of the children of Abraham (3:28-29; 4:4-7, 28-31; 5:2-6; 6:15). This "separatism," therefore, is also Paul's target, that which he in-

---

by the biblical standard" (see also idem, *Paul and Palestinian Judaism,* 1, that Paul, being "Jewish," "explicitly contrasts himself and Peter with the Gentile sinners [Gal 2:15]"). Sanders fails here to consider Paul's rhetoric; the apostle points to "the standard distinction" (*Law and the Jewish People,* 72) between Jews and "gentile sinners" in order to expose it as fallacious. Sanders, to be sure, knows that Paul "puts everyone, whether Jew or Gentile, in the same situation" (ibid., 69; see also 72), but he fails to carry this through in regard to Gal 2:15. Against Sanders here, see Eckstein, *Verheißung,* 9–10, who rightly indicates that 2:15-17 in terms both of "structure and content" (10) is parallel to Phil 3:4-8. In both texts (see also Romans 2–3) Paul starts with his former "self-estimation" based on his relationship to the law and then, "with an abrupt turn," indicates how "knowledge" of Christ (Phil 3:8; cf. Gal 2:16a) brings about a "fundamental shift" (10) in that understanding of the law and thus in his own self-understanding. This will be important for understanding the dying of the "I" in 2:19-20 (see below).

   9. Dunn has written extensively on this theme; for example, "Pharisees, Sinners, and Jesus," 61–81; "Incident at Antioch," 129–63; and "Works of the Law," 215–32, in *Jesus.*

tends to expose as a "perverting of the gospel" (1:7) both in the present passage and throughout the letter.[10] It is thus important to establish the provenance and rationale of this mentality.

Separatism

As a phenomenon of postexilic Judaism, separatism, under-stood to be Israel's awareness of being socially and religiously distinct from the Gentiles, is well documented, both in Scripture and in apocryphal literature.[11] The grace of election necessarily set Israel apart, and the Hebrew Scriptures as a whole reflect this fact (see n. 11). We must be careful, of course, not to read back into ancient times the problem that arose urgently only in the Hellenistic period, but on the other hand we must not imagine that the

10. Dunn, "Echoes of Intra-Jewish Polemic," 464, believes that "gentile sinners" is probably not Paul's language but that of the James group in Antioch. This, of course, is not impossible, but in that case there is a lot of tension between such language and the Synoptic tradition of Jesus as "friend of tax collectors and sinners" (Luke 7:34), where "sinner," according to Dunn, "is used more or less as a synonym for 'Gentile'" ("Pharisees, Sinners, and Jesus," *Jesus*, 73f.). Peter, in his eating with Gentiles perhaps showed the influence of Jesus' association with "sinners," but if so, could James have been so ignorant of Jesus' practice? Or is it that James did not connect Jesus' behavior with the later issue? In any event, I favor the view that "gentile sinners" is *Paul's* caricature of his opposition.

11. For example, Deut 7:1-6; Ezra 9:1–10:44; Neh 13:3-30; Ps 147:19-20; Jubilees 22–23; 2 Macc 6:12-16; Wis 12:19-22; 13:1–16:10 and passim (e.g., note "our enemies" versus "your [God's] children," 16:8-10). During the Maccabean rebellion three sets of laws emerged as touchstones of fidelity to the covenant: Sabbath, circumcision, and food (e.g., 1 Macc 1:41-63; 2 Macc 6–7). See Dunn, "Incident at Antioch," *Jesus*, 137–48, dealing especially with food laws. The vocabulary in Hebrew texts, followed consistently by the LXX, also demonstrates Israel's awareness of its distinctiveness from other nations. Israel is regularly designated עַם ("people," singular! e.g., Exod 1:20; Num 11:29; Deut 7:6), the other nations as גּוֹיִם ("nations," e.g., Exod 34:10; Lev 25:44) or occasionally the plural עַמִּים("peoples," e.g., Josh 4:24; Ezra 10:12). In the LXX עַם is translated λαός, and גּוֹיִם as ἔθνη. The New Testament follows the LXX's usage, and Paul himself makes full use of this distinction in terms.

separatist attitude of Paul's period had no precedent in ancient times (Deut 7 and Neh 13!).[12] There were in fact substantive theological reasons deriving from ancient traditions why Jews of the Hellenistic period felt the necessity of defining themselves as Israel over against the Gentiles and, indeed, sometimes of fighting to the death for that identity (e.g., the Maccabees).

Hellenism, sometimes by violence, more often by cultural attraction, threatened to swamp Israel with alien cultures and gods. As a response, some Jews, whose efforts ultimately issued in the Mishnah,[13] applied the priestly code, originally intended to regulate only the temple cult and its ministers, to the life of ordinary Jews.[14] In the era of our concern there were developed "rules governing what food may be eaten, under what circumstances and with what sort of people; whom one may marry and what families may be joined in marriage." The purpose of these rules was to form "a protective boundary, keeping in those who were in, keeping out those who were not." Such rules, of course, excluded "the non-Israelite from participation . . . and raised high those walls of separation and underlined such distinctiveness as already existed."[15]

12. It should be noted that "the shifts and changes in social and cultural and political life and institutions captured by the word 'Hellenization'" were a reality for Israel "long before the conquest of Alexander" (Neusner, *Judaism,* 72).

13. On the Pharisees as the probable originators of the Mishnaic code, see Neusner, *Judaism,* 70–71; and idem, *Politics to Piety,* 78–90.

14. Neusner, *Judaism,* 71–72; and idem, *Politics to Piety,* 83–90. For a general description of the Pharisees, see Dunn, "Pharisees, Sinners, and Jesus," *Jesus,* 62–71.

15. All quotes from Neusner, *Judaism,* 69, 70, and 74 respectively. See also E. P. Sanders, *Paul and Palestinian Judaism,* 206–12, who stresses the "not ungenerous" attitude of the Rabbis (210). This generosity is well demonstrated by Fredriksen, "Judaism," 533–48, but the very discussion shows the reality of the distinctiveness of Jews over against Gentiles. It is also important, of course, to remember the *spectrum* of Jewish responses to Gentiles, enabling a wide range of relationships. On this, see also Dunn, "Incident at Antioch," *Jesus,* 142–48; Segal, *Paul the Convert,* 201–7; Bright, *History of Israel,* 442–46, for a very balanced assessment of "the tension between universalism and particularism" (443).

Not surprising, given the persecution to which Jews were often subject, this separatist mentality developed very negative views of Gentiles. It was in this context that the distinction between "Jews by birth" and "sinners of the gentiles" prevailed. Thus 1 Macc 1:34 characterizes Israel's oppressors as "a sinful nation (ἔθνος ἁμαρτωλόν), lawless men." Among the Greek additions to Esther, Esther in prayer reminds God, "You know that I hated the glory of the lawless and that I abhor the bed of the uncircumcised and of every foreigner" (Esth 14:15-17 *RSV*). Similarly negative is 3 Maccabees, whose theme is summed up in 5:13: "Then the Jews . . . praised their holy God and begged him . . . to show the might of his all powerful hand to the arrogant gentiles." This book's strongly anti-Gentile tone follows the experience of Jews being persecuted by "abominable, lawless gentiles" (6:9). Wisdom of Solomon, though more philosophical in tone, also knows of Gentile persecution (15:14; 17:2) and describes Gentiles in markedly harsh terms: "For they were an accursed seed from the beginning" (12:11; see 12:3-11). In several such texts, as Dunn points out, "sinner," "lawless," and "gentile" are parallel terms; this is also true in New Testament texts.[16]

Among New Testament writers it is ingenuously assumed that "gentile" is synonymous with "sinner."[17] This is apparent in the parallelism of "tax collectors" and "gentiles" in Matt 5:46-47 (see also 6:7, 32; 10:5; 18:17). Similarly 1 Pet 4:3 describes the time before faith as the time when "the will of the gentiles" was done, who indulged in "licentiousness, passions, drunkenness, revels, carousing and lawless idolatry" *(RSV)*. Also telling is Luke's interchanging of "gentiles" and "lawless ones" in Luke 18:32; 24:7; Acts 2:23. But of all New Testament writers, the one most clearly aware of Jewish separatist notions is Paul. For him

---

16. See Dunn, "Incident at Antioch," *Jesus,* 150–51.

17. It is true, of course, as E. P. Sanders points out (*Law and the Jewish People,* 171–79), that the New Testament sometimes thinks of three groups: Jews, Christians, and pagans, the latter being designated ἔθνη ("gentiles"). But, of course, the fact that the outsiders/pagans, who are guilty of "such immorality" (1 Cor 5:1; also 1 Pet 4:3), are designated as Gentiles, speaks volumes.

Gentiles are the prototypical "sinners";[18] their receiving of righteousness by faith alone constitutes in large measure the eschatological scandal over which unbelieving Israel has stumbled (Rom 9:30-33 with 10:10-13).[19] That is why the gospel for Paul can be summed up in terms of the "gospel beforehand" to Abraham, "In you shall all the gentiles be blessed" (Gal 3:8). His awareness of "the dividing wall" between Jews and Gentiles (Eph 2:14) is graphically demonstrated in his use of the words Ἰσραήλ ("Israel"), λαός ("[God's] people") and ἔθνος ("gentile nation").

Of the sixteen instances of "Israel" in Paul, none includes Gentiles with the possible exception of Gal 6:16.[20] All of the eleven instances of λαός are direct quotes from the Old Testament; all but one are in the singular and denote Israel. Predictably, the one plural usage (Rom 15:11) denotes Gentiles, being parallel in the psalm to ἔθνη (Ps 116:1 LXX; *RSV* 117:1). Romans 9:25-26 is the exception that proves the rule, for there Paul applies to Gentiles the words of Hosea to restored Israel, thus interpreting the prophet as foretelling the time of the Gentiles' elevation to the λαός-status of Israel. Λαός ("people [of God]") is what Israel is by God's election; by definition the Gentiles could never be such except by the eschatological redeeming action of God.[21] This brings us to ἔθνη, which is used forty-four times, all being plural (except Rom 10:19 quoting Deut 32:21) and all referring to Gentiles. Most telling here are the texts that show that for Paul, even as an apostle, "gentiles" denotes those who "by na-

18. 1 Thess 4:5; cf. Gal 4:8-9; 1 Cor 5:1; 12:2; Rom 2:14; 9:30.

19. The "stone of stumbling" is, of course, Christ (10:11), but it is Christ in his role as "Lord of all" who dispenses with the "difference" between "Jew and Greek" (10:12).

20. In light, however, of Paul's consistent usage elsewhere, Burton's conclusion (*Epistle to the Galatians,* 358) regarding Gal 6:16 has much to be said for it: that it refers "not to the Christian community but to Jews . . . the pious Israel, the remnant according to the election of grace (Rom 11:5)." This is supported by Mussner, *Galaterbrief,* 417 and note 61; Bruce, *Epistle to the Galatians,* 275. For a different view see Lightfoot, *Galatians,* 225; Schlier, *Galater,* 283, note 2.

21. The other instances of λαός in Paul are Rom 10:21; 11:1-2; 15:10; 1 Cor 10:7; 14:21; 2 Cor 6:16.

ture," as it were, are "sinners" (see n. 18; also Col 2:13; Eph 2:11-12). Both Paul and his opponents take such vocabulary for granted. Beker properly notes that "both Paul and the Jew already know from their heritage the self-evident sinful condition of the Gentile; it is a point that does not need to be argued."[22] The classic expression of this in Eph 2:11-18 is fully consistent with what Paul has to say on the matter: the Gentiles, "those named 'uncircumcision' by those named 'circumcision' . . . were alienated from Israel and strangers to the promise of the covenants, without hope and without God . . . once far off but now brought near by the blood of Christ . . . who broke down the barrier of the dividing wall . . . that is, the law . . . that he might create in himself the two to be one, a new humanity."

Paul's own one-time attachment to a separatist mentality almost certainly explains his preconversion persecution of the church. It is further attested by the ease with which he describes the exalted status of Israel (Rom 9:4-5) and his own former "advantages" (κέρδη) as a Jew (Phil 3:4-7; 2 Cor 11:22). So also the Judaizers came to faith in Christ with the presumption of the religious advantage of Jews over Gentiles (see Rom 2:17-20) and thus with a separatist mentality. In 2:15 Paul uses language that sums up that thinking in a nutshell, albeit negatively. The difference between the apostle and his opponents is that the latter have not extricated themselves from this mentality and the practices of law which it demands.[23]

---

22. Beker, *Paul the Apostle*, 80. None of the forty-four uses of ἔθνη ("gentiles") denotes Israel. Romans 4:17-18 might include Israel, but the focus is certainly on Abraham as "father of many *gentile* nations." Other significant uses include Rom 1:5; 2:14; 3:29; 9:24, 30; 11:11-13, 25; 15:9(x2), 16(x2); Gal 1:16; 2:8-9; 3:14.

23. The question naturally arises whether or not Paul continued to observe the law after his call to apostleship. Davies, *Paul and Rabbinic Judaism*, 321, argues that "throughout his life" Paul was "a practicing Jew." He goes so far as to say that "at great inconvenience to himself," Paul even observed the Jewish food laws while he was a prisoner, although "he could accept food only from his practicing Jewish friends" (74 and note 3). This, however, is clearly contradicted by Gal 2:11-14 and, for that matter, by 1 Cor 9:19-23. In Rom 15:1 Paul aligns himself with the "strong" in faith who dis-

Even for them, however, there has been a shift in thinking. With the coming of Christ the law does not stand alone as the touchstone of faithful membership in the people of God; now faith and law function together in that capacity. They also probably shared with Paul and other Jews the general expectation that at the "end" Gentiles would recognize Israel as God's people and come to Jerusalem to worship Israel's God (e.g., Zech 8:20-23).[24] That general expectation would only be intensified with the experience of Gentiles joining the community of the Messiah. On this much there would be agreement between Paul and the Judaizers. The devil, as usual, was found in the details. There were some Jewish Christians, like Paul, who made no demands on these Gentiles other than they should believe in Jesus' death "for our sins." Some insisted on minimum requirements regarding food laws (e.g., James). Others, like the "believers from the party of the Pharisees" (Acts 15:5) made more radical demands, including circumcision. The Galatian opponents clearly shared the views of the latter, and it should be noted that they were not alone in doing so.[25]

---

regard laws about food and holy days (14:1-6, 14!). Galatians 1:13-15 and Phil 3:4-8 attest Paul's former "zealous" devotion to the law. E. P. Sanders, *Law and the Jewish People,* 192, takes the more defensible position that Paul "kept attending the synagogue . . . and obviously he submitted to the thirty-nine stripes" (a Jewish punishment, see 2 Cor 11:24). This indicates that "both Paul and the Jews who punished him regarded the Christian movement as falling within Judaism." This is surely correct and helps explain the harshness of this internecine struggle.

24. See Isa 2:2-4; 25:6-10; 49:1-6; Pss 22:27-28; 47 (see especially v. 9); 86:8-9. On this, see Hamlin, s.v. "Nations," *Interpreter's Dictionary of the Bible,* 3:515–23, especially 517; and E. P. Sanders, *Judaism,* 290–95, stressing the "wide variety" of views.

25. See the observations of Koester, "Gnomai Diaphoroi," 143–48. See also Dunn, "4QMMT and Galatians," 147–53. MMT has its name from a key Hebrew phrase (מקצת מעשי התורה) meaning "some works of the law." This recently published Qumran text seems to personify extreme separatism (see below, under "Works of Law," and nn. 35 and 37). Comparing it with Galatians, Dunn finds possible points of connection in (*a*) Peter's "separating himself" in Antioch (2:12); (*b*) use of Deuteronomy 27–30 and the

In the Galatian opponents this mentality can properly be called "separatism," because their teaching presupposed a clear theological distinction between themselves and the Galatians. The Judaizers believed that their status before God, as members of the Abrahamic covenant, was superior to that of the Galatians. Their purpose in Galatia, however, was essentially positive, to enable the Galatians also to attain to the inheritance of Abraham. It is doubtful, in my view, that they or James would have reduced their message to the negative language of 2:15. The harsh antithesis, "Jews" versus "gentile sinners," more probably represents Paul's distilling of their thinking to its most narrowly harsh terms. Be that as it may, this language serves Paul well. Its division of humanity into those privileged before God over against those who are "without hope and without God" (Eph 2:12) represents a clear target at which he can aim that truth that the gospel proclaims, that Christ died for the sins of *all* humankind and that the law, which has fostered the ancient division between Jews and Gentiles, no longer governs humanity. This brings us to 2:16.

2:16 The Polemical Announcement of Justification by Faith

"[We ourselves, though Jews by birth and not sinners of the Gentiles,] who know that no one is justified by works of law but through faith in Jesus Christ, we also came to faith in Christ Jesus, in order to be justified by faith in Christ[26] and not by works of law, for no one will be justified by works of law."

---

concern with covenantal curses and blessings (3:10); *(c)* the phrase "works of law"; *(d)* use of Gen 15:6 (3:6); and *(e)* the calendar of feasts (4:10). The point is *not* that Paul knew or directly reacted to 4QMMT or to Qumran itself but that "MMT preserves a vocabulary and manner of theologizing which left its mark on a wider spectrum of Jewish thought and practice, and that it was just this sort of theologizing and practice which confronted Paul in Antioch and which he wrote Galatians to counter."

26. The case for taking πίστις Χριστοῦ as subjective genitive ("the faithfulness *of* Jesus") has been made by, among others, Barth, "Faith of the Messiah," 363–70; Hooker, "ΠΙΣΤΙΣ ΧΡΙΣΤΟΥ," 321–42; and Johnson, "Rom 3:21-26 and the Faith of Jesus," 77–90. The latter is an attempted refutation of Hultgren, "Πίστις Χριστοῦ Formulation in Paul," 248–63, but

A JEWISH-CHRISTIAN CONFESSION AND ITS PROVENANCE

Beginning in verse 16—and continued in the protasis of verse 17—Paul describes the experience, as he sees it, of Jewish Christians when they became believers. To do so he calls upon the common "awareness" (εἰδότες, "knowing"), which Jews attained under the gospel.[27] Followed by εἰδότες, the ἡμεῖς (emphatic "we") of verse 15 suggests that the content of verse 16a is a confession Paul and other Jewish Christians had in common.[28] Indeed, it further suggests that the confession predated Paul essentially as formulated here, including the negative element "not by law."[29] Such a confession is reflected elsewhere in the

Hultgren's observations on syntax clearly win out in my view, as also do exegetical considerations, on which see Dunn, *Romans 1–8*, 166–67; Eckstein, *Verheißung*, 18–19; Fitzmyer, *Romans*, 345–46; Westerholm, *Israel's Law*, 111f., note 12. Galatians 2:16, with the explication of πίστις Χριστοῦ by "we believed in Christ Jesus," is an important indicator that the phrase should be taken in the usual sense. Note also Phil 1:27, πίστις τοῦ εὐαγγελίου, and Col 2:12, πίστις τῆς ἐνεργείας τοῦ θεοῦ, and other texts cited by Fitzmyer (345).

27. Pace Burton, *Epistle to the Galatians*, 119, who sees εἰδότες as expressing "the reason for the ἐπιστεύσαμεν ['we believed'] of the principal clause"; "By his [Paul's] experience under law [he] was forced to abandon it" (118); similar is Winger, *By What Law?* 133. But Paul's use of εἰδέναι elsewhere establishes that he speaks here of a "knowledge" that *follows* the faith experience: for example, Rom 5:3; 6:9; 7:14; 8:22; 1 Cor 3:16; 6:2-3, 15; 2 Cor 4:14. See Kertelge, "Zur Deutung," 216; Mussner, *Galaterbrief*, 168; Schlier, *Galater*, 89, n. 4; Wilckens, "Aus Werken," *Rechtfertigung*, 88.

28. Gaston, *Paul and the Torah*, 70, denies that "Paul means to include Jewish Christians like Cephas in the 'we's' of verse 16" and says it is "even more doubtful if Cephas or the Jerusalem church would have agreed with the formulation." For Gaston, 2:16 is the exclusive language of "the Gentile mission." This completely ignores the context of 2:11-14 and the natural meaning of "we" in light of that context.

29. That 2:16a is a Jewish-Christian confession, see Betz, *Galatians*, 115–16, note 28. Dunn, "New Perspectives on Paul," *Jesus*, 195f., comes to the same conclusion from the manner in which the confession likely functioned among Jewish Christians to distinguish their beliefs from those of other Jews and from the language of "being justified," which is essentially Jewish and covenantal. Mussner, *Galaterbrief*, 168, sees the formulation as

New Testament, in Acts 13:38b-39; 15:10-11 (see Luke 18:9-14); and James 2:14-16. There are undeniable linguistic connections between these texts and Gal 2:16 (see Rom 3:20), suggesting that at an early date Jewish Christians distinguished themselves from other Jews with regard to faith in Jesus and the consequent relativizing of the law.[30] Accordingly, 2:16a in all essentials was probably accepted by the Judaizers, but if so they certainly understood it differently than did Paul.[31]

The confession enabled Jewish Christians to distinguish their beliefs from those of the larger Jewish population. In its origins it did not intend to abrogate the law but to relativize it, setting the law in its place beside Christ: viz., "No one is justified by law (alone!), but (also!) by faith in Jesus Christ."[32] Those who believe in Christ, it is said, do not abandon the law, which he fulfilled (see Matt 5:17-19). The law, after all, as even Paul

---

Paul's. I believe that the focus on "works" may have been introduced by Paul, but at least "not by law" must predate him.

30. To be sure, these texts could be reflections (possibly misunderstandings) of Paul's preaching as is maintained, with regard to Acts, by Haenchen, *Acts of the Apostles,* 412 and 446. But Haenchen is too quick to answer no to Bauernfeind's question ". . . does not Paul himself, in Gal 2:15-16, imply as Peter's opinion what [Peter] says here [Acts 15:11]?" (446, n. 4). The coincidence of sources here is impressive. The impossibility of the law (Acts 15:10, 13:38b) is not the sum total of Luke's rejection of it as a means to salvation; rather, the law is excluded because in Christ there is "forgiveness of sins" and "righteousness" (13:38-39). James certainly reflects knowledge of the confession and reacts against a misunderstanding of it (notably Jas 2:14, 18, 20–26).

31. E. P. Sanders, *Law and the Jewish People,* 19, makes this point with regard to the simple formulation "faith in Christ," but there is no evidence of debate on this point. It was the *consequences* of faith for law-observance that focused the debate. This is apparent throughout the New Testament (see, e.g., Matt 5:17-19; Mark 2:1–3:6; 7:1-23 [note 2:19-20, 27–28; 7:19]; Acts 21:20-25; Jas 2:14-26).

32. Dunn, "New Perspectives on Paul," *Jesus,* 195, properly points out that ἐὰν μή ("except") in 2:16a does not as such exclude the law but merely qualifies it. On this combining of faith and law, see Beker, *Paul the Apostle,* 43; Bultmann, *Theology of the New Testament,* 1:280; Burton, *Epistle to the Galatians,* 167.

knows, bears witness to Christ (Rom 3:21; Acts 10:43 and passim) even as Christ confirms the law's validity (Rom 3:31). Over against other Jews, Jewish Christians maintained that the law was not by itself sufficient for salvation but that faith in the Messiah was also necessary. The compelling nature of this position is to be noted. Most important at this point, however, is the corollary of this position in the Judaizers' thinking. For them Gentiles cannot come to faith in Christ with the same status as Jews, for as Gentiles they are outside of the covenant of the Messiah, which demands observance of the law. If Gentiles were to be part of the covenant, therefore, certain prescriptions of law, including circumcision, must be fulfilled. In the absence of this observance they could not truly be heirs of Abraham, members of the people of God. Paul's interpretation of the confession, of course, is radically different. His manipulation of the confession aims to bring out this difference and thereby to undermine the interpretation of the opponents.

PAUL'S MANIPULATION OF THE CONFESSION

Ἄνθρωπος *("Human Being")*

In the discussion of 1:4a we noted that the "sins" for which Christ died are, according to Paul, the sins of all humanity equally. In other words "our" in 1:4a includes the "we" (i.e., Jewish Christians) of 2:15-17. In 2:16a the confession declares that "no ἄνθρωπος is justified by works of law." In its original context ἄνθρωπος, possibly equivalent to Aramaic אֱנָשׁ ("human") or Hebrew כָּל־חָי ("any living being," see Ps 143:2), would have been without emphasis and certainly would not intend to place Jews and Gentiles in the same position before God. Paul's context, however, throws ἄνθρωπος into a new light. The division of humanity into "Jews" and "gentiles" contrasts with the confession's statement about *any* "human being." If δέ ("but") is original to verse 16a, then the contrast between the division of humanity in verse 15 and "human being" in verse 16 is even sharper.[33] In any

---

33. It is taken as original by both Nestle and United Bible Society, though they place it in brackets. Lightfoot, *Galatians,* 114, and Schlier,

event, in Paul's context ἄνθρωπος calls attention to the common
plight of all humans before God. There are none who can appeal
to the law, and that means that faith in Christ is the sole hope of
salvation for every "human being."[34]

Ἔργα Νόμου *("Works of Law")*

Paul's manipulation of the confession becomes evident with
this phrase in that it is repeated twice in such a way that the antithesis between "law" and "faith" is unmistakably brought forward. This raises the possibility that Paul elaborated on the
simple ἐκ νόμου ("from law") or the like of the original formula
(cf. ἐν νόμῳ ["by law"], 3:11; 5:4). This possibility is enhanced
when we note that apart from Paul ἔργα νόμου is extremely rare[35]
and yet is *a favorite Pauline phrase in polemical contexts* (Rom
3:20, 28; cf. 3:27; 4:2, 6; 9:12, 32; 11:6; Gal 3:2, 5, 10). Further,
the fact that in those contexts ἔργα *can sometimes stand alone as
an abbreviation for the whole phrase* indicates how determinative that word is for the meaning of the phrase, enhancing the

---

Galater, 88, are among those who accept it as genuine; Dunn, "New Perspectives on Paul," *Jesus,* 204, note 25, regards it as "unlikely." The issue
cannot be decided for certain one way or the other.

34. Schlier, *Galater,* 89, note 5, says that here, as in Rom 3:28; 1 Cor
4:1; and 11:28, ἄνθρωπος can only be equivalent to τίς ("someone"). Schlier
is probably correct about the latter two texts, but in Rom 3:28, as here, the
context possibly gives ἄνθρωπος a certain sharpness; the same may be true,
in my opinion, of its occurrence in Rom 1:18, 4:6; and 7:24a.

35. See the survey of Lohmeyer, *Probleme paulinischer Theologie,*
37–48, briefly duplicated by Tyson, "Works of Law," 423–25. Until very recently, Kertelge's observation in 1968 ("Zur Deutung," 214) that the Hebrew
phrase תּוֹרָה מַעֲשֵׂי ("works of law") "is not verifiable in the literature" held
good. However, the phrase is now clearly attested in an extremely sectarian
Qumran document (4QMMT). See note 25, above; also see Abegg, "Paul,"
52–55 and 82; the same issue of *Biblical Archaeology Review* (56–61) contains the composite Hebrew text of MMT with a translation by Qimron and
Strugnell (see line 27, on 60–61); Eisenman and Wise, *Dead Sea Scrolls Uncovered,* 180–200, also containing Hebrew text and translation (see line 30,
on 199–200); Kampen, "4QMMT," *Reading 4QMMT,* 138–43.

possibility that it was introduced by Paul.[36] The emphasis upon
ἔργα is unmistakable in Rom 3:27-28; 4:2, 6; 11:6; Gal 3:10-12;
and in the present verse. Clearly what Paul attacks has everything
to do with the law's demand for the performance of its prescriptions, its ἔργα. The antithesis to Paul in regard to "works of law"
is Qumran.

Although rare, the usage of the phrase in Qumran may not
be without significance for understanding Paul,[37] especially if its
general context there and related language are taken into account.
4QMMT in particular and Qumran texts in general represent the

36. These points, emphasized here in italics, are missed by E. P.
Sanders, *Law and the Jewish People,* 46, when he says, "In the phrase, 'not
by works of law' the emphasis is not on *works* abstractly conceived but on
law, that is, the Mosaic law." Sanders sees no critique by Paul of the law's
demand for performance; what Paul attacks is "the notion of Jewish privilege
and the idea of election" (47, and idem, *Judaism,* 264). But the "notion of
Jewish privilege" is completely dependent on possession of and obedience
to the law (e.g., Deut 4:7-8; also note Rom 2:17-20). What stands behind
their sense of privilege—the real object of Paul's attack—is their demand
that if Gentiles wish to attain the same status then they must obey the law's
prescriptions, its ἔργα. If ἔργα has no punch to it, then why is it included?
Westerholm, *Israel's Law,* 117–18, is quite right that "works of law" and
"law" are often "coterminous" (118—e.g., Rom 3:20), but this does not render ἔργα superfluous. To the contrary, it supports the thesis Westerholm
(119) argues so well that Paul (with reference to Rom 4:1-5) demonstrates
"that the broad category of 'works' cannot be a factor in salvation in order to
exclude the subcategory, 'works of law.'" In Galatians also, a misplaced
focus on "deeds" as constitutive of the divine-human relationship is the object of Paul's attack.

37. So far the phrase is not attested outside Qumran. On *Testament of
Dan* 6:9 (ἐκδιδάσκων διὰ τῶν ἔργων [νόμου] τὸν νόμον κυρίου) as an "un-
doubtedly Christian" interpolation, see R. H. Charles, *Testaments of the
Twelve Patriarchs,* xlix and 142; but to the contrary, see Charlesworth, *Old
Testament Pseudepigrapha,* 1:810. For other instances or analogous phrases
within Qumran documents, see Kampen, "4QMMT," *Reading 4QMMT,*
138–39 and notes 40 and 41; Dunn, "Works of the Law," *Jesus,* 220. As
Kampen indicates (n. 40), the supposed instance in 4QFlorilegium 1.7 (pace
Eckstein, *Verheißung,* 25) almost certainly reads מעשי תודה ("acts of
thanksgiving"), on which see also Martinez, *Dead Sea Scrolls Translated,*
136; idem, "4QMMT in a Qumran Context," *Reading 4QMMT,* 24.

extreme edge of Jewish separatism in the Second Temple period. They also represent, in comparison with liberal Christian Judaism (i.e., Paul), the far opposite end of the spectrum in regard to interpretation of the law. For the writers of 4QMMT, not only are Gentiles and their offerings to be barred from the Temple, so also are "the bastard and the man with crushed testicles"[Deut 23:1-6] and the deaf and the blind.[38] The law here is constantly understood in terms of "works." The blind are barred, according to 4QMMT, because they "cannot see so as to avoid polluting mingling," and the deaf because they "hear neither law, nor statute, nor purity regulation."[39] It was because of incorrect performance of law that the sectarians of 4QMMT "separated" themselves from the rest of "the people."[40] This same extreme separatism characterized the Qumranites as a whole. The Judaizers are far from such extremism, but their separatist attitude toward Gentile believers and their general focus on doing the "works of the law" are not unrelated. As opposed to 4QMMT, their "texts," so to speak, in addition to the Pentateuch, would be Jubilees, 4 Ezra, and 1–4 Maccabees.[41] In contradistinction to the tradition of strict

38. Eisenman and Wise, *Dead Sea Scrolls Uncovered,* 194–95; see also Martinez, *Dead Sea Scrolls Translated,* 77–79 and his emphasis that "the contents [of Qumran texts] are surprisingly uniform" (xlix); what we are dealing with, for the most part, is "sectarian theology and customs." Of course, that very sectarianism warns against seeing Qumran as in any way typical of Judaism as a whole. Paul and Qumran are the opposite ends of a wide spectrum.

39. Eisenman and Wise, *Dead Sea Scrolls Uncovered,* 195. For a different translation, see Martinez, *Dead Sea Scrolls Translated,* 78.

40. On whether this "separation" was from Israel as a whole or represented a further break among the sectarians themselves, see Abegg, "Paul," 54; see also Dunn, "4QMMT and Galatians," 147–48.

41. *Jubilees* and 1–2 Maccabees could have been available as *written* "texts," but certainly 4 Ezra and (probably) 3–4 Maccabees were not. The point is that such texts bear witness to the concern for strict observance of the law, which, it seems, also characterized the Judaizers. The traditions of the Maccabean martyrs (e.g., 2 Maccabees 6–7) and *Jubilees'* interpretation of the law of circumcision (*Jub* 15:25-32)—even the angels were circumcised!— must have been particularly influential. Eisenman and Wise, *Dead Sea Scrolls Uncovered,* 182–83, regard MMT as comprising "two letters,

law observance apparent in these texts and in the Judaizers' teaching, ἔργα νόμου, for Paul, is a sharply *negative* characterization of the law.

This means that νόμος *in this context* must be carefully distinguished from νόμος in texts like 4:21b ("hear the law") and 5:14 ("the law is fulfilled"; also Rom 3:21). In these latter texts νόμος is used in a broad positive sense as equivalent to "scripture," the revelation of God's salvific design (γραφή in Gal 3:8; Rom 15:4). In Gal 2:16, however, and in fact throughout the first part of Galatians (through 4:10) νόμος is used more narrowly to designate the requirements demanded by the law, "the sum of specific divine requirements given to Israel through Moses."[42] In Galatians this latter sense of νόμος is dominant and is treated by Paul in a thoroughly negative fashion. This is the law which "I destroyed" (2:18) in coming to faith and to which "I died that I might live to God" (2:19). As a system that demands "deeds" of obedience, the law can even be portrayed as a "curse" from which Christ, by his death, "redeemed us," that is, all humanity (3:13-14). This is not because the ἔργα themselves are either good or bad[43] but because the law thus understood determines the divine-human relationship in terms of its prescriptions rather than in terms of faith (3:11-12). The law in this negative sense is characterized by its demand of obedience to its ἔργα and as such, it should be stressed, determines the entirety of the existence of its adherents.[44]

---

something like Corinthians 1 and Corinthians 2," which, "if placed in the first century [C.E.], where [they] would prefer to place it," might have "Agrippa I (c. AD 40)" as addressee. This would make MMT's reach, and thus its influence, rather more far reaching than I am envisaging.

42. Westerholm, *Israel's Law,* 108. See his excellent discussion (106–21), which brings a lot of clarity to a difficult topic, though it will become apparent that I differ with him at some points. I will deal with the two senses of νόμος in some detail in chapter 5.

43. Properly stressed by Westerholm, *Israel's Law,* 120–21. I would emphasize, however, that though doing "works of law" is not bad in itself, neither does such obedience bring justification. In other words, even the one who might be "blameless" in regard to law-observance is not ipso facto, in Paul's view, "righteous" before God (Phil 3:6-9).

44. See Böttger, "Paulus": Paul thinks of the law here "as a unity in

The genitive νόμου defies any simple definition.[45] The best
clues for understanding the phrase are to be found in its antithesis
to πίστις Χριστοῦ ("faith in Christ") and in its synonymous restatement in 3:12, where "the one who does them shall live by
them [=ἔργα]" is antithetical to "the one who is righteous by faith
shall live." In Paul's view, the Judaizers make "being righteous
[before God]" (δικαιοῦσθαι)—albeit in the context of covenant—
dependent on performance of law. Against this Paul insists on the
gospel's radical claim that to receive the gift of righteousness it is
only necessary to have faith. Ἔργα νόμου defines the divine-
human relationship in terms of performance of the law's demands; "faith in Christ," which has to do with ἀκοὴ πίστεως (3:2,
5), sees the relationship in terms of the obedient acceptance of
God's gift.[46] For Paul,

---

all its parts," even though "the special role of the 'ceremonial' laws, particularly circumcision," must be recognized as "a component of the covenant"
(83), which itself completely "determines the existence of the circumcised"
(84). That is why, for Paul, one must "die to the law" (93–95). See also
Winger, *By What Law?* 137, and his definition of "Jewish νόμος," 104.

45. The issue is discussed extensively by Lohmeyer, *Probleme
Paulinischer Theologie,* 33–37, and Tyson, "Works of Law," 424–25, making use of Lohmeyer's findings. See also Dunn, "Works of the Law," *Jesus,*
220. The phrase is perhaps to be rendered as an objective genitive, "the service of the law" or "nomistic service" (Tyson), but genitive of origin is also
possible, the "works" being "obligations set by the law, the religious system
determined by the law" (Dunn). Gaston, *Paul and the Torah,* 100–106, argues for subjective genitive, which is impossible in light of texts like Gal
3:12; against Gaston, see also Westerholm, *Israel's Law,* 116–17.

46. Ἀκοὴ πίστεως (literally, "hearing of faith") is a very important
phrase for understanding what Paul understands faith to be. The key to the
phrase is ἀκοή, which in 3:2-5 stands over against "works" just as "faith"
stands over against "law" (see Betz, *Galatians,* 133, n. 50; Kieffer, *Antioche,*
46). Ἀκοή is probably best rendered by "hearing." The "true parallel" here
is ὑπακοὴ πίστεως in Rom 1:5 (Lightfoot, *Galatians,* 135), which is epexegetic genitive ("obedience which is faith"). The focus in Gal 3:2 and 5 also
falls on faith as acceptance of the gift *as opposed to* the performance of the
law's demands. Thus, for example, Burton, *Epistle to the Galatians,* 147,
paraphrases ἀκοὴ πίστεως as "a believing-hearing acceptance of the
gospel," and Mussner, *Galaterbrief,* 207, is similar: "obedient acceptance of

faith is not the *prerequisite* and *condition,* which humans of themselves must satisfy in order to gain salvation; it is, rather, the *mode (Art und Weise)* by which God grants to humanity a share in his own righteousness. *Fides qua creditur* is therefore not the *condition,* but the *manner* of receiving salvation; for Paul righteousness is gained not *propter fidem,* but *per fidem.*[47]

In 2:16 as elsewhere (3:11-12; Rom 3:27-28) "faith" stands over against "doing" in a programmatic fashion, for Paul is dealing with first principles, specifically with what is the basis of the divine-human relationship. For Paul, the Judaizers' theology gives human action, as defined by law, too great a focus and thus, on the basis of law, distorts the divine-human relationship and divides humans from one another.

That Paul is working out this critique of the law at the level of fundamental principles and thus intends to expose "works" in general as an inadequate basis of the divine-human relationship is clear both in Galatians and Romans. In Gal 2:19-21 Paul disqualifies the law radically: "I died to the law that I might live to God. . . . [I]f justification is through law, then Christ died for nothing." Law as such here is denied any place in determining human status before God. This is not because either the Mosaic law, or any other, is necessarily evil in itself or because law necessarily "leads to legalism, self-righteousness and self-estrangement" (partially agreeing with Sanders). Nor is it simply because "it

---

the preaching of faith." Paul, then, takes pains to distinguish faith from ἔργα νόμου, for it is in no sense a "work." Faith, for him, describes from the human side the relationship to God created by the love of Christ (Gal 2:20). Faith partakes of the character of gift (see Schlier, *Galater,* 93; Bultmann, *Theology of the New Testament,* 1:319). That is why faith, like grace (e.g., Rom 4:4; 11:6)—which describes the relationship from God's side—stands as the opposite of works, and Paul can speak of "the coming of faith" (Gal 3:23), which is identical with the domain of grace (5:4). None of this denies that the law, for the opponents, was "gift" (e.g., Deut 4:7-8), but for Paul the relationship presumed by the law's demands is quite different from that of faith.

47. Eckstein, *Verheißung,* 19; he properly stresses (18–19), against Betz, *Galatians,* 117, that faith for Paul is to be understood in terms of *fides qua* (faith as relationship) rather than as *fides quae* (faith as creed).

lacks Christ . . . [and] does not provide for God's ultimate purpose, that of saving the entire world through faith in Christ" (disagreeing).[48] That may be true, but Paul's central critique is that the law cannot fulfill its promise of "life" (3:11-12, 21) and thus leads its adherents, Jew or Gentile, into illusion. In 3:1-22 as I shall argue, Paul so distances the law from the Spirit, and from the Abrahamic blessing and its promises, that its appearance can be referred to as an illegitimate intrusion (3:15-17) between the promise and its fulfillment in Christ. This denigrating of the law is rhetorical and can only be assessed in the context of the Galatian crisis. Paul's reason for it is the way the law is being seen to function by the Galatians in their relationship with God. Its "social function" for Jews is not the primary issue for Paul.[49]

48. E. P. Sanders, *Law and the Jewish People,* 46 and 47 respectively. This goes along with Sanders' argument in *Paul and Palestinian Judaism,* 482–84, that in Gal 2:21; 3:2-5, and 10–12, "what is wrong with the law" for Paul is simply that "it does not rest on faith," but he can only uphold this by ignoring Paul's polemical contrast between "faith" and "doing," which is obvious both in 3:10-12 and 2:16. The basic error in Sanders' view of Paul, as I see it, is his insistence that what dominates Paul's thinking regarding the human plight and salvation is "the transfer [by faith] from one lordship to another" (497; see also 500 and passim), whereas Paul's concern, in my opinion, is with the *qualitative* shift in the divine-human *relationship.* Paul sees the gospel as refocusing the relationship on "grace" and "faith" as those are understood apart from the law (as with Abraham; see Romans 4; Galatians 3); he therefore rejects the opponents' teaching, which cannot conceive of "grace" and "faith" apart from obedience to the law's demands. This means that Paul attacks the law directly with regard to the *manner* in which it construes the relationship as being based on obedience to its demands.

49. Dunn, "Works of the Law," *Jesus,* 216–19 and 238 (see also ibid., "New Perspectives on Paul"), has made "the social function of the law" the key to understanding Paul's critique of the law. In Gal 2:16, according to Dunn, "What [Paul] is concerned to exclude is the *racial* not the *ritual* expression of faith; it is *nationalism* which he denies not *activism*" ("New Perspectives on Paul," 198; see also "Works of the Law," 228f.). The law's "social function" is indeed a crucial aspect of the context of the debate, but Paul deals with the law's theological role, its power to convince the Galatians that without "deeds of law" they are not "seed of Abraham." For Paul this is an illusion produced by the law's own demands. The problem, then, is

Romans 4:2-5 is further indication that Paul thinks of any "works," whether propounded by Moses at Sinai or Peter in Jerusalem, as radically excluded *if they are made the basis of human relations with God.* The point of the passage, says Westerholm, is to exclude "the broad category of 'works'" in order to show that "the subcategory 'works of law'" must also be excluded. This links with 3:27-28, where *any* human "boasting" before God is excluded, whether by Jews (2:17-20) or Gentiles (11:17-21). The "boasting" of Paul's opponents must indeed have had to do with "Jewish pride in [their] status as the people of the one God," as Dunn says,[50] but a distinction has to be made between the *fault* of Paul's opponents as he sees them, on the one hand, and the *mode of Paul's response* on the other. How the law functioned for Paul's opponents—its social function to enable Jews to maintain their identity, on which Dunn has shed so much light—does not perfectly match Paul's critique of the law (see n. 49). The "social function" of the law is not the point for Paul but its *theological* function. It is the law's claims upon the *entire world* that Paul must contest, not merely how it functions for his opponents or within parts of Judaism. "Righteousness was reckoned" to Abraham, as the prototype for all nations (Gal 3:6-8), of one "who did

---

not merely the illusion of Jewish nationalism but the illusion of "doing," and that is a universal problem. For critique of Dunn on this, see also Winger, *By What Law?* 137, note 57; Westerholm, *Israel's Law,* 117.

50. Dunn, "Works of the Law," *Jesus,* 238, responding (unsuccessfully, in my view) to Westerholm's critique (see preceding note). Hays, *Echoes of Scripture,* 54–57; idem, "Have We Found Abraham?" 76–98, sees Romans 4 as Paul's *denying* that Abraham was "our forefather according to the flesh" (against this reading of Rom 4:1, see Dunn, *Romans 1–8,* 199). Such a denial, however, in no way serves Paul's purpose. Christ's own descent "according to flesh" from David (1:3) and "the patriarchs" (9:5) is happily affirmed by Paul; and in Rom 9:6-13 it is not the *fact* of physical descent that is argued but simply its (in)significance. What Paul denies is that physical ancestry or any of Israel's gifts and privileges is any guarantee of privilege before God (9:8). The proper focus on Abraham as the father of all nations (4:9-12) *depends on* Paul's prior focus, which Hays wants to avoid (*Echoes of Scripture,* 56; "Have We Found Abraham," 89–90), on Abraham's being "justified" without "works."

not work, but who believed in the [God] who justifies the ungodly" (Rom 4:5). "Ungodly" here stands for those "without
works"—not the evil necessarily, simply those who have no status before God—and in antithesis to those (of any nation) who do
have "works" and who might imagine that thereby they have a
basis for "boasting." Dunn confuses, it seems to me, how the law
functioned sociologically among the opponents with how Paul
thought of it theologically.

It is not enough, therefore, with Dunn, to take ἔργα νόμου
as denoting primarily those laws that separated Israel from the nations, enabling Israel to maintain its identity in the face of persecution and the pressures of assimilation. Dunn is surely correct
that those laws—circumcision, Sabbath, and food laws—were
prominent "boundary markers" for many Jews in this time period
and that they were of particular importance for Paul's opponents
in Jerusalem, Antioch, and Galatia.[51] And of course I agree with
Dunn that Paul attacks separatism. The issue is on what basis he
does so. Behind separatism lies the belief that law grants to Israel
and thus to Jewish Christians a status before God to which Gentiles can attain only by themselves obeying the law. The Galatians
are close to accepting this belief, and thus that is the point Paul
must refute. What the law affirms about Jews is not a problem for
Paul, as his affirmations of Israel's election and gifts indicate
(Rom 3:1-2; 9:4-5). It is what the law, in the Judaizers' teaching,
denies about Gentiles that is the problem. And what is denied is
their standing before God on the basis of "works of law" they
have not performed. Just as in Antioch the nature of the meals was
not the point for Paul but rather Peter's (i.e., the law's) implicit
denial of the full status as believers of Gentiles "for whom Christ

51. Dunn, "New Perspectives on Paul," *Jesus,* 191–95, and "Works of
the Law," ibid., 219–23. In responding to the critiques of Stuhlmacher and
Westerholm, Dunn, "New Perspectives on Paul ," 210–11, and "Works of the
Law," 223 and 238, insists that in his understanding "'works of law' denote
all that the law requires of the devout Jew" (223) and not only Sabbath, circumcision, and food laws. I accept this. My disagreement with Dunn centers
on his making the "social function of the law" (238) into the hermeneutical
key for Paul's theology of the law.

died," so also in Galatia the law's function as an "identity marker" for Jews is neither denied nor problematic. It is rather the law's own fundamental claim to determine for *all humanity* the basis of the divine-human relationship that Paul must expose as a denial of God's new eschatological deed in Christ, of offering "right-eousness" as a "gift" to all simply on the basis of faith. As de-manded in the Judaizers' teaching, ἔργα are a denial of grace, and thus must be radically excluded.[52]

After the main clause, to which I shall turn in a moment, ἔργα νόμου appears again in the purpose clause. The repetition heightens the antithesis. Not only did "works" play no part in "our" coming to faith, neither did we look to it to do so. The faith-event is thought of here solely in terms of faith in Christ and of what God accomplishes through him. And, anticipating exegesis of 2:19, what this will come to mean is that law is excluded not only from the *event* of faith but also from the *living* of faith, that is, from "living to God."[53] Confirmation that ἔργα νόμου has a polemical edge to it comes with the further repetition of the phrase in the psalm citation, but first the sentence's main clause.

The Main Clause and Its Purpose Clause

The assertion of the main clause is deceptive in its simplicity: "We too became believers in Christ Jesus." Both grammatically and theologically all else is subordinate to this. The polemical intent is no less evident than was the case with the repeated ἔργα νόμου.

---

52. Dunn, "Works of the Law," *Jesus,* 239, misses the point of West-erholm's critique when he says: "To deduce [like Westerholm presumably] from this analogy [viz., Rom 4:4-5] that Paul regards 'working' as wholly negative and 'reward' as entirely excluded for the Christian makes nonsense of Romans 2:10, 13 and 1 Corinthians 3:8, 14." First, Westerholm, *Israel's Law,* 120, does not see "working" as "negative"; quite the contrary. Second, Paul's rejection of "works" as such does not leave him without direction for ethical exhortation (see Westerholm, *Israel's Law,* 198–216), a point I will elaborate with reference to 2:19-20.

53. Against Sanders, *Law and the Jewish People,* 93–114, who says that "Christians are judged according to how well they fulfill the law" (112). Against this, see Westerholm, *Israel's Law,* 198–205.

With καὶ ἡμεῖς ("even we") Paul takes up "we Jews by birth" from verse 15a, driving home the point that he is speaking of Jewish Christians, who in the time previous to believing in Christ considered themselves privileged over against "sinners of the gentiles." The inceptive aorist main verb points to the event of conversion.[54] "Coming to faith" was a transforming event, a rescue "from the present evil age" (1:4). It was this event that led to the conviction enunciated in verse 16a and to the "discovery" contained in the protasis of verse 17. It was an event that so radically transformed their lives as Jews that they ought now to be able to say, as the apostle said of himself (1:13-16), that they have "died to the law"; all that matters is Christ (2:19-20; cf. Phil 1:21; 3:8-11).

The main clause, therefore, has significant echoes at other points in the letter. In the first instance it harks back to the aorist participle καλέσας of 1:6, by which Paul reminded the Galatians of their own "call" to faith. It also evokes "the gospel which we proclaimed" and which the Galatians "received" in 1:8-9. In the more immediate context it anticipates κατέλυσα ("I destroyed") in 2:18, where the faith-event is seen as equivalent to abrogating the law's power. In this connection the main clause also anticipates "I died" in 2:19 and beyond that is evoked by "you received" in 3:2 and by "you became known by God" in 4:9. These aorist verbs repeatedly bring Paul's readers back to the event of their conversion, and in every instance the transforming power of that event is at the forefront, as it is in the purpose clause of 2:16.[55]

That ἵνα δικαιωθῶμεν ("so that we might be justified") in the purpose clause has to do with the creation of a new eschato-

54. Schlier, *Galater*, 94, maintains that "we came to faith" also has baptism in mind. Baptismal language is clear enough in 2:19, as we shall see, but even there it is not baptism as such that is important (similarly 3:26-29) but rather the transforming power of the one event of "coming to faith" and "being made righteous." Contra Schlier, on this point, see especially Eckstein, *Verheißung*, 20 and note 117.

55. Under the analysis of 2:18 we will see how these aorists regularly contrast with the present-tense verbs in their immediate contexts to highlight the difference between the original faith-event and the presently threatened apostasy.

logical reality hardly needs saying. It has already been prepared for by 1:4b, and its meaning will soon be developed further in 2:19-20. It is this new eschatological reality that shows up the bankruptcy of the law. The power of the law is in "the present evil age"; it is a power of bondage (3:23-25) that has nothing to do with the freedom of believers in Christ (5:1-4). The latter statements, especially 5:1-4 ("you" = Galatians; see also 4:8-9), speak directly to the Galatians' threatened apostasy, but in 2:16 Paul is describing for the Galatians' benefit the experience of *Jewish* believers. They also experienced a transformation when they came to faith, but in their case what Paul has in view is their rescue from the bondage of the illusion created by their understanding of the power of the law. That is why he speaks of their experience in terms of a conviction ("knowing," v. 16a) gained by faith. This same experience of coming to a new awareness is also presupposed in εὑρέθημεν καὶ αὐτοὶ ἁμαρτωλοί ("we also were found to be sinners") in 2:17. The recounting of the Jewish-Christian experience in this regard carries within it its own warning to the Galatians not to be fooled in the same way. It is no accident that Paul warns the Galatians of the "bewitching" to which they are falling prey (3:1; cf. 4:21; 5:7-8).[56] What is peculiar about this theme in Galatians is that Paul's direct polemic against the law as such places the blame for the illusion not primarily with the opponents but with the law itself, for what the law claims it cannot in fact accomplish (3:11-12). This brings us to the psalm citation.

The Psalm Citation (Ps 143:2)

The separatist vocabulary of verse 15 and the Jewish-Christian confession of verse 16a represent common vocabulary that both

---

56. Internecine religious polemics, of course, invariably are characterized by one side claiming that the other misunderstands or, worse yet, "perverts" (1:7) the religious tradition in question. That Paul regards the Judaizers as misunderstanding the law is beyond all dispute (e.g., Rom 10:2-3). Their misunderstanding, for him, corresponds to his own before his call (Phil 3:3-9), when he swapped one estimate of himself with its concomitant view of the law for another. Paul presumes on this misunderstanding also in Rom 9:30–10:3 and 2 Cor 3:7-18.

the Judaizers and Paul knew from their Jewish and Christian background. The radical disagreement between them is veiled at first by this vocabulary. Paul's polemical intent is present, to be sure, but it breaks into the open only gradually, first with ἄνθρω-πος, then progressively by the repetition of the profession's content in the purpose clause and especially with ἔργα νόμου. It is with his free citation of Psalm 143 (142 LXX)[57] that Paul shatters any remaining ambiguity due to common vocabulary. His overturning of its natural meaning renders it a foreign element for those who think in the Judaizers' terms.

As understood by the opponents and the nearly convinced Galatians, the psalm is far from abrogating the salvific significance of the law. The psalmist knows, of course, that in a lawsuit with God no human can stand "justified" (δικαιωθήσεται) and thus at the beginning and end of the prayer appeals to "your [God's] righteousness" (ἐν τῇ δικαιοσύνῃ σου, vv. 1 and 11). On the other hand, the psalmist knows what the Judaizers also will not deny, that God's righteousness to Israel has been shown precisely in the giving of the law, a gift not granted to Gentiles (e.g., Ps 147:19-20 = LXX vv. 8-9; Deut 4:5-8).[58] It is unthinkable within this tradition to deduce from one's poor human standing before God that one ought to eliminate the law as a means of

57. Mussner, *Galaterbrief,* 174, doubts that this should be regarded as an actual "citation," since by no means the whole of Ps 143:2 is quoted. He holds to this in spite of Schlier's objection (*Galater,* 94, n. 5), which he (Mussner) quotes, that verse 16c would be "superfluous if not recognized as a quotation." Mussner says further (175) that the "scripturally unlearned" Galatians would not have recognized these words as a quotation from Scripture, and (n. 37) that Paul's overturning of its natural meaning excludes it as either a "quote" or a "scriptural argument." But that, of course, would put into question Paul's use of numerous other texts, including Deut 27:26 in 3:10 and Gen 13:15 in 3:16.

58. On this, see Mussner, *Galaterbrief,* 170–71, stressing, from Old Testament, apocryphal, and Qumran texts, that for Jews "faith" and "works of law" constitute a "vital synthesis"; also see E. P. Sanders, *Paul and Palestinian Judaism,* 84–101, showing from Tannaitic literature that the rabbis interpreted the commandments of the law as part and parcel of the covenant of God's love for Israel.

"being righteous before God." Thus the psalmist prays, "Make known to me, O Lord, the *way* in which I should walk (v. 8). . . . Teach me to do your *will*" (v. 10), where the vocabulary leaves no doubt that it is the doing of the *law* that is intended.[59] The opponents, even as believers in Christ, continue to stand in this tradition. They cannot conceive of the gospel except in terms of the law and its ἔργα. For them, unless the prescriptions of the law are obeyed there is no hope of being found "righteous" before God either now or at the final judgment. The righteousness of faith presupposes the righteousness of the law.

Paul no longer holds such an understanding of δικαιοῦσθαι, and thus he ignores the context of the psalm citation. Indeed, by the addition of ἐξ ἔργων νόμου ("by works of law") he not only ignores it, he also reverses its meaning. For the psalmist, humanity's one hope of attaining "righteousness" is the law's guidance in the divine "way" and "will." Paul, however, detaches God's "will" from the law and defines it purely in terms of Christ's death "for our sins" (1:4c). Paul's freedom with the Scriptures here will be repeated many times in this letter (e.g., 3:10-13). Such freedom demonstrates that for him the helplessness of the law, on the one hand, and Christ as the one hope for all humankind, on the other, are what Psalm 143 and the Scriptures in general truly assert. This brings us to the issue of what Paul means in this letter by δικαιοῦσθαι ἐκ πίστεως.[60]

---

59. In Ps 119:1 (LXX 118:1) "way" stands in synonymous parallelism with "law," as does "will" in Ps 40:9 (LXX 39:9). This exact parallelism is not found in Psalm 143, but these examples and others (e.g., Pss 1:1-2; 18:22-24 [LXX 17:22-24]) make it apparent that by "way" and "will" is meant the "law" of God. Eckstein, *Verheißung,* 28–29, contrasts LXX Psalm 142 here with LXX Pss 7:9 and 25:1, where appeal is made to "my righteousness" and "innocence" as grounds for God's help, and thus concludes that Paul does not so much "completely change the sense" (29) of Psalm 142 as draw out "its deepest religious meaning" (quoting Oepke, *Galater*, 60). This is true from Paul's perspective, but not from that of the opponents.

60. On the choice of ἐκ ("from"), see Mussner, *Galaterbrief,* 147: "The reason that the apostle on this occasion writes ἐκ instead of διὰ πίστεως ["through faith"] is that he is already under the influence of the quote from Hab 2:4 which he cites at 3:12."

JUSTIFICATION BY FAITH

Paul's Preference for Positive Assertions

In the study of 1:4 and its developments in the letter I noted that the ὅπως ("so that") clause introduces positive assertions that describe the reality and characteristics of the age of faith. The traditional formula revolves around the remitting of sins, but Paul's description of the salvific effect of Christ's death is more positive. This preference stands out when we note that the vocabulary of forgiveness is almost completely absent from his letters.[61] The "for our sins" formula looks to what has been *removed;* Paul prefers to speak of what has been *created.* He does not dwell on the removal of sins, since this is not adequate to express the new eschatological reality created by the gospel. Accordingly 1:4b, as we have seen, is made to anticipate the letter's vocabulary of "life" (2:19-20; 3:11; 5:25), "freedom" (2:4; 4:21–5:1), "redemption" (3:13; 4:5), "inheritance" (3:7-9, 18, 29), "adoption" (4:5-7), and "new creation" (6:15). It is primarily in these terms that Paul conceives of the life of faith. This is not unimportant for understanding Paul's preference for the language of justification by faith, the primary vocabulary of the *propositio* and thematic of the letter as a whole (3:6, 8, 11, 21, 24; 5:4, 5), for it too is part of Paul's positive vocabulary for the new existence of those who belong to Christ.[62]

---

61. In stark contrast to Luke-Acts, ἄφεσις ("forgiveness") never occurs in Paul's letters and only twice in the deutero-Pauline tradition (Eph 1:7; Col 1:14). The verb ἀφιέναι ("forgive") occurs only at Rom 4:7, a quote from Psalm 32 (LXX 31:1). Paul's nearest equivalents are the exceptional usage in Rom 6:7 (δεδικαίωται ἀπὸ τῆς ἁμαρτίας, "has been freed from sin") and the phrase διὰ τὴν πάρεσιν τῶν προγεγόνοτων ἁμαρτημάτων ("by passing over sins previously committed") in Rom 3:25, which is probably from the tradition.

62. E. P. Sanders, *Paul and Palestinian Judaism,* 499, also notes the absence of "repentance and forgiveness" from Paul, but he sees "righteousness by faith" as "primarily a negative argument against keeping the law" (492) and says that the "primary thrust" of the argument in Galatians 2–3 is "negative" (493). Sanders is not wrong, in my view, to assert the negative, polemical edge of "righteousness by faith"; it has everything to do with Paul's exclusion of the law, but his focus on "the participatory categories" as

The Hebrew Antecedents of Δικαιοῦσθαι *("Be Made Righteous")*

צֶדֶק *("Righteousness") as a Relational Term*

צֶדֶק, and its cognates, which stand behind Paul's concept of justification/righteousness, have to do with describing a person's behavior according to the demands of a given relationship.[63] This is illustrated graphically in Gen 38:26, when Judah says of Tamar, "She is more righteous than I" (צָדְקָה מִמֶּנִּי = LXX δεδικαίωται Θαμαρ ἢ ἐγώ). That the norm of צֶדֶק is the relationship rather than an abstract objective norm is shown here in that Tamar's צֶדֶק consists in her fidelity to her dead husband in a totally unlawful, even immoral, fashion (Deut 23:17).[64] Nevertheless, with regard to the relationship she was in the right. The term's essentially relational meaning, whether used of humans or God, is confirmed by the words with which it is regularly paralleled, such as חֶסֶד ("compassion"), אֱמֶת ("faithfulness," e.g., Pss 33:5; 85:10-13; 143:1, 11-12), and מִשְׁפָּט ("justice," 89:14), themselves all relational terms. When צֶדֶק is applied to God it has to do with divine fidelity to the covenant, often in spite of Israel's infidelity (e.g., Deut 32:4-9; Neh 9:32-37; Ezra 9:15; Dan 9:4-14).[65]

"the heart of Paul's theology" (502), along with his view that "transfer from one lordship to another" dominates Paul's soteriology (497), causes him to miss the term's positive aspect.

63. Properly stressed by Achtemeier, s.v. "Righteousness in the Old Testament," *Interpreter's Dictionary of the Bible,* 4:80–81; Von Rad, *Old Testament Theology,* 1:370–74; and Kertelge, *Rechtfertigung,* 16–20. With no difference of meaning the noun is sometimes written צְדָקָה.

64. Von Rad, *Genesis,* 359, provides the background that shows that Tamar's was no act of ordinary prostitution; nevertheless it remained "repulsive to Israel"; "Tamar, in spite of her action which borders on a crime, is the one justified in the end" (362), and that was "because she had shown loyalty to her relationship to this family" (idem, *Old Testament Theology,* 1:374). See also 1 Sam 24:17f.; 26:23; Prov 21:26; 29:7; and Ezek 18:5-9, similarly illustrative texts.

65. On "righteousness of God" in the pre-Pauline church kerygma, specifically in Rom 3:24-26, see Kertelge, *Rechtfertigung,* 48–62; on the parallel terms see Von Rad, *Old Testament Theology,* 1:372, note 6. Since God's צֶדֶק was known in salvific deeds for Israel, the latter are sometimes

צֶדֶק *as a Forensic, Eschatological Term*

The relational emphasis of צֶדֶק means that in a legal situation the judge's decision was based not so much on a legal codex as on the particulars of the relationship in question. In Isa 5:7 the divine judge examines Israel with regard to its care for the oppressed, but in place of מִשְׁפָּט and צְדָקָה, Jahweh finds מִשְׂפָּח ("bloodshed") and צְעָקָה (the "outcry" [of the poor]). Doom, therefore, is pronounced on those "who acquit the guilty (מַצְדִּיקֵי רָשָׁע, hiphil participle) for a bribe and deprive the innocent of their right (צִדְקַת צַדִּיקִים, v. 23, *RSV*)." Here both the verb and the noun have a place in the legal forum, the factitive form of the verb (mostly hiphil; sometimes piel) denoting the declaration of innocence (also Deut 25:1; Isa 53:11), the noun denoting the state of innocence in the context of the trial (also Job 6:29; Ps 35:27). This forensic sense is also illustrated in Judah's pronouncement over Tamar. As Von Rad points out, "Judah assumes competence as judge."[66]

A similar declaratory forensic use of the term, this time employing the adjective (צַדִּיק), occurs in Ezek 18:5-9. In this instance also it is significant that the conditions of צֶדֶק include not only the observances of law but also supererogatory actions not definable by law, such as giving bread to the hungry and clothes to the naked. In other words, the forensic usage presupposes the basic relational sense of the term. With regard to the declarative forensic sense, Bultmann points to such texts as Pss 37:6; 17:2, 15; 51:14: "A man has 'righteousness' or 'is righteous,'" says Bultmann, "when he is acknowledged to be such . . . when he is

---

called צִדְקוֹת יהוה ("the triumphs of the Lord" *[RSV]* Judg 5:11; 1 Sam 12:7; Mic 6:5). God's צֶדֶק, says Von Rad, is "always a saving gift. It is inconceivable that it should ever menace Israel" (372, n. 7, and 377).

66. Von Rad, *Genesis,* 360. It should be stressed, however, that the forensic sense of the term is only one aspect of its meaning, "for it [צֶדֶק] embraces the whole of Israelite life, wherever men found themselves in mutual relationships" (idem, *Old Testament Theology,* 1:373). In Gen 38:26 the qal form is used because Judah is quoted directly. A report of his pronouncement would use the hiphil form, הִצְדִּיק אֶת־תָּמָר ("he declared Tamar to be righteous").

. . . 'pronounced righteous.'"[67] The one who is not so vindicated, even if innocent, clamors to be pronounced righteous, as is most apparent with Job (9:2; 13:18; 33:32 and passim; cf. Isa 43:25-26; 53:11). In the absence of that vindication one's righteousness is in doubt (Job 27:5; 32:1-2).[68] Accordingly, especially in the factitive forms, the verb bears the meaning "vindicate," "save," or "deliver" in that it denotes the rescue of the oppressed, even if the latter were not entirely innocent of wrongdoing.

It is in Second Isaiah (Isaiah 40–55) that this meaning of the root (to save) comes most strongly into play (see also Psalm 85). In Isa 50:7-9 it stands parallel with עָזַר ("help"), with God as subject of both verbs, and in 51:5-6 the noun צְדָקָה is paralleled with יְשׁוּעָה ("salvation"). Second Isaiah's eschatological and universal vision also lends to צֶדֶק a meaning that provides clear precedent for Paul's notion that in Christ God creates for all nations a new existence definable in terms of "righteousness."[69] Isaiah 45:20-25 provides a good example of this. The invitation to

---

67. Bultmann, *Theology of the New Testament,* 1:272.

68. E. P. Sanders, *Paul and Palestinian Judaism,* 494, rejects Bultmann's view (*Theology of the New Testament,* 1:270ff.) that "in Judaism righteousness is a forensic/eschatological term," since within Palestinian Judaism "the term 'righteous' was applied to those who were proper members of the covenant. . . . They do not wait to be declared righteous; the righteous are alive and well." Sanders provided the evidence for this much earlier in his book (e.g., 204 and passim). That same evidence, however, indicates that righteousness is both forensic and eschatological (e.g., 201–5, 380–82). Sanders' concern is to show that present righteousness does not *earn* future righteousness (204), which is well and good, and that "the formal meaning of righteousness" is *not "the same* for Paul and Judaism" (494, my emphasis), a point I accept. But that the term both in Jewish literature and in Paul is forensic and eschatological is beyond dispute. Along with its basic relational sense, these are the aspects of the term that hold it together in Paul and prevent it from becoming the fragmented concept that Sanders takes it to be (492–95).

69. On the universalism of Second Isaiah see Von Rad, *Old Testament Theology,* 2:243–44. Paul, of course, is not only dependent on Second Isaiah for his view; he also appeals to Gen 18:18 (Gal 3:8), and note LXX Ps 86:5 in Gal 4:26. In Rom 9:25ff. he particularly appeals to Hosea 2. It is especially noteworthy, however, that Paul describes his own call to be "apostle to the gentiles" (Rom 11:13) in the language of Second Isaiah (Isa 49:1 in Gal 1:15).

salvation goes out to all the nations (vv. 20, 22) from the God who is צַדִּיק וּמוֹשִׁיעַ ("righteous and who saves," v. 21). From God's mouth has gone forth צְדָקָה (v. 23), and "in the Lord all the off-spring of Israel יִצְדְּקוּ ("shall triumph"=*RSV*; literally= "shall be righteous," v. 25).[70] In line with this, 54:17 sums up the Lord's promises of salvation as צִדְקָתָם מֵאִתִּי ("their salvation from me"). Also noteworthy is 51:1-8, where צְדָקָה is coupled with יְשׁוּעָה no less than three times (vv. 5, 6, 8) and where the object of God's salvation is not only Israel but "the peoples" (vv. 4–5; note LXX ἔθνη ἐλπιοῦσιν). The passage ends with "My צְדָקָה will be forever and my יְשׁוּעָה to all generations."

In these texts צדק has two distinct but closely related senses. It is, first, God's righteousness and fidelity to the whole of crea-tion and to the covenant with Israel. And second, it is the right-eousness that God creates within Israel and "the peoples." This righteousness is a new eschatological reality, synonymous with vindication and salvation. Righteousness rained down from heaven causes righteousness to spring up from the earth (45:8); a new relationship is formed between God and humanity (54:9-17).[71] In further texts, particularly in Third Isaiah, צדק has a

70. *RSV* (and *NRSV*) strangely and misleadingly inserts the word "in" into the translation of 45:23: "From my mouth has gone forth *in* righteous-ness. . . . " It *should* read, "From my mouth has gone forth righteousness, a word that shall not return." This is not unimportant, for like the "word" of 55:11, the "word, righteousness," spoken by God, accomplishes its purpose, that is, "all the offspring of Israel יִצְדְּקוּ" (45:25, LXX δικαιωθήσονται, "shall be vindicated"). God's צדק creates צדק within Israel and ultimately within all nations (51:4-5).

71. To be accurate I should stress that Old Testament visions of the end focus on Israel; the inclusion of the *nations* is indeed apparent in some prominent texts, as noted, but there are at least as many texts that envision judgment on and even the destruction of the nations, including within Sec-ond Isaiah (e.g., Isa 49:22-26; also Mic 5:5-15; Dan 7:23-27). Gentile na-tions are included insofar as they attach themselves to Israel (Isa 56:1-8; Zech 8:20-23). The biblical writers clearly distinguished between righteous and unrighteous Gentiles (see Fredriksen, "Judaism," 544). My description focuses on the positive ideas about Gentiles that evidently were picked up by New Testament writers and Paul in particular.

sense not emphasized in the texts quoted, namely, that Israel must "do righteousness" (56:1) as a moral requirement. This meaning is apparent in Ezek 18:5, which has been mentioned, and is not uncommon in the Old Testament.[72] It also finds a place in the letters of Paul (e.g., Rom 6:13, 19; 2 Cor 9:9-10; Phil 1:11).

THE LANGUAGE OF JUSTIFICATION IN PAUL

Paul's Language Over Against His Opponents

It is the language of Second and Third Isaiah that, in my view, provides the primary background for Paul's understanding of the confession that δικαιοσύνη is God's gift, received by faith apart from the law. For Paul the gospel is the eschatological revelation of the "righteousness of God" (Rom 1:17; 3:21-22). Its purpose is that all who believe in Christ δικαιωθήσονται (3:24-26; Gal 2:16; 3:8, 24). The universalism of Second Isaiah is emphatically taken up in Paul's understanding of the gospel. That Paul uses the language of this prophet to describe his own call to preach the gospel to Gentiles is good reason for believing that Second (and Third) Isaiah's use of צדק had formative influence on Paul. Most important is the prophet's vision of God's righteousness being exercised in a new and decisive way to effect a new situation on earth, the righteousness, according to Paul's interpretation, of all humanity.

For both Paul and his "contemporaries among [his] people" (Gal 1:14) "righteousness" was covenant language. Within the Judaism of Paul's heritage, righteousness was maintained by obedience to the law, what Sanders has called "covenantal nomism."[73]

---

72. It is clearly found in Deuteronomy (e.g., 6:25; 24:13), as Von Rad, *Old Testament Theology,* 1:379 and 383, indicates. Within Isaiah 40–66 it is only with what moderns call Third Isaiah (56–66) that צדק gains a clear ethical meaning (56:1; 58:2; 59:9). Paul, of course, recognized no distinction between Second and Third Isaiah. From the latter texts, Deuteronomy and elsewhere, he knew that "righteousness" also had to do with moral demands on the human recipients of the righteousness of God (e.g., Rom 6:1-23).

73. E. P. Sanders, *Paul and Palestinian Judaism,* especially 419–28. Sanders rightly rejects the idea that Paul's theology is a new form of

Paul is also well aware of the primacy of grace in Israel's consciousness; indeed, he affirms it and relies upon it for his own argumentation against "righteousness by law" (e.g., Rom 4:1-17; 9:6-13; Gal 3:6-18). The law functioned within the Judaism of Paul's experience as a fundamental aspect of the relationship with God, but Israel's obedience to the law was not the foundation of the relationship. Its foundation was God's gift, and there is no reason to believe that the opponents denied this or that Paul only came to this conviction after his call to be "apostle to the Gentiles." It was a conviction he must have known also as a Pharisee, as texts like Rom 3:1-2 and 9:1-4 indicate; God's righteousness consists in fidelity to Israel even if Israel was unfaithful (Rom 3:3-4). For Paul's Jewish contemporaries, therefore, and specifically for his opponents, "righteousness" in the sense of obedience to the law's demands was simply Israel's obligation under the covenant of grace with God and as such was a requirement for salvation.[74] It is this indispensable role of the law in the divine-human relationship that Paul the apostle no longer accepts.

Paul's disagreement with the Judaizers, therefore, has to do, first, with how their understanding of the law must now be radically changed in light of God's action in Christ, which reaches out beyond Israel to the whole world. It goes without saying that Paul emphasized the *universality* of God's offer of salvation in a way that far exceeded even the most universal vision of Israel.[75] Paul

---

"covenantal nomism" (511–15), but he does so primarily because of his insistence that "participationist transfer terms" dominate Paul's soteriology (514). Sanders thereby eliminates any direct critique of the law by Paul.

74. See Westerholm's (*Israel's Law,* 143–50) excellent statement of this point, properly taking especially Räisänen to task for his denial that Judaism understood the law in this way. That salvation was at stake is particularly clear if one takes seriously a generalizing statement like Jubilees 30:21-23: "If they transgress . . . they will be blotted out of the book of life."

75. See E. P. Sanders, *Paul and Palestinian Judaism,* 497: "Jewish expectations" about Gentiles being "brought in at the eschaton" have to do "with obeisance to the Jewish law and the worship of the one true God on Mount Zion, not the universalizing of the way of access to salvation," and certainly not "the abolition of the law."

also emphasizes the *present reality* of righteousness as a gift that anticipates the future judgment far more than the Scriptures or any sector of contemporary Judaism. Bultmann notes, "The first difference from Jewish usage is that Paul asserts of this forensic eschatological righteousness that *it is already imputed to man in the present* (on the presupposition that he has faith)."[76] Ernst Käsemann disputes that this is so very unique to Paul, but even he concedes "that Paul lays the strongest emphasis on the present nature of salvation."[77] And Paul does so nowhere more clearly than in Galatians, including in the statements on justification (see 3:7-9, 24-29; 4:5-7), even though 2:16-17 and 5:5 also envisage future judgment.

Paul's sharpest disagreement with his contemporaries has to do with the new radical understanding of grace to which he has come in light of the Christ-event, an understanding that leads him to direct and harsh criticism of the law and of the manner in which it functions in the thinking of his opponents. Paul does not deny the reality of grace within his opponents' consciousness, but he has come to the point of denying that it is linked with the law in the manner they assume. For them the law, just like God's other salvific actions for Israel, was a manifestation of divine grace. For Paul, however, in light of God's action in Christ, specifically with

76. Bultmann, *Theology of the New Testament,* 1:274. Note Sanders' disagreement on this point, to which I have referred (n. 68, above). In Jewish literature those obedient to the law are called "righteous" and look forward to the reward of "righteousness" in the world to come. I am not disagreeing with Sanders on this when I state that the presence of righteousness is more pronounced in Paul than among his Jewish contemporaries. The difference is apparent in Paul's statements that "the justified . . . have peace with God" (Rom 5:1); the event of justification was a "dying to sin" so as no longer to "live in it" (6:2). By the power of the Spirit, righteousness in the believer is an anticipation of the blessings of the eschaton (Gal 3:1-29), and it enables life now, "in the flesh," to be lived "dead to sin" and law but "alive to God" (2:19-20). This is the *positive* reason why "repentance and forgiveness" language are absent from Paul. See Beker, *Paul the Apostle,* 215–18, on sin, in Paul, as "an impossible possibility."

77. Käsemann, "Righteousness of God," *New Testament Questions,* 178.

respect to Gentiles, it is now apparent that the law was never intended to have a determinative role in the covenant between God and Israel, much less in the "new covenant" (2 Cor 3:6), which also includes the Gentiles. The law, therefore, is not on a par with the call of Abraham or the election of Jacob (i.e., Israel; see Rom 9:6-13). On the contrary it was secondary, "added because of transgressions" (Gal 3:19-25; see Rom 4:15), and as such was to be in effect for only a limited time.

"The law" being spoken of here, of course, is the law in that narrow sense of a system of requirements that defines "righteousness" in its own terms and therefore necessarily excludes those— most especially Gentiles—who do not live by its prescriptions and thus inevitably come under its curse (3:10-13). When Paul excludes the law as a means of δικαιοῦσθαι, therefore, he is not denying the covenant or God's gifts to Israel; he denies simply that the law has the essential role in the covenant, which the opponents claim for it. From the beginning, Paul asserts, the covenant did not have to do with "works" as such but was grounded in "grace" and in "promise" (Rom 4:1-18; 9:6-13; Gal 3:6-29), terms he interprets "apart from the law." In insisting on "grace," so understood, as the true foundation of the original covenant, Paul can attack the law, as understood by the opponents, as an illegitimate intrusion (3:15-17) and its definition of righteousness as an illusion (3:11-12) to which the Galatians are in danger of falling victim. But what "even we" *Jewish* Christians "know" by faith, says Paul, is that "works of law" are of no avail in attaining righteousness before God. Anything contrary to this "knowledge" does not conform to "the truth of the gospel" (2:14; see 5:7-8). What this will lead to is that the ἐγώ ("I") that defined itself in terms of the status granted by observance of law must "die" in order to "live to God" (2:19). In 2:16 Paul prepares for this by emphatically excluding "works of law" as a means of attaining δικαιοσύνη. This is the negative edge of the doctrine of justification, but it also has a clear and important positive edge.

Justification as New Creation

Justification by faith is a *present* reality (3:23-29) just as surely as it is also waiting final fulfillment (5:5).[78] It is to be noted that in 2:16 all three instances of δικαιοῦσθαι are in the passive voice (cf. 3:8), indicating that it is God's action that is in view. The tenses and moods vary between present indicative, aorist subjunctive, and future indicative. The latter, of course, is dictated by the psalm (LXX), but the question remains how all these are coordinated in terms of the present and the future. Of the present indicative Bultmann says that it is not "a genuine present, but the timeless present of didactic statement and may therefore apply, in spite of the tense, to the decision of God in the coming judgment." This accords with Bultmann's interpretation of justification in Paul as having primarily declarative forensic force,[79] as opposed, say, to Schlier's understanding that δικαιοῦν *also* bears the notion of "transforming power" ("'gestaltende Macht'").[80] We shall turn to this in a moment. For now it must be conceded to Bultmann that the use of the verb in 2:16, including the present tense, is clearly forensic and eschatological. Paul has in view God's eschatological verdict upon believers, a future event with present effect. This is confirmed by the aorist and future tenses, both of which envisage both present experience and the situation at the

78. For full discussion of this balance between present and future regarding justification, see Bultmann, *Theology of the New Testament,* 1:274–79; Kertelge, *Rechtfertigung,* 128–34.

79. Bultmann, *Theology of the New Testament,* 1:274 and 276 respectively. Ridderbos, *Galatia,* 99, says: "The *not justified* [of 2:16] is used in the typically Pauline forensic sense. It expresses neither an ethical change or influence, nor a *iustum efficere* in the sense of causing someone to live a holy, unimpeachable life; it expresses, rather, the juridical judgment of God, in which man is protected from the sanction of the law in the judgment of God, and thus goes out acquitted." This quasi justification ("'as if' he were righteous," Bultmann, 277) is properly rejected by Bultmann and stands in radical contrast to Schlier (see following note and n. 86, below).

80. Schlier, *Galater,* 90, in stark contrast to Ridderbos (preceding note). Subsequent discussion will make it clear that I favor Schlier's emphasis. See the very balanced discussion on this by Kertelge, *Rechtfertigung,* especially 113–34.

coming judgment.[81] Paul's quotation from Psalm 143 in Rom 3:20 includes the words "before thee [=God]" making unmistakable Paul's understanding of the forensic and eschatological sense.[82]

The question arises, however, whether the forensic and eschatological connotations of the word are all that Paul has in mind. How far does the present reality of righteousness go? Bultmann's view is that "the righteousness which God adjudicates to man (the righteousness of faith) is not 'sinlessness' in the sense of ethical perfection, but is 'sinlessness' in the sense that God does not 'count' man's sin against him (2 Cor 5:19)." But for Bultmann this righteousness is not a mere "as if." This and other misunderstandings of the term, he maintains, all see in δικαιοῦσθαι "the ethical quality of a man, whereas in truth it means his relation to God." Accordingly the grace of God in the gospel addresses to every person "the decisive question: Will you surrender, utterly surrender, to God's dealing—will you know yourself to be a sinner before God?"[83] This is all undeniable, in my view, but "freedom," "adoption" and "new creation" have to do with more than recognizing oneself as a sinner. Though all of these terms denote gifts of the eschaton, the specific thrust of Galatians is that the

81. Dunn, "New Perspectives on Paul," *Jesus,* 207f. explains the coordination among the tenses in 2:16 very well. His response (1c) to the critique of Räisänen ("Paul's Break with Judaism," 543–53), who maintains that δικαιοῦσθαι in Gal 2:16 is simply a "transfer term," is very telling.

82. The psalmist employs a simple forensic metaphor; Paul envisages a forensic and *eschatological* situation. Ziesler's thesis (*Meaning of Righteousness,* 1) that in Paul as in the term's Hebrew and Greek background "the verb 'justify' is used relationally, often with the forensic meaning 'acquit,' but that the noun, and the adjective δίκαιος, have behavioral meanings" cannot be consistently carried through, as is apparent with the noun in Gal 5:5 (see also 2:21) and with the usage of the verb and its development in 2:16-20. E. P. Sanders, *Paul and Palestinian Judaism,* 493f., says: "Dr. Ziesler has now indicated to me that he does not disagree with the position that righteousness is *more than* ethical uprightness. He had been concerned to emphasize that it meant at least uprightness against the view that it refers to imputed 'fictional' righteousness." I agree with this latter emphasis.

83. Bultmann, *Theology of the New Testament,* 1:276, 277, and 285 respectively.

eschaton can be experienced *now;* the age of faith has come (3:23-25). The point is that the intent of Paul in *this* letter and its crisis situation must be taken into account; particularly in Galatians δικαιοῦσθαι has to do with "transforming power."[84]

Schlier argues persuasively for this on the basis of Paul's general usage.[85] But even within the brief confines of 2:15-21, verses 19-20 develop the meaning of δικαιοῦσθαι in a direction that goes beyond simple forensic-eschatological justification. Being "crucified with Christ" means that, for the believer, the old order has been destroyed (see Rom 7:1-6). The very "self" (ἐγώ) of the believer died "in order to live to God." It is not merely that "sins" are removed and the punishment due under the law is annulled. Rather, the believer is rescued "out of the present evil age," so that the law itself is rendered null and void and the relationship with God is based, as with the ancient covenant, "apart from" Sinai, on grace and faith. Accordingly, the ἐγώ, which was in slavery under the law's dominion, is now replaced by the ἐγώ, in which "Christ," not "self" as understood from the law, is Lord, and faith in him is the watchword of life "in the flesh." The forensic-eschatological sense of δικαιοῦσθαι, while accurate, is not in itself adequate to describe what Paul means by "I no longer live, Christ lives within me."[86]

84. Ibid., 78, recognizes that "adoption" is not only "a longed-for goal" as in Rom 8:23, but also "a present thing" as in Rom 8:15f. and Gal 4:6f., but understandably he does not see the particular thrust of Galatians with respect, for instance, to the Spirit: that whereas elsewhere the present experience of the Spirit points to *future* fulfillment, in Galatians it is the guarantee of the *presence now* of "blessing" and "adoption" (3:14; 4:6).

85. Schlier, *Galater,* 89–91.

86. On the "effective" as well as "forensic" sense of justification by faith in Paul, see especially Kertelge, *Rechtfertigung,* 113–34. He properly asserts that recent scholarship has gone beyond discussion of "two conceptual categories separate from one another," either "forensic" ("juridical") or "effective" ("mystical," "ethical," 114); "The declaring of sinners to be righteous has not only forensic but, as forensic, also *'effective'* significance" (123). "Effective" is more fully defined as follows: "For Paul 'justification' denotes the 'enactment,' legally established by God in the present time, for the salvation of all humans. The *enactment-character* of God's saving work

This positive viewpoint answers the needs of the Galatian situation no less than the negative assertion "not by works of law." Indeed these correspond to one another as the good news and the bad news, so to speak, of Paul's gospel for Galatia. Whereas the "bad news" undermines the Judaizers' separatism and their exalting of the law, the "good news" for the Galatians is that what they experienced by faith was a real eschatological event, a crossing of the boundary line between the age dominated by sin and law and the dominion of God's grace. Käsemann, it seems to me, is quite correct in his assertion that what distinguishes Paul's theology from both "Christian enthusiasts" and "Jewish apocalyptists" is not so much "realized eschatology" as "the unprecedented radicalization and universalization of the promise in the doctrine of the justification of the ungodly."[87] The Galatian opponents could not envisage that God would justify the Gentiles by faith *apart from the law,* but this is precisely what Paul asserts. God in Christ is establishing a new relationship with all peoples without distinction in which the barriers of the law are destroyed and there is created from all nations one people. As already noted, Paul uses far more vocabulary than the δικαιο-root to explain this conviction, but we cannot understand Paul's use of "justification" language unless we appreciate its place within this positive vocabulary.[88]

---

is articulated, to be sure, by means of the juridical-forensic structure of the concept of justification. But God's enactment does not consist in a decree which remains merely extrinsic, rather it signifies the actual establishing of a new reality by God. Nevertheless the new existence of the justified, which is brought about by God, is not to be thought of as a static condition ("Verfaßtheit") in humans, but as a *relationship ("Beziehungsrealität").* In other words, it is an existence which consists in nothing other than a divine-human relationship, which is newly created by God, and which is characterized by the lordship of God and the obedience of humans" (127). As such, "righteousness by faith" in Paul can be seen as connected to his ethical instruction.

87. Käsemann, "Righteousness of God," *New Testament Questions,* 178. The phrase "realized eschatology" is used and placed in quotes by Käsemann. It was coined, as far as I know, by Dodd, *Parables of the Kingdom,* 35.

88. It is appropriate in this context to consider insights from the debate between Käsemann, "Righteousness of God," *New Testament Questions,*

In my view, 2:16 points to the dual cutting edge of the
gospel, its power, on the one hand, to "destroy the wisdom of the
wise" and, on the other, to "bring into existence what has no existence" (1 Cor 1:19, 28; Rom 4:17). To be sure, this requires further development both in the *propositio* and in the coming
probatio, which is duly provided. The terms, however, are established here that make the gospel "a word on target"[89] for the Galatian churches. With 2:16, however, Paul has not yet finished with
the gospel's negative edge, its undercutting of the opponents'
separatist notions. It is in fact the latter that is most markedly pursued in 2:17.

2:17 The Consequence of the Law's Impotence
for the Law's Adherents

But if, in seeking to be justified in Christ,
we also were found to be sinners,
does that make Christ an agent of sin? By no means!

---

and Bultmann, "ΔΙΚΑΙΟΣΥΝΗ ΘΕΟΥ," 12–16, on the phrase δικαιοσύνη
θεοῦ. The debate focuses initially on the genitive θεοῦ; is it "subjective
genitive" (Käsemann) or "genitive of origin" (Bultmann)? As far as that
goes, Bultmann has the better textual support (e.g., Rom 5:17; 9:30; 2 Cor
5:21; Phil 3:9). The difference comes to expression when Bultmann says,
"To be sure the gift of δικ. θεοῦ is based upon God's action, but δικ. does
not designate the action as such, but rather its result" (14). For Käsemann
"the righteousness of God" is primarily God's *action,* so that "the essential
meaning of the gift" is "the lordship of Christ" ("Righteousness of God,"
176). Käsemann is irrefutable when he says in relation to Gal 2:20, "The gift
which is being bestowed here is never at any time separable from its Giver.
It partakes of the character of power, insofar as God himself enters the arena
and remains in the arena with it," a point Bultmann (14–15) essentially accepts. Käsemann's corrective (176) concerning the gift, "which is an entity
in itself," is therefore vindicated, but if what is changed by God's action is
the divine-human relationship, then it is easier to see that righteousness is indeed a gift "from God" transforming the individual, which yet entails as
much a divine "claim" and "demand" as it does "promise" and "hope" (Bultmann, 15).

89. Beker, *Paul the Apostle,* 12.

2:17 AS REFLECTIVE OF THE GALATIAN SITUATION

Our earlier investigation of the Jerusalem and Antioch incidents persuaded us to maintain that Paul composed them and the *propositio* with the Galatian situation as the primary target of his theological statements. We have found this to be consistent with the polemical intent of 2:15-16, in which Paul manipulates both separatist vocabulary and the confession of justification by faith according to the needs of the Galatian crisis. In the verse of our present concern it will be no less important to adhere to our initial conviction. In the history of interpretation it is verses 17–18 that are most pulled back and forth by interpreters between Antioch and Galatia. Bruce and Ridderbos, for example, see Antioch as no particular help at this point, while Feld and Mussner see it coming to the fore.[90] The interpretation here will pursue the thesis that these verses refer primarily to the Galatian crisis, with Antioch—particularly with respect to verse 18—remaining illustrative of what Paul attacks (viz., the "rebuilding" of the law).

Those who interpret verse 17 primarily against the background of Antioch regularly take the conditional clause to be "unfulfilled" (i.e., "we" were *not* "found to be sinners") and the apodosis to be a *reductio ad absurdum*.[91] Mussner, for example, takes verse 17a as a reference to Peter's table fellowship with the Gentile Christians at Antioch. By his withdrawal from that fellowship Peter has implied that it was a sinful action. He engaged in it, however, on the conviction that justification is to be sought in Christ alone. The further implication of Peter's withdrawal, continues Mussner, is that Christ is the one who promoted the sinful action, an absurd conclusion that neither Peter nor the Judaizers

90. Bruce, *Epistle to the Galatians,* 141; Ridderbos, *Galatia,* 101; Feld, "Christus Diener," 120–21; Mussner, *Galaterbrief,* 176.

91. In this category belong Beyer and Althaus, "Galater," *Die kleineren Briefe des Apostels Paulus,* 20; Bonnard, *Galates,* 54; Cosgrove, *Cross and the Spirit,* 137f.; Dunn, *Epistle to the Galatians,* 141f.; Ebeling, *Truth of the Gospel,* 128–30; Kieffer, *Antioche,* 54–55. An exception to this is Burton, *Epistle to the Galatians,* 125. On "simple" or "real" conditional clauses, see below.

could accept.[92] Very similar is Kieffer: "In associating with gentile Christians and thus renouncing legal prescriptions they [Peter and the rest] believe that they have become sinners."[93] Among other problems, the obvious weakness of this is that it has to equate unsegregated table fellowship with "seeking to be justified in Christ." This equation, however, by no means arises clearly from the text. It can be established only on the presupposition that Paul has the Antioch incident as his primary focus, and even then it is tenuous. Seeking justification in Christ and table fellowship are quite separate moments in the Christian experience, and the former is an unlikely way of referring to the latter, whether for Paul or anyone else.

From the flow of the text it is better to see verse 17 as arising from the statement of principle in verse 16 and to understand the objection ("Is Christ then an agent of sin?")[94] as deriving from the opponents, who cannot accept Paul's radical interpretation of this principle as applying *equally* to Jews and Gentiles.[95] The objection appears in another form in Rom 3:8; 6:1 and 15. It is not unlike the complaint against Jesus' association with sinners (Matt

92. Mussner, *Galaterbrief,* 176f.

93. Kieffer, *Antioche,* 55; see also Dunn, *Epistle to the Galatians,* 141: "The surprising discovery for Paul (and Peter) was evidently that their eating with Gentiles caused them to be regarded as 'sinners,' even by their fellow believers"; also Cosgrove, *Cross and the Spirit,* 133, "Was the custom of Peter and the other Jewish Christians to eat with the uncircumcised Gentile believers *wrong?*" But Paul's text is: "If, in seeking to be *justified in Christ,* we were found to be sinners." There is no reference here to "eating with Gentiles."

94. Regardless of how the particle ἀρα (on which see Kieffer, *Antioche,* 53f.) is taken (whether illative [ἄρα] or interrogative [ἆρα]), the objection must be in the form of a question. This is apparent from Paul's use of μὴ γένοιτο ("by no means"). See Mussner, *Galaterbrief,* 176 and note 45; Oepke, *Galater,* 60.

95. That the objection derives from the opponents is a fairly common view: see Betz, *Galatians,* 120; Burton, *Epistle to the Galatians,* 127 (these both also ascribe v. 17a to the opponents, which I do not); Duncan, *Paul to the Galatians,* 67f.; Oepke, *Galater,* 60; Ridderbos, *Galatia,* 101; Schlier, *Galater,* 95f. Feld, "Christus Diener," 121, takes verse 17 as *Peter's* words to Paul in *Antioch.*

9:11; Luke 15:1-2) that an easy acceptance of those outside the law not only transgresses the law but promotes that transgression in the name of grace.[96] Grace without law, the opponents would assert, quickly becomes cheap grace, and Christ is thus made "an agent of sin." Such an objection to Paul's preaching could be persuasively argued and would certainly demand some response from Paul, which he provides both in this letter (5:13–6:10) and even more extensively in Romans (notably 2:1-16; 6:1-23). The evident reality of the objection in Romans (3:8, "some are saying . . .") and its similarity to that in Galatians make it apparent that we are dealing with an objection from real opponents rather than with a *reductio ad absurdum* produced by Paul.

On the other hand, the similarity of the objection in the two letters should not blind us to the different handling of it in Galatians over against Romans. In Romans the premise to the objection has to do with the radical nature of grace (5:20, "Where sin abounded, grace abounded the more"), in Galatians, with human bondage under sin ("Even we were found to be sinners"). The premise in Galatians, I suggest, corresponds to the crisis in that situation. Paul is battling with a Jewish-Christian separatist mentality. Against that, a major weapon for him is the assertion that *all humans alike* are enslaved in bondage to sin (3:22). Verse 16 has prepared for this with its exclusion of the law, and verse 17 seals the matter with its assertion that "even we" Jews "were found" in the light of the gospel to be "sinners" no less than the Gentiles. Humanity's common enslavement to sin is a crucial notion underlying the *probatio* (3:10, 21-25). It suits Paul's purpose well to

96. See Schlier, *Galater*, 95f. Tannehill, *Dying*, 56, disagrees with Schlier on this: in light of Judaism's well-known system of repentance and forgiveness, "the assertion that Christ is made a servant of sin must rest on some other basis than the fact that Christ accepts those who were sinners but have decided to do better." But this misses the point. Probably Jesus himself, and certainly Paul, proclaimed God's acceptance of sinners *apart from the terms dictated by the law.* E. P. Sanders, *Jesus and Judaism,* 206f., says, regarding Jesus' ministry to sinners, that he offered them inclusion in the kingdom "even though they did not make restitution, sacrifice, and turn to obedience to the law." See also the remarks of Meier, *A Marginal Jew,* 2:149f., essentially accepting Sanders' thesis.

introduce the opponents' objection with the premise that Jewish Christians also have been exposed as "sinners."[97] Thus, though the objection derives from the opponents, its premise derives from Paul, being equivalent to Rom 1:18–3:19, which culminates in the resounding assertion "There is no difference; all sinned and come short of the glory of God" (3:22-23). Galatians 2:17 takes the ground from beneath the feet of his separatist opponents and thus conforms perfectly to the demands of the crisis as Paul sees it. But our line of interpretation cannot be substantiated simply by viewing these verses in a Galatian as opposed to an Antiochian context. We must turn therefore, to the linguistic issues in this verse.

THE LINGUISTIC ISSUES IN 2:17

"Seeking to be justified in Christ" (v. 17a)

The δέ ("but") signals a new point of departure in the argument.[98] Nevertheless, Paul resumes the content of verse 16, as δικαιωθῆναι makes clear; it is still a matter of "our" purpose "to be justified" before God. The participial phrase ("seeking to be justified in Christ")[99] is equivalent to the main verb and purpose clause of verse 16 ("we believed in Christ in order to be justified

97. Ἀμαρτωλοί ("sinners") means the same in verse 17 as in verse 15 in that it denotes one's lost *status* before God. In verse 15, with respect to Gentiles, they are "sinners" by virtue of being "lawless," outside the covenant of Israel; in verse 17 it means that regardless of law-observance Jews also have no preferential standing before God but like Gentiles, are to be saved, like Abraham, only by grace received by faith. It is not, however, without an ethical aspect; the opponents' question is whether "the teaching of justification destroys the substance of the spiritual-ethical relationship with God," Oepke, *Galater,* 61.

98. See Zerwick, *Biblical Greek,* 157, no. 467, on δέ as having "'progressive' or 'explanatory' force"; also see Blass and Debrunner, *Greek Grammar,* 232, sect. 447, no. 8.

99. Contra Betz, *Galatians,* 119, note 60, ἐν ("in [Christ]") should be taken as instrumental rather than as denoting "participation in 'the body of Christ.'" As Burton, *Epistle to the Galatians,* 124, points out, "ἐν with δικαιόω usually has its causal and basal sense," as in 3:11; Rom 3:24; 5:9.

by faith").[100] The interpretation of ζητοῦντες ("seeking") has to proceed from this resumptive purpose and from its relationship to aorist infinitive δικαιωθῆναι and aorist indicative εὑρέθημεν, for which it prepares ("seeking . . . we were found . . .").[101] It overloads ζητοῦντες to see in it a reference to Antioch,[102] even more so to see it as changing "the meaning of the verb δικαιωθῆναι."[103] The governing aorists, particularly εὑρέθημεν, indicate that Paul still has in mind the event of coming to faith. By εὑρέθημεν Paul says that when Jewish Christians came to faith they "were found" before God—and thus recognized themselves—to be sinners.[104]

100. This is properly pointed out by Betz, *Galatians,* 119, and Schlier, *Galater,* 95, note 5.

101. The only real equivalent in Paul to ζητοῦντες is in Rom 10:3, where "seeking," parallel to ἀγνοοῦντες ("being unaware of"), denotes the misguided search of unbelieving Jews who "pursue" (9:31) righteousness, thinking that it derives from "works," whereas in fact it derives from "faith" (9:32). Ζητοῦντες in Gal 2:17, of course, denotes the "seeking" for righteousness of *believing* Jews, but in the case of the Galatian opponents, they remain in the illusion that the law provides them with a status before God that is denied to Gentiles; in both cases the "seeking" is fraught with illusion due to misplaced reliance on the law. In Romans Paul primarily blames "unbelief" for this; in Galatians he blames the law itself. On Paul's recognition by faith of the "illusion" of the law, see Keck, "Paul as Thinker," 31.

102. Contra Tannehill, *Dying,* 56.

103. Contra Brinsmead, *Response to Opponents,* 71..

104. In Paul the passive instances of εὑρίσκω ("find") have various senses. The basic meaning is found in Rom 10:20, quoting Isa 65:1. Beyond that the sense is sometimes clearly forensic and eschatological, having to do with that which will only come to light before the judgment seat of God (2 Cor 5:3; Phil 3:9). Other instances are also forensic but look more to a present "finding" that will yet have consequences at the end (1 Cor 4:2; 15:15; 2 Cor 11:12), which seems also to be the sense here. Yet further instances speak simply of that which becomes apparent by the light of experience and are more or less equivalent to the verb "to be" (Rom 7:10; 2 Cor 12:20; Phil 2:7). A "middle or intransitive force" for εὑρέθημεν here ("we found ourselves"), as suggested by Burton, *Epistle to the Galatians,* 125, and Schlier, *Galater,* 95 and note 7, is not impossible but in light of the context and Paul's general usage seems unlikely. The force of the passive suggests God's action in and through the gospel. The recipients of the action were the Jewish

This discovery corresponds to the "conviction" of verse 16. The new "conviction" about the law has its counterpart in the unveiling of a verdict on "ourselves," who were under the law. Thus it is apparent that verse 17 furthers the argument of verse 16 by speaking not in terms of the law but of Jewish Christians' experience when they abandoned the law as the measure of justification. Their new "knowing" implies that their previous convictions about the law, and themselves as its adherents, were mistaken. If the law could not δικαιοῦν, then they were not δίκαιοι but, like the Gentiles, were "sinners." The powerlessness of the law raises the issue of the plight of those who most emphatically relied upon it as the norm of the divine-human relationship.[105] This is what verse 17 describes with obvious polemical intent. Confirmation of this exegesis comes with analysis of the conditional clause.

"If we also . . . were found to be sinners"

Interpreters are very much divided on the interpretation of the conditional clause. Grammatically it is ambiguous, since the protasis is "simple" but the apodosis contains neither a verb nor ἄν.[106] Tannehill makes the pertinent observation that in the absence of ἄν "the reader will most naturally supply a present verb

---

Christians themselves, who accepted the verdict upon their previous existence. Wilckens, "Aus Werken," *Rechtfertigung,* 90, note 26, is therefore correct in saying that "with εὑρέθημεν an experience is described which comes upon Jewish Christians with their conversion."

105. On "rely" as appropriate in translation of 3:10 and for understanding Paul's opponents, see below, under exegesis of 3:10.

106. ῎Αν is an untranslatable particle that occurs in the apodoses of various types of conditional sentences. Since verse 17a is a "simple" conditional clause, whether or not Paul regards its content as "fulfilled" can only be determined from the context; see Zerwick, *Biblical Greek,* 102f., no. 303; also Blass and Debrunner, *Greek Grammar,* 188–89, nos. 371–72. Those who favor, as I do, that Gal 2:17 is a "fulfilled" condition, include Bruce, *Epistle to the Galatians,* 140f.; Burton, *Epistle to the Galatians,* 127; Duncan, *Paul to the Galatians,* 67; Lightfoot, *Galatians,* 116f; Oepke, *Galater,* 92; Ridderbos, *Galatia,* 101; Schlier, *Galater,* 95; Tannehill, *Dying,* 55; Wilckens, "Aus Werken," *Rechtfertigung,* 92; Winger, *By What Law?* 144; Hahn, "Gesetzesverständnis," 53f. and note 76.

in the apodosis and interpret the whole sentence as a reference to reality."[107] This is also what the context seems to demand. What we found to be most surprising about the harsh antithesis of verse 15 was *not* that Paul described "gentiles" as "sinners"—that we found to be quite typical—but that he seemingly excluded "Jews by birth" from that description, which is quite untypical (Gal 3:22; Rom 2:17–3:22). Already in verse 16, with the attack on "works of law" Paul has begun to expose the fallacy of Jewish privilege under the law. Now in verse 17 it would be quite incongruous for him to retreat from this aggressive posture and reaffirm the separatist notion of verse 15 by dissociating Jewish Christians from the sinful plight of humanity. The application of "sinners" to Jews in verse 17 resolves the enigma of separatist vocabulary from Paul in verse 15. "Sinners" within a "fulfilled" condition indicates that Paul set up separatism as a target for destruction. In that sense verse 17 is the denouement of the strange antithesis of verse 15.

The confirmation that Paul regards the content of verse 17a as "fulfilled" is found in the apostle's use of μὴ γένοιτο ("By no means!").[108] Of the fifteen uses of the phrase in the New Testament,[109] fourteen are found in Paul's letters. In Gal 6:14 and Luke 20:16 the phrase has a different function, not being part of a diatribe. In all other instances it is part of a diatribe, answering the

107. Tannehill, *Dying,* 55.

108. Elsewhere in Paul, as I shall explain, this phrase *always* denies an improper conclusion drawn from a *true* ("fulfilled") premise. Attention to or neglect of this significance of the phrase virtually draws the line between those who take the clause to be "fulfilled" and those who do not. This meaning is completely missed by the interpreters listed in note 91, above, who take the clause to be "unfulfilled." To that list we can add: Betz, *Galatians,* 120; Bultmann, "Zur Auslegung," 395f.; Mussner, *Galaterbrief,* 177; E. P. Sanders, *Law and the Jewish People,* 68. Cosgrove, *Cross and the Spirit,* 138, is an exception here, but his argument for Paul's shift in usage ("Epictetus, . . . also shifts his use of [the denial phrase] in just one case") is hardly compelling. Particularly good on the significance of the phrase for verses 17 and 18 is Oepke, *Galater,* 60.

109. They are Luke 20:16; Rom 3:4, 6, 31; 6:2, 15; 7:7, 13; 9:14; 11:1, 11; 1 Cor 6:15; Gal 2:17; 3:21; 6:14.

questions of real or imaginary opponents.[110] And in all of these instances it denies a conclusion that an opponent improperly draws
from *premises that Paul takes to be correct.* With regard to 2:17,
this means that μὴ γένοιτο denies the improper conclusion that
Christ is "an agent of sin." The thesis, however, on which that
false conclusion is based is a thesis affirmed by Paul: "In seeking
to be justified in Christ we also (we Jews under the law) were
found to be sinners." Paul has the objection of the opponents follow immediately ("Is Christ, then, an agent of sin?"),[111] which he
quickly disavows and then launches into the reasons (vv. 18–20)
why he must disavow it.

2:18 To Return to the Law Is to Betray Christ

> For if I build again that which I destroyed,
> then I show myself to be a transgressor.

THE FUNCTION OF THE VERSE IN RELATION TO 2:15-17

The first problem here is the function of the verse, and that
involves how the connective γάρ ("for") is to be taken. Those interpreters who understand verse 17 as an "unfulfilled" condition
often take verse 18 as its antithesis: "we" are not found to be sinners in seeking justification in Christ (or in eating with Gentiles),
but—here's the antithesis—there is sin in reestablishing the authority of the law, which Christ has set aside.[112] In this interpreta-

110. The opponents are probably "imaginary" only in 1 Cor 6:15; see
Oepke, *Galater,* 60.
111. The objection would more likely be raised to Paul's law-free
gospel in general (see Ridderbos, *Galatia,* 101), as in Rom 6:1, 15, than to
the specific assertion that Jews are sinners just as the Gentiles. The latter, as
I have said, is introduced by Paul at this point because it suits so well his purpose of undermining the separatist mentality of the opponents.
112. For example, Bultmann, "Zur Auslegung," 397; Bonnard,
Galates, 55; Kieffer, *Antioche,* 61f.; Lietzmann, *An die Galater,* 16; Mussner, *Galaterbrief,* 177–79, who begins by saying, "The verse gives the reason (note γάρ) why the one who returns to a life of law thereby shows
himself to be a transgressor of the Torah and thus a ἁμαρτωλός." This is

tion γάρ does not so much substantiate the immediately preceding denial phrase as look back to the protasis of verse 17. It is in line with this that γάρ is sometimes taken as equivalent to "but" and the whole verse understood as a parenthesis.[113]

We have already seen, however, why verse 17 is not to be taken as an "unfulfilled" condition. There is no antithesis, therefore, between the protasis of verse 17 and the apodosis of verse 18. On the contrary, verse 18 is concerned only with substantiating the denial phrase. Again, Paul's well-established diatribe style confirms this. In three other instances where γάρ follows μὴ γένοιτο (Gal 3:21; Rom 9:14f.; 11:1) it clearly performs its usual function of substantiating what immediately precedes, that is, the denial phrase. Indeed, whenever Paul uses μὴ γένοιτο, with the possible exception of Rom 7:7, he immediately substantiates the denial in one way or another.[114] The natural conclusion is that 2:18

---

questionable on two counts: first, not ἁμαρτωλός but παραβάτης ("transgressor") is used in verse 18. The latter word "throws off the studied ambiguity of ἁμαρτωλός" (Lightfoot, *Galatians,* 117); παραβάτης gets away from the issue of adherents of the law as such to the issue of a particular transgression against God's action in Christ (see below). Second, from Paul's general usage, the function of verse 18 is simply to substantiate the denial phrase of verse 17c by stating *that* the one who rebuilds the law thereby becomes a transgressor; it does not, however, give a reason for that assertion. The "reason" for the assertion of verse 18 is supplied in verse 19.

113. This is especially true of Lambrecht, "Line of Thought," 495. Lambrecht's interpretation is rightly contested by Kieffer, *Antioche,* 60f., who, however, sees verse 18 as explicative both of 17b *and* c, which, in my view, is incorrect. Against this interpretation, see also Eckstein, *Verheißung,* 42; Winger, *By What Law?* 145, notes 92 and 93.

114. See Kümmel, "Individualgeschichte," 168. Oepke, *Galater,* 60, notes that after the denial phrase in Paul there follows "a concise counter assertion or, if followed by γάρ (Rom 9:14f.; 11:1; Gal 3:21), substantiation of the denial." See also Lightfoot, *Galatians,* 117; Winger, *By What Law?* 145. Elsewhere, after μὴ γένοιτο there appear ἀλλά ("but," Rom 3:31; 7:7, 13; 11:11), δέ (Rom 3:3f.), ἐπεὶ πῶς ("since how," Rom 3:6), and in three cases, asyndeton (Rom 6:2, 15f.; 1 Cor 6:15f.). In Rom 7:7 Paul does not *immediately* substantiate the denial, since the ἀλλά clause and its sequel (vv. 7–12) explain what *is* the connection between law and sin; the substantiation is postponed until 7:13.

intends simply to provide a reason why Christ is not "an agent of sin." It does so by an *e contrario* argument.[115] Using Schlier's paraphrase, the line of reasoning is as follows: "Christ is not an agent of sin when he justifies the sinner, for I become a sinner if I reestablish the law."[116]

The first-person singular appears here as abruptly as did the first-person plural in verse 15.[117] The latter, highlighting the experience of Jewish Christians in becoming believers, dominated verses 15–17, just as this switch dominates verses 18–20. What seems to be clear is that Paul no longer wishes to focus on the experience of Jewish Christians as such[118] but moves on to apply the lesson of their experience to believers in general and particularly to those in Galatia who "wish to be under law" (4:21). In substantiating μὴ γένοιτο Paul switches the focus from the opponents' charge against his teaching to a reprimand of his own, both against them and against the Galatians' threatened apostasy. Kümmel misses this when he describes verse 18 as the behavior of some purely hypothetical Jewish Christian.[119] Again, the conditional clause is "simple" and in this case is clearly "unfulfilled" with respect to Paul, but it is equally clear from the context that it

115. Burton, *Epistle to the Galatians,* 130; Byrne, *Sons of God,* 145; Eckstein, *Verheißung,* 42.

116. Schlier, *Galater,* 96; see also Kümmel, "Individualgeschichte," 168. As Schlier's paraphrase suggests, this interpretation requires some stress on ἐμαυτόν ("myself"), but Paul is not thereby referring to himself (as also in 1 Cor 6:15 and elsewhere).

117. Kümmel, "Individualgeschichte," 168, argues that the switch is merely stylistic (see his n. 39 listing others of like mind). Mussner, *Galaterbrief,* 178, on the other hand, argues that it is "more than merely stylistic" and sees in the unstressed "I" of verse 18 a reference to Peter and in the emphatic "I" of verse 19 a reference to Paul, on which see also Kieffer, *Antioche,* 62. I would agree that more than style is involved here.

118. On the other hand, Kümmel, "Individualgeschichte," 167, goes too far when he says that the Galatians "could hardly notice that the behavior of Peter mentioned in verses 12–14 was to be associated with verse 18." To the contrary, Peter's behavior is the necessary backdrop to illustrate the mistake of the Judaizers and the threatened apostasy of the Galatians.

119. Ibid. On 2:18 as having primarily Galatia in view, see especially Eckstein, *Verheißung,* 45–46.

is a threatening reality among the Galatians and, insofar as it describes the behavior of Peter and others, is "fulfilled." Thus, as Mussner concedes, the "I" of 2:18 (and of 2:19) has a "more than individual" reference.[120]

Mussner, however, as I have mentioned (n. 111), also sees in the unemphatic "I" of 2:18 a reference to Peter, and in the emphatic "I" of verse 19 a reference to Paul. Such a reference to the two apostles cannot be denied outright, but it can be no accident that the contrasting possibilities represented in these verses ("rebuild" the law versus "die to the law") line up neatly according to the options Paul places before the Galatians. Verse 18, to be sure, is illustrative of the "false brothers" in Jerusalem and of Peter and company in Antioch, but in the context it must have in mind above all the threatened apostasy of the Galatians.

THE FUNCTION OF 2:18 IN THE GALATIAN CONTEXT

That Galatia is the primary focus of this verse can be substantiated by noting the correspondence of language between 2:18 and those passages where Paul addresses the Galatians directly with regard to their impending apostasy. This is most apparent in the echoes between "*build* again" (πάλιν οἰκοδομῶ) and the "again" (πάλιν) phrases in 4:8-9 ("Are you *turning* again . . . do you *wish* again to be in slavery?") and 5:1 ("Do not *submit* again to the yoke of slavery"). Furthermore, these present-tense verbs (in *italics*) describing the Galatians' near apostasy stand starkly over against the aorists ("destroyed [the law]"; "acknowledged [by God]"; "set [you] free"), by which Paul reminds the Galatians of their initial conversion. This same pattern is also

120. Mussner, *Galaterbrief,* 178. See also Tannehill, *Dying,* 56f., who sees in "I" "Peter and the others mentioned in vss. 11–13" but also recognizes a general reference to "the Christian who falls back into dependence on the law." Burton, *Epistle to the Galatians,* 130f., and Oepke, *Galater,* 61, both believe there is reference here to Peter in Antioch but that Paul has "tactfully" avoided direct reference to him, but then one wonders where the tact was in 2:11-14! Lagrange, *Galates,* 50, tries to take the spotlight off Peter completely, but that flies in the face of the context. Peter, in my view, is illustrative of what remains primary for Paul, the near apostasy in Galatia.

found in 1:6-9 ("God called" and "we preached the gospel" over
against "you are deserting") and in 3:2-3 ("you received the
Spirit" over against "are you ending with the flesh?"). In the present verse the contrast is between "I destroyed" and "I build
again." This, of course, will be important for deciding what the
"transgression" consists of for Paul (below). It is appropriate also
to note the connection between 2:18 and 2:21. There is a clear
analogy between "if I build [the law] again, I show myself to be
a transgressor," and "if righteousness is through the law, Christ
died in vain." Both speak of the law in terms that reflect the Galatian crisis,[121] and both abhor the thought of granting the law an authority that in Christ has been exposed as illusory.

The vocabulary of "building" and "destroying" the law is
rabbinic: "For the scribes and students of the law 'builders of the
law' [is] a term of honor."[122] Paul's purposes, of course, are
polemical, and there is no doubt that the Judaizers would find his
language scandalous, as he must have known.[123] In his mind, however, abrogating the law as decisive for the divine-human relationship was necessary for the accomplishment of a very positive
purpose. What was destroyed was not only the law as an illusion
of righteousness but also the law's other fault, about which Paul
is no less concerned in this letter, its power to divide humanity.
Dunn is surely correct that the "imagery" of 2:18 has to do with
the "wall," which marked Israel off from the other nations.[124] For

121. There is virtual unanimity on this point among interpreters. Lightfoot, *Galatians,* 114, says, "Paul's thoughts and language have drifted away
from Peter at Antioch to the Judaizers in Galatia." Kieffer, *Antioche,* 78, and
Mussner, *Galaterbrief,* 146, 184, who both interpret in terms of Antioch,
concede the same point as Lightfoot. I would only stress that the Judaizers,
and the Galatian situation, have been in the forefront all along.

122. Kieffer, *Antioche,* 65; see also Byrne, *Sons of God,* 145 and note
27; Mussner, *Galaterbrief,* 178.

123. Paul's more circumspect statements about the law in Romans
(e.g., 2:13; 3:31; 7:12) suggest that he knew this and perhaps even regretted
the difficulties his harsh statements in Galatians caused. Those difficulties
must have included difficulties for himself also, since Galatians could be
used against him by his opponents (see chap. 5, below).

124. Dunn, *Epistle to the Galatians,* 142. It is probably also the case

Paul, the divisions within humanity, most notably those between Jews and Gentiles but others also (3:28), are eliminated by Christ's death for all. Three times in this letter Paul declares the division between Jews and Gentiles to be null and void for believers (3:28; 5:6; 6:15). The rebuilding of the law, then, is not only a denial of the original act of faith in Christ, it is also a reestablishing of the division between "Jews by birth" and "gentile sinners" which Christ healed. In this respect 2:18 certainly brings to mind Peter's "separating" and "withdrawing" at Antioch and justifies Paul's assessment of him as "condemned." But Peter, we must remember, is tinged with the colors of the Judaizers; Antioch is narrated in terms of Galatia. The same is true of 2:18; it has in mind primarily the rebuilding of the law in Galatia and the consequent threat of apostasy *from Christ.*

TO REBUILD THE LAW IS TO BETRAY CHRIST

It is already clear that in my view the "transgression" consists in the "rebuilding," not in the "destroying," of the law. Most interpreters adopt this view or something like it.[125] This is demanded by

---

that *what* was destroyed includes "a reference to the food laws," which occasioned the Antioch conflict (ibid.). Nevertheless, Winger, *By What Law?* 146, is correct to say that "Paul eschews the particular." The apostle deals here as elsewhere with the fundamental principle that is at stake, not with particular commandments. Eckstein, *Verheißung,* 49, also insists that Paul "argues at the level of principle." Further, he argues instructively that in verse 18 Paul does not think primarily either of "food laws" or the Sinai Torah; rather, what faith "destroyed" was "the *conviction*" that "anyone is made righteous by works of law" (v. 16, my emphasis). Accordingly, the object of destruction was "not the νόμος itself . . . but rather the illusion of" being justified by works of law (50). For the most part I agree with this, except that in Galatians what Paul sees as destroyed by faith are not only the *illusions* regarding "Jewish self-evaluation" and "the meaning and function of the Sinai-Torah" (49) but also the *power* of the law to govern human existence (3:13-14, 23–25; 4:5), and thus it is truly the *law itself* that is destroyed for believers.

125. For example, Brinsmead, *Response to Opponents,* 72; Bruce, *Epistle to the Galatians,* 142; Burton, *Epistle to the Galatians,* 131; Dunn, *Epistle to the Galatians,* 142f.; Eckstein, *Verheißung,* 52; Hahn, "Gesetzesverständnis,"

the immediate context, because verses 16, 19, and 21 argue expressly for the exclusion of the law. It is also demanded by the context of the letter as a whole (e.g., 4:9; 5:1-4). If Paul were to locate the "transgression" in the law's destruction, then he would be in agreement with his opponents![126] It is also clear, as I have indicated, that the content of the supposition ("rebuilding the law") describes above all the threatened apostasy of the Galatians. In that regard aorist κατέλυσα ("I destroyed") corresponds to their initial faith experience and thus is reminiscent of "God called you" in 1:6 and anticipates "I died to the law" and "I have been crucified with Christ" (2:19). The event of faith, when God's call was heard and accepted and the Spirit was received (3:2-5), was also the event of the law's destruction. It ought to be evident, therefore, that to "rebuild" the law is to betray God's call in Christ, and it is that *betrayal of Christ* that comprises the "transgression" of 2:18.

In spite of this the vast majority of interpreters would agree with Tannehill that "in verse 18 it is clearly a question of transgression of the *law*."[127] In favor of this it is pointed out that παραβάτης ("transgressor") and παράβασις ("transgression") are

53, n. 76; Kieffer, *Antioche,* 64; Kümmel, "Individualgeschichte," 168; Lambrecht, "Line of Thought," 494; Lietzmann, *An die Galater,* 16; Ridderbos, *Galatia,* 103; Tannehill, *Dying,* 56f.; Westerholm, *Israel's Law,* 206; Wilckens, "Aus Werken," *Rechtfertigung,* 93 and note 35. On the other hand, Betz, *Galatians,* 121; Bultmann, "Zur Auslegung," 398; Schlier, *Galater,* 97f., interpret 2:18 by way of Rom 4:15 ("Where there is no law, there is no transgression") so that the "transgression" is the *result* of reestablishing the law's power to determine what is sin. For Mussner's rather complex interpretation, see note 130, below.

126. Nevertheless, a number of interpreters see it this way: Beyer and Althaus, "Galater," 21; Cosgrove, *Cross and the Spirit,* 138; Lightfoot, *Galatians,* 117; Oepke, *Galater,* 94; Segal, *Paul the Convert,* 202. Some interpreters seem to see the "sin" in both the destroying and the rebuilding of the law: for example, Lagrange, *Galates,* 50; Mussner, *Galaterbrief,* 178f.; Schmithals, *Paul and James,* 75f., but Paul's polemic against the law is clear and unequivocal.

127. Tannehill, *Dying,* 56f. (my emphasis). This is completely taken for granted and so is hardly ever questioned: for example, Dunn, *Epistle to the Galatians,* 143, says: "That 'transgressor' meant 'transgressor of the law' would be self-evident"; see also Eckstein, *Verheißung,* 51–52.

used by Paul only in the context of the Mosaic law (Rom 2:23, 25, 27; 4:15; Gal 3:19). But, first, there is an exception to this in Rom 5:14 ("the transgression of Adam"), which shows that παράβασις includes any act of disobedience against God, even in the absence of "law." This accords with Gal 2:18.[128] Second and more telling is the context, both the immediate context of the *propositio* and the wider context of the letter.

With regard to the *propositio* it ought to be clear that the argument of verse 18 follows directly from the "conviction" enunciated in verse 16 that justification is not by works of law but by faith in Christ. Verse 18, as I have argued, presents Paul's counterargument to the opponents' objection that the apostle's preaching of justification by faith alone makes Christ "an agent of sin." The conviction that Christ and not the law confers justification leads directly to the assertion that for believers to return to the law is to betray Christ. With the denial phrase and its substantiation in verse 18 Paul asserts that Christ is not "an agent of sin" in exposing the helplessness of the law and the plight of those who relied on it; rather, the transgressor is the one who returns to the law and thus renders Christ's death "useless" (2:21). This latter statement of 2:20-21, we may remind ourselves, evokes the letter's opening statement on the content of the gospel (1:4).

From that opening statement the entire letter is consumed with the thought that if the Galatians seek justification by law, then they betray what Christ did for them when "he gave himself for our sins." This is what is meant with the language of "betrayal" and "perversion" of "the gospel of Christ" (1:6-7). This same concern is apparent in 2:4 with the description of the "false brothers" who intend to "enslave us" and thus destroy "the freedom we have in Christ Jesus." The same is true of 3:1-5 with the identification of "Christ crucified" as the content of preaching that occasioned receiving the Spirit, the antithesis of which is

128. That παραβάτης in Gal 2:18 does not have the sense it bears in Romans 4–5, see Winger, *By What Law?* 149, note 105. Winger (148) takes "I show myself a transgressor" as "parallel to" what is said of Peter in 2:11, "he stood condemned." I accept this except that, to repeat, the primary reference of 2:18 is to Galatia, not Antioch.

"works of law." So also 4:8-9 presupposes that to "turn again" to the law is to turn away from God. In all of these texts (see also 5:1-4; 6:12-14) the thought is not at all of transgression of the law but of a betrayal of God's action in Christ.[129] In this context it would be strange for Paul to have in mind that by a return to the law believers transgress the *law*. Rather, to return to the law denies "the grace of God" and declares that "Christ died in vain" (2:21), the very opposite of the confession of the churches. Interpreters forget the decisive impact of the Galatian situation when they take 2:18 as they commonly do. But if that situation and the main concerns of the letter are taken into account, the conclusion seems inevitable that 2:18 maintains that to return to the law is to be a transgressor against Christ.[130] The reason why this is true is set out in verse 19.

---

129. Not even 5:3 is concerned with transgressions against the law. The purpose of Paul's warning the Galatians that if they are circumcised they must then keep "the whole law" is not to set out the conditions of a genuine alternative to the way of faith, as though Paul could envisage that perhaps some Galatians might attain justification by law! His purpose rather is to issue "a kind of threat" (E. P. Sanders, *Law and the Jewish People,* 27), not unlike his portrayal of the law in 3:10 as a threatening, oppressive power (see below). Such a threat, of course, would be nonsense to Jews but might have some influence with Gentiles (ibid., 29).

130. In agreement with this interpretation are Duncan, *Paul to the Galatians,* 69; and Ziesler, *Meaning of Righteousness,* 173 and note 1. Eckstein, *Verheißung,* 52, comes close to this interpretation when he says, "The realm of grace in Christ and the realm of the Sinai-Torah are mutually exclusive (Gal 2:21; 5:2-4), so that turning to the law *per se* means turning from Christ," but then he goes on to say that "as a result [of returning to law], humans can only appear, faced with the law, as what they are since Adam, independently of Christ: people under the power of sin." This reads too much into 2:18. When talking of the sins of believers, Paul never—even when it might seem most appropriate to do so (e.g., 1 Corinthians 5–6)—points to the law as the offended party. And certainly when the issue is apostasy from Christ, it would make no sense to him to invoke the law (Gal 5:2-4). Mussner, *Galaterbrief,* 178f., recognizes that to "rebuild" the law is a "disavowal" of the "original faith-decision," but he also sees it as the moment when table fellowship with Gentiles is shown to be transgression of the law. He (rightly) sees sin against *Christ* in the rebuilding of the law and (wrongly) sin against the *law* in its destruction.

2:19 A Further Description of the Experience
of Being Justified Apart from the Law

For I, through law, died to law,
that I might live to God; I have been crucified with Christ

PARTICIPATION IN CHRIST AS AN INTERPRETATION
OF JUSTIFICATION BY FAITH

This verse pointedly takes up the antithesis established in verse 16, provides further substantiation of μὴ γένοιτο, and represents, with verse 20, the initial development of 1:4, anticipating the letter's focus on the salvific power of Christ's death and the present realization of the blessings of the eschaton. It is worth noting again that these emphases derive from the polemical situation of the letter. The opponents are causing the Galatians to doubt their standing before God. Paul responds by pointing, above all, to what Christ's death and faith in him have accomplished: Spirit, inheritance, adoption, and freedom. All of these are anticipated with "I live to God; I have been crucified with Christ," and were prepared for with the confession of 1:4, "Christ died for our sins, that he might rescue us from the present evil age." The "rescue," as I have emphasized, has in Paul's mind a primarily positive focus, looking more to "new creation" than to "sins" removed. All of this is not without implications for understanding "justification by faith," which is still very much a part of the context.

The connective γάρ, as in verse 18, makes verse 19 a reason for the truth of what has preceded. Oepke, however, considers that the verse "is not appropriate to provide a reason either for verse 18 or for μὴ γένοιτο of verse 17c." Accordingly, in his view, this is "one of the rare cases where γάρ does not provide a reason for what precedes, but emphasizes by a conceptual shift the importance of what follows."[131] Oepke's view is doubtful, not least

131. Oepke, *Galater,* 62. Similar usages occur, he suggests, in Rom 4:3, 9; 14:15. I would not agree about Rom 4:3, much less about Gal 2:19. G. Ebeling, *Truth of the Gospel,* 136, considers this same possibility without

because the argument runs smoothly if γάρ is taken in its usual way. In this connection it is important that ἀπέθανον ("I died [to the law]") corresponds to κατέλυσα ("I destroyed [the law]") of verse 18. The argument of verses 18–19 is that it is sinful to rebuild the law, which I "destroyed" by faith *because* (γάρ, v. 19) thereby my "dying to the law, so as to live to God" is reversed. "Living to God," of course, is only possible by being "crucified with Christ," and this makes verse 19 a reason not only for the assertion of verse 18 but also for the denial phrase of verse 17c; far from being "an agent of sin," Christ is rather the instrument of my "living to God." Whereas verse 18 grounded the denial phrase by pointing to Peter's and the Galatians' error, verse 19 does so by pointing to Christ's accomplishment.[132]

Contrary to Oepke, emphatic ἐγώ provides both a link and a contrast with verse 18. In the latter, unemphatic "I" referred to the Galatians and Peter; in verse 19 emphatic "I" refers, as I shall argue, to all believers but also to Paul himself as an illustration of authentic Christian experience.[133] Second Corinthians 10–13 aside, Galatians contains a more sustained personal and emotional appeal to its readers than is usual in Paul's letters.[134] He not only speaks at length about himself in terms of narrative information (1:11–2:14) but also speaks poignantly of his inner turmoil and physical sufferings (4:12-19; 5:11; 6:14, 17).[135] This

---

favoring it. Better, in my view, are Lightfoot, *Galatians,* 119; Mussner, *Galaterbrief,* 179; and Schlier, *Galater,* 98, who represent the common view.

132. See Kümmel, "Individualgeschichte," 169; also Eckstein, *Verheißung,* 59.

133. This is essentially the view put forward by Mussner, *Galaterbrief,* 178f. With slight reservation I accepted Mussner's view in the exegesis of 2:18. The balanced view expressed well by Kieffer, *Antioche,* 67 (see also Oepke, *Galater,* 62), that ἐγώ is inclusive both of Paul's personal experience and of what was true for all believers is also the view adopted here.

134. In 1 Corinthians only 15:8-11 and perhaps 2:1 convey any obvious emotion; texts like 1:12; 3:4; 4:15; and 5:3 are discursive. Second Corinthians 10–13 is, of course, sustained in its emotion. Romans shows little emotion, since Paul was personally unknown to most there.

135. On the personal and emotional force of 4:12-20 and of 6:17 ample background information is provided by Betz, *Galatians,* 220f. and 323f. re-

gives reason to believe that ἐγώ in 2:19-20 does intend to draw attention to Paul himself, but it does so in order to present him as a paradigm of the believer's experience, which the Galatians should recognize as true also of themselves.[136] This will become clear in examining 2:19 as baptismal language (see below). The death of the ἐγώ, also described as the "crucifying of the flesh" (5:24; see 6:14) or simply as being "justified by faith" (2:16), was their experience also, particularly by baptism.

This new description of the experience of faith presupposes the description already given in 2:16, including its emphasis on the negation of the law.[137] The parallelism of the two main verbs

spectively. The former has "the rhetorical character" of "a personal appeal to friendship" (221), the second that of a *"conquestio"* that "points out the defendant's 'worth, his manly pursuits, the scars from wounds received in battle'" (323). In this regard, however, Paul is restrained ("reduced to a minimum," says Betz).

136. Schweitzer, *Mysticism of Paul,* 3, 101–40 (n. 125), interprets Gal 2:19-20 (and other texts) in terms of Paul's "mysticism"; the elect who die and rise with Christ enjoy "the preordained union . . . with one another and with the Messiah which is called 'the community of the saints'" (101). Those "in Christ" can already enjoy "the resurrection mode of existence before the general resurrection of the dead takes place" (see 115f.). This has not, however, been generally accepted. Among other things, it short-circuits Paul's emphasis that Christ is the "first fruit" and believers *wait* for *future* resurrection (e.g., Rom 6:4-5; 8:11; 13:11-12; 1 Cor 15:12-22). Balanced thoughts on this are offered by Kieffer, *Antioche,* 72–75. Segal, *Paul the Convert,* 34–71, has given an extended interpretation of Paul in terms of mysticism, comparing "Paul's Mystical Reports" (34) with Jewish texts from Ezekiel 1 and its interpretations in "merkabah mysticism" (40) to Philo, the books of *Enoch,* the *Ascension of Isaiah,* and others (39–52). Many of these texts, of course, postdate Paul, but Segal's point that Paul himself is evidence of "first-century Jewish mysticism" (58, see also 61 and elsewhere) nevertheless remains plausible. The point to be made, however, is that Paul's "mysticism," if that is an appropriate term (see 34), never exists for itself, not in 2 Cor 3:18–4:6 and 12:1-5 nor in Gal 2:19-20; it is employed only in service of Paul's theology and communities. For Segal, it is Paul's mystical, "(ecstatic) conversion" that accounts for his apostolate to the Gentiles and for his unique revaluing of Torah and Judaism (70–71).

137. See Mussner, *Galaterbrief,* 179, note 58, on this connection between 2:16 and 2:19.

("we came to faith," and "I died") followed by their purpose clauses ("so that we might be justified" and "so that I might live") indicates that the latter interprets the former.[138] The faith experience of Jewish Christians, says Paul, was a "dying to the law," and the resultant "righteousness" is not merely a hope for future judgment (see 5:5) but is also a present experience of "living (in a new relationship) to God" apart from the law. Χριστῷ συνεσταύρωμαι ("I have been crucified with Christ") appended to the main statement ("I died to the law") sums up and provides the reason for the truth of that statement. The perfect tense ("I *have been* crucified") brings out that the union with the crucified is an ongoing reality, and the linguistic and conceptual links with 5:24 and 6:14 are important for recognizing that 2:19 envisages an ontological and moral transformation of the believer.[139] Such "trans-

138. As 3:11-12 and (especially) 3:21 also show, this suggests that δικαιοῦσθαι can be understood in terms of "life," meaning both "life now in the flesh" (2:20) and eschatological life (3:11-12). E. P. Sanders, *Paul and Palestinian Judaism,* 493–95, revises his earlier view that "the 'real' meaning of righteousness . . . is *life*" (493) and asserts that Paul "does not use the righteousness terminology with *any one* meaning. It may be used as the equivalent of salvation and life; or it may refer to acquittal in the present for past transgressions, or to future vindication in the judgment (Rom 2:13)" (495). This goes along with Sanders' rather negative view of the doctrine of "righteousness by faith," that it is "not a set doctrine—it is only one formulation among many—and it serves a primarily negative purpose" (viz., to exclude "works of law," 493). The negative, polemical purpose of the doctrine cannot be denied, but its equally positive edge, to denote what is accomplished by the Christ-event, is demonstrated, in my view, in Sanders' own list of "the terms which are parallel to 'righteousness'" (492f.). As for it not being "a set doctrine," Stuhlmacher, *Reconciliation,* 78, developing his own understanding of "righteousness" (see his n. 16), accepts that "the Christian tradition . . . that blazed the trail for Paul already used our expression to designate both God's own righteous action and the result of this action." This "synthetic" meaning, he says, was preserved by Paul, and interpreters "must ponder from passage to passage where the apostle's accent lies" (81).

139. "Ontological" is said in the context of Paul's view, present in his cultural milieu, that the human plight has to do not merely with a subjective, existential disorder but also with a cosmic disorder; not only are humans sinful (Rom 3:23) but the universe itself is in "bondage to corruption" (Rom

formation," however, and the participation in Christ (or Christ "in me," v. 20) on which it is based, are alike founded on the doctrine of justification by faith. The faith-event, referred to here as "dying to the law," leads to union with Christ and (ethically) "living to God."[140]

8:21). These two are closely related; humans are liberated from the cosmic powers (e.g., Rom 8:2, 38–39; Gal 1:4) by Christ's death. To be sure, the "powers" are not yet completely subject (1 Cor 15:24-28), just as humans remain in peril of becoming "enslaved again" (Gal 4:9), but just as the "rescue" was real, so also is the present "transformation" (2 Cor 3:18). This is what Gal 2:19-20 presupposes. On the "ontological character of new creation," see Stuhlmacher, "Ontologischen Charakter"; Beker, *Paul the Apostle,* 189–92. On the ethical dimensions of "justification by faith" in Paul, see, for example, Keck, "Justification of the Ungodly and Ethics," 200, who says, "Paul's significance for ethics does not lie in his answer to the question, What am I to do? but rather in the way *he transforms the situation of the doer*" (my emphasis); Furnish, *Theology and Ethics in Paul,* 162–203; Stuhlmacher, *Reconciliation,* 83–85. Pace Eckstein, *Verheißung,* 69, the ethical understanding of Gal 2:19 is confirmed as "primary" by its echo in 5:24 as also by its parallel in Rom 7:4, in which note καρποφορεῖν ("bear fruit," cf. Rom 6:22; Gal 5:22; Phil 1:11; Col 1:10).

140. Although E. P. Sanders, *Paul and Palestinian Judaism,* 504, recognizes that "in Gal 2 Paul had clinched the argument about righteousness by faith with participationist language" and knows that "righteousness by faith and participation in Christ ultimately amount to the same thing" (506), nevertheless—consistent with his view that righteousness by faith "serves a primarily negative purpose" (n. 131)—he insists that "the heart of Paul's theology" is not expressed "with the juristic categories" (righteousness by faith) but with "the participatory categories, even though he himself did not distinguish them this way" (502, emphasis omitted). To this end, he says that "Paul's 'juristic' language is sometimes pressed into the service of 'participationist' categories, but never vice versa" (503). As examples of this, Sanders cites Gal 3:25-29 and 2:20 (504). Neither is supportive of Sanders' position, in my view. In both of them "participatory categories" are "pressed into service" to explicate and draw out the meaning of righteousness by faith. In 2:16-20 righteousness is clearly the basis of participation. With regard to 3:25-29, it curtails Paul's argument to say that "the basis of the lack of distinction between Jews and Greeks with regard to salvation, and consequently the basis for Paul's view that the law should not be obeyed by Gentiles is that 'all are one [person]'" (457). This strips Gal 3:28 from its context. To be sure, Paul's "language . . . becomes completely 'participationist'"

In 2:16 the new divine-human relationship was denoted by "justification by faith," but the new relationship can be described in various ways, including the language of participation, or in terms of receiving the Spirit (3:2-5), being blessed (3:9), receiving the inheritance of Abraham (3:18, 29), being adopted as God's children (3:26, 4:4-7), "acknowledging" or, better, "being acknowledged by" God (4:8-9), and being set free (1:4; 5:1). The basis of all of these, however, is the same: it is God's "call" in the preaching of the gospel and the gift of justification by the death of Christ for those who respond to God's summons with the obedience of faith. Participation presupposes faith. Thus 2:19 is an alternative expression for the transformation of the believer already described with "justification by faith."

THE FUNCTION OF THE VERSE IN THE CONTEXT OF THE GALATIAN CRISIS

Like 2:16 and those other texts in which Paul reminds the Galatians of their conversion, 2:19 goes back to faith's beginning and to the transformation then achieved. In 2:16 Paul describes this beginning in terms of justification; in 2:19 he does so in the language of baptism.[141] The linguistic connections to the baptismal language of Rom 6:1-11 are unmistakable. The latter is an extended explication of baptism as death "to sin" and life "to

---

(504), but the latter derives from "the coming of faith" (3:23-25), which is shorthand for the confession of 2:16. Both juristic and participatory categories are essential to Paul's theology; it distorts the picture to subordinate the one to the other, as Sanders does, particularly since Paul *"himself did not distinguish them this way"* (502). Gundry, "Grace, Works," 30–32, also criticizes Sanders on this point; he properly concludes that "the dynamics of union with Christ are pressed into the service of forensic justification as well as vice versa" (32).

141. That Paul has baptism in mind here is the common view: see, for example, Beyer and Althaus, "Galater," 21; Brinsmead, *Response to Opponents,* 73f.; Hahn, "Gesetzesverständnis," 54; Kertelge, *Rechtfertigung,* 239–42; Mussner, *Galaterbrief,* 180f. For a different view see Betz, *Galatians,* 123; Bonnard, *Galates,* 56; Tannehill, Dying, 59.

God."[142] Romans 6 surely represents actual baptismal language rather more closely than Gal 2:19-20; it conforms well to the language of the confession that "Christ died for our sins."[143] On the other hand, it is doubtful that "dying to the *law*" is original to the context of baptism, and this indicates that the language of 2:19-20 represents Paul's accommodation to the Galatian context. It goes along with this that ἁμαρτία ("sin") occurs only three times in Galatians (1:4a; 2:17b; 3:22).[144] In this letter it is νόμος which is viewed almost exclusively as the cosmic power that defies the grace of God (also "flesh" in 3:3 and 5:13-24). The apostle, then, interprets baptism in a new way for the Galatians in light of the Judaizers' teaching. Baptism is now seen as "dying to *law*" by

142. Datives of disadvantage and advantage respectively, just as in Gal 2:19. Of these datives of advantage in Paul (e.g., Rom 6:10-11; 7:4; 14:7-8), including Gal 2:19, Ebeling, *Truth of the Gospel,* 138, says that "though devoting one's life to God may be included," they mean more than that, in that "life itself is so intimately related to the power of God, so surrendered to His sovereignty, that it receives itself from God as a life absolutely dependent on God." The opposite of "living to God" is living "to law"; the latter defines the self as privileged (2:15; Rom 2:17-20), the former defines life as "centered" on God (see 139) where all privilege based on law has been taken away (Phil 3:3-9). This is important for understanding both Paul's positive assertions about the life of faith and his critique of the law as that which deludes the self (see below).

143. Romans 7:1-6, on the other hand, with its vocabulary of "dying to the law," is "a specifically Pauline variation of the common Christian notion that, in baptism, the Christian shares in the destiny of Christ and, being crucified with him, dies to *sin*" (Räisänen, *Paul and the Law,* 58). Galatians 2:19 is similar in this respect. In other words, Paul edits the traditional language here. Tannehill, *Dying,* 59, misses this when he says that "the phrase 'through law'" precludes a reference to baptism.

144. This contrasts markedly with Romans, where ἁμαρτία occurs forty-eight times, forty-one instances coming between 5:12 and 8:3, seven in 6:1-11 alone. Thus with respect to critique of the law Romans focuses sin as a power (7:7-13) as well as human sinfulness (1:18–3:20; see also 9:30–10:4; 11:11-12) to account for the law's failure, whereas Galatians, to repeat, focuses the critique on the deceptive power of the law itself. Proportionately, νόμος is even more frequent in Galatians (thirty-two times) than in Romans (seventy-four times).

"being crucified with Christ." This prepares for what will be made explicit in verse 20: Paul is harking back to the confession of the churches that Christ "gave himself for our sins in order to rescue us from the present evil age" (1:4). It now becomes clearer that in contrast to the age of faith and of freedom, the evil age is the age of the law. The extent of this polemic against the law, just how oppressive it has been, in Paul's harsh portrait, becomes most apparent with the phrase διὰ νόμου ("through law").

This phrase is notoriously difficult.[145] How can it be that the law itself is the instrument (διά) of my death to the law?[146] The

145. For example, Burton, *Epistle to the Galatians,* 133, says that Paul "has in mind the experience under the law . . . which he describes at length in Rom., chap. 7. . . . [It] taught him his own inability to meet its requirements and its own inability to make him righteous." Similar to this is Lightfoot, *Galatians,* 118 (see following note), but against this, Romans 7 is about human bondage to *sin* and the law's inability, not about the law as instructor in any sense. Lagrange, *Galates,* 51, opts for the interpretation of Ambrosiaster ("by the law of faith he died to the law of Moses") and equates "law of faith" with the Sermon on the Mount. Bonnard, *Galates,* 56, however, (quoting Sieffert), properly points out that "Paul never uses the word 'law' alone, without special qualification, to speak of the law of Christ." Dunn, *Epistle to the Galatians,* 148, says that διὰ νόμου in 2:19 means the same as in 2:21, "both having in mind the understanding [of the law] over-exemplified in Paul's previous life-style" when "at the bidding of the law as he then understood it," he had persecuted the church (1:14) and thus come "face to face with the risen Christ," so that "the law ceased from that time to exercise the same hold over him" (143). But seeing a reference back to 1:14 in this way reads a great deal into διὰ νόμου, especially since the baptismal language of "dying with Christ" suggests a more straightforward explanation. Winger, *By What Law?* 150–52, denies that διά means either "because of" or "by means of": "Since the [latter] stronger senses are not explained or required by the context of 2:19, the weak sense is indicated; ἐγὼ διὰ νόμου is then a way of saying, 'I having νόμος,' . . . 'I as a Jew.' In short, Paul repeats the point made in 2:15." But this takes the heart out of Paul's rhetoric, and it begs the question to say that the more obvious sense of διά cannot be accounted for in the context. Against this, see Eckstein, *Verheißung,* 60, also his discussion of various interpretations (59–66).

146. There seems to be an obvious interpretation in 3:24, παιδαγωγὸς . . . εἰς Χριστόν, which is sometimes taken as purposive ("pedagogue *for* Christ") rather than, as it is, temporal ("*until* Christ"). For example,

needed clue is provided by the asyndetic assertion Χριστῷ
συνεσταύρωμαι ("I have been crucified with Christ"). This reference to the manner of Christ's death, and of the believer's death
with him, anticipates 3:13, where the law is seen to curse the crucified. As in 4:4b-5, so also in 3:10-13 and 2:19, Christ and humanity suffer a common fate; both come under the curse of the
law.[147] Christ "became an accursed thing" because the law declares the body of the criminal "which hangs on a tree" to be
cursed. It must be removed lest it pollute the land (Deut 21:23).[148]
Humanity comes under the law's curse because humans do not
abide by the law's commands (3:10) and, furthermore, are deceived by its promise of life (3:11-12, 21).[149] The law acknowledges

---

Fitzmyer, "Paul and the Law," 79, says that the law "schooled man in prepa-
ration for Christ." But in the ancient world, as Betz, *Galatians,* 177f., explains at length, the "pedagogue" was a "disciplinarian," not a "schoolmaster"
(see also Lightfoot, *Galatians,* 148f.), and Paul seems to have in mind simply that restraining role of the law *until* "the coming of faith" (3:23; 4:1-5)
and not any educative role.

147. Thus ὑπὲρ ἡμῶν ("for us") in 3:13 is not vicarious (contra Räisänen, *Paul and the Law,* 59, and E. P. Sanders, *Law and the Jewish People,*
25); Christ does not deflect the curse by receiving it "in our stead"; rather,
he "became subject [like all other humans] to law that he might redeem those
subject to law" (4:4b-5). Christ entered into the human condition (4:4a,
"born of a woman") and in his death, subject to the law's curse (3:13), reveals that the law does not speak for God with regard to the essence of the
divine-human relationship. The difference between Christ and humans is
that the latter come under the law's curse as sinners, as 1:4 assumes, whereas
Christ does so as "innocent." It is in regard to Christ as "innocent" that 3:13
links with 2 Cor 5:21, but the difference between these verses is instructive.
The latter speaks of *God's* action in making Christ "to be sin," whereas Gal
3:13 regards the curse as the *law's* verdict in contradistinction to the verdict
of God.

148. Paul's different wording of LXX Deut 21:23 (=κεκατηραμένος
ὑπὸ θεοῦ πᾶς κρεμάμενος ἐπὶ ξύλου) is best accounted for as his accommodation to the wording of Deut 27:26 in 3:10 (note ἐπικατάρατος) *and* to
his desire to dissociate the law's verdict from that of God (omission of ὑπὸ
θεοῦ), the latter as noted by Burton, *Epistle to the Galatians,* 165. See also
following note.

149. For the sake of clarity it might be useful briefly to anticipate the
coming exegesis of 3:10-13, below. For Paul "the curse of the law" functions

only those who abide by its definition of "justification" (3:11). As the crucified, Christ, though innocent, is ranged with the sinners whom the law cannot tolerate. Those who by faith "have been crucified with Christ" are similarly cursed by the law and thereby become dead to it. Thus the law itself is the instrument of believers' death to the law.[150]

The offensiveness of this image in the Judaizers' framework is unmistakable. This is also true of the antithesis, "I died to the law that I might live to God." Law-observant Judaism in any age presupposes, as Ebeling says, that "living to the law means living to God, and consequently dying to the law must be tantamount to dying to God." But Paul is intent on dissociating the law from God, as 3:1-21 will confirm. Ebeling, however, says, "It is important to Paul, especially in this context, that there not be the slightest hint of degradation of the law."[151] But this misses the

---

in two ways corresponding to the "sin" of two groups of sinners. The curse falls first on the transgressors of the law, the disobedient envisaged in 3:10 paradigmatically represented by "sinners of the gentiles." Writing to Gentiles Paul has primarily this group in mind when he thinks of the law's curse in 2:19 and 3:13. The punch of 3:13 is that the Messiah is ranged with these sinners even though he is innocent. The other "sinners," so to speak, are the law-abiding Judaizers, who imagine that the law's verdict of Lev 18:5 applies to them. For Paul, however, that is an illusion. They do not understand the law and thus are under the curse of deception; what the law promises (3:12) it cannot deliver (3:21). They do not know it, but they are "sinners" just as the Gentiles are (2:17; 3:22), and thus for both alike salvation is to be found only by faith in Christ.

150. Recent interpreters regularly note the connection between 2:19 and 3:13 and interpret 2:19 accordingly: for example, Bultmann, "Zur Auslegung," 397; Cosgrove, *Cross and the Spirit,* 139; Ebeling, *Truth of the Gospel,* 147; Eckstein, *Verheißung,* 66; Kieffer, *Antioche,* 68f.; Oepke, *Galater,* 62; Schlier, *Galater,* 100f.; Tannehill, *Dying,* 58. E. P. Sanders, *Law and the Jewish People,* 25f., typically tries to disarm the aggressiveness of Paul's image: for him, "Gal 3:13 . . . has a subsidiary place in explaining how the curse (3:10) is removed," but it "is not actually an argument against righteousness by the law." But Paul's radical dissociation of the law's verdict from that of God is a very powerful argument against righteousness by the law.

151. Ebeling, *Truth of the Gospel,* 147; see also Eckstein, *Verheißung,*

point of what Paul is doing precisely in this Galatian context. In Romans, especially 7:12, Paul seems to want to maintain the law's high standing, but even there the law is still the instrument, in sin's hand, of human illusion and death (7:7-13). Still, Ebeling has a point. Even in Galatians Paul appeals to the law as witness of the gospel (e.g., 3:8; 4:21; cf. Rom 3:21) and affirms that believers "fulfill" the law and, by implication, must do so by love of one another (5:14). As γραφή ("scripture"; 3:8, 22) the law reveals God's intention and will. But this idea, always presupposed by Paul, is not in view in 2:19. At this point he is intent on showing that the law, *as understood and preached by the Judaizers,* a view of the law he once accepted himself (1:13-14; Phil 3:4-9), is false and indeed is inimical to God's intentions for the salvation of both Jews and Gentiles.

This view is characterized by the Judaizers' confidence in the promise of Lev 18:5, "The one who does [works of law] shall live by them." As believers the Judaizers did not depart from this conviction and are now convincing the Galatians of it. For them the law was conjoined *with* Christ in God's plan of salvation. The confession of 2:16a did not, in their view, mean "dying to the law." To the contrary, the law maintains its usual function as the means of living the covenant and is simply conjoined with faith in Christ. This has the inevitable corollary that their presuppositions about "Jews" over against "sinners of the gentiles" have remained essentially intact. That is the basis of the separatism that makes itself felt in Galatia even as Paul writes. That supposed privilege of "Jews by birth," conferred by belonging to the covenant and being obedient to the law, is now becoming the envy of the Galatians. The opponents' strategy is working ("that you may come to envy them," 4:17c, *NEB*). It is against this privilege that Paul asserts, "I, for my part, died to the law." The "I" of the Judaizers,

---

66, who focuses the law's "condemnatory" role so that "the law itself does not wish to be seen as a way of salvation." This, however, flies in the face of both what the *opponents* claim for the law *and* what the law claims for itself (Lev 18:5), which Paul in 3:11-12 and most directly in 3:21 says is false. The offensiveness of Paul's imagery is also noted by Beyer and Althaus, "Galater," 21; Mussner, *Galaterbrief,* 180.

and now of the nearly convinced Galatians, has a specific content and orientation. Assertions about the law have translated into assertions about "self." The death of the "I," therefore, means not only the end of the law's rule over "me," but also means the end of self-assertion.

The theme of self-assertion as a fault of adherents to the law is not well developed in Galatians, but it is present. In the immediate context we have seen it already in Paul's tongue-in-cheek espousal of separatism in 2:15, which he proceeds to expose as illusory in 2:17. Even "we Jews by birth" are shown in the light of the gospel to be "sinners," utterly dependent on grace alone no less than are "sinners of the gentiles." The inability of the law (2:16) has consequences for those who placed their confidence in the law. That confidence was misplaced, and self-estimation based on adherence to law was an illusion. In Rom 2:1–3:31 and Phil 3:4-11 the theme of self-assertion as an illusion of the law's adherents is somewhat more developed, and especially in Philippians it is apparent that the faith-event as the end of self-assertion was also Paul's personal experience.[152]

152. On Romans 2–3, suffice it to say for now (see chap. 5) that its primary purpose is the indictment of Jewish transgression of law in support of the theme of universal sinfulness (3:9-23), which is crucial to the argument in Romans (not so Galatians). Transgression of law, however, also has to do with "hardness" and "an unrepentant heart" (2:5). That this includes a misguided "reliance upon law" is apparent from 2:17-20, with its string of verbs sarcastically describing the self-image of one who, from knowledge of the law, "knows the will" of God and is convinced of superior status, above those who are "blind," "foolish," and mere "children." It strains credibility beyond breaking to think that Paul regards this knowledge and boasting as correct with respect to the law. It is this "boasting" (= reliance on "works" as the means to righteousness and "privilege") that is excluded in 3:27 "by the law (= principle) of faith." And it is that misguided "pursuit" of the law, "as though [righteousness were] by works" that Paul laments in 9:31-32. Thus E. P. Sanders (*Law and the Jewish People,* 30) is quite correct that "the brunt of the argument is in favor of the equality of Gentiles and against the assumption of Jewish privilege" (I also agree with his critiques of Beker and Hübner; ibid., 33), but Paul also rejects the *basis* of that "assumption," namely the conviction that law produces righteousness. Paul indeed commends "zeal for pious works" (ibid., 156)—zeal in itself is good—but in his

Sanders, of course, rejects such an interpretation of Philippians 3. In his view it is simply a matter of a shift from one dispensation to the other:

> Paul does not say that boasting in status and achievement was wrong because boasting is the wrong attitude, but that he boasted in things that *were gain.* They *became loss* because, in his black and white world, there is no second best. His criticism of his own former life is not that he was guilty of the attitudinal sin of self-righteousness, but that he put confidence in something other than faith in Jesus Christ.

But, as Gundry has shown, this flies in the face of the text.[153] There is, of course, a shift in regard to the *object* of faith (from law to Christ), but crucial also is the new understanding of self which that shift entails. For Paul, true believers "boast in Christ Jesus and *do not trust* in flesh" (Phil 3:3). The "anyone else" of 3:4b clearly designates the Philippian opposition, which "supposes [it has reason] to trust in the flesh."[154] That *attitude* toward covenant obedience and status is what, for Paul, defines the fault of the opponents. Thus it is not, as Sanders would have it, that the former dispensation simply has been "surpassed" by the new one.[155] What is wrong is the opponents' misguided convictions about law, which they imagine ("trust") grants them a status that in fact it cannot give. If such "trust" was appropriate, Paul would have even more grounds for it, he says, than they do (Phil 3:4b),

---

opponents it is "not enlightened" *(NRSV).* As elsewhere, Sanders is correct in what he asserts but wrong in what he omits.

153. E. P. Sanders, *Law and the Jewish People,* 44; see also 139–41. See Gundry, "Grace, Works," 13–15.

154. That the issue is not merely the transition from one "dispensation" to another (*what* to believe) but also a critique of "attitude" (*how* to believe) is apparent from Paul's focus on "trust," with the alternatives being "the flesh" (three times in 3:3-4) or "boasting in Christ." To "trust in the flesh" would be seen as wrong by the opponents as well as by Paul (e.g., Ps 56:4), and to go from trust in flesh to trust in God would be seen as a fundamental conversion of heart, not merely as a transition from something "good in itself" to something better.

155. For example, E. P. Sanders, *Law and the Jewish People,* 139.

and so would have all the status they might claim, and more (3:5). To undermine their stance, Paul recounts his own conversion from such "trust in the flesh," and the status it provided, to the position of "regarding" those "gains" as "loss" and indeed as "rubbish." Parallel to the goal of "gaining Christ" is "that I might be found in him." The conversion is from an illusory view of self to one based on "knowledge of Christ Jesus." This parallels what Paul says of himself, and all believers, in Gal 2:20, "I live, yet no longer I, rather Christ lives within me." The specific "gain," which Paul came to "regard as loss because of Christ," is "*my own righteousness which is from law.*" "My own righteousness," therefore, is an illusory righteousness that results from "trusting in the flesh" and, for Paul, is in fact no righteousness at all.[156]

Sanders asserts that "the righteousness which comes by law, which is therefore the peculiar result of being an observant Jew, . . . is *in and of itself a good thing* ("zeal," Rom 10:2; "gain," Phil 3:7), but which is shown to be 'wrong' ("loss," Phil 3:7f.) by the revelation of 'God's righteousness,' which comes by faith in Christ."[157] But Sanders here confuses "zeal" for the law with "righteousness by law," whereas Paul keeps them distinct (Rom 9:30-32; 10:2-3). Righteousness, of course, is good in itself, but "righteousness *by law*" is a nonentity for Paul. Also "good" are Israel's pursuit of "the law of righteousness" (Rom 9:31)[158] and its

---

156. Contra Sanders, ibid., 140 (see next note).

157. Ibid., 44f. Sanders sees Philippians 3 in terms of "two righteous-nesses": "The only thing that is wrong with the old righteousness seems to be that it is not the new one; it has no fault which is described in other terms. Paul has confidence in the old righteousness, but, as we said above, his 'fault' as a zealous Pharisee was not his attitude, but boasting in a 'gain' which he later saw as 'loss'" (140). Sanders has to say that "Paul has confidence in the old righteousness" because his insistence on a purely "dis-pensational" shift will not allow him to see Paul as finding fault with the *mindset* of his "former way of life in Judaism" (Gal 1:13). But Philippians 3 and Rom 2:17ff. make it undeniable that "thinking" and "judgment" are im-portant aspects of what Paul finds wrong both in his own past and in his pres-ent opposition.

158. The phrase "law of righteousness" (νόμον δικαιοσύνης) in Rom 9:31 is somewhat surprising, as the commentaries regularly note. I take it to

"zeal for God" (10:2). These, however, are misguided in that they proceed "as though [righteousness were achieved] by works" (9:32b) and thus fail to attain their goal (9:31b). Though zeal is good, righteousness is not achieved because it is pursued in the wrong way ("by works") and thus becomes the righteousness of the pursuer ("my own righteousness") rather than true righteousness, the "righteousness of [or "from"] God" (Rom 10:3; Phil 3:9). In Rome, Philippi, and Galatia the righteousness of the opponents is an illusion precisely because it derives from a misguided trust in the law's power to define righteousness. That is why in Philippians 3 Paul can designate "my own righteousness" as "rubbish," and in Galatians 2:19 that is why "I" must "die to law." In both cases what that also means is the end of a false understanding of self.[159] In 2:20 Paul speaks further of the demise of this "I" and of the life that every believer must live in union with Christ.

---

be a positive use of the word "law" (as in Rom 3:21b; Gal 4:21b), unlike its negative usage in Rom 3:21a, Gal 4:21a and in most of Galatians. I will deal with Rom 9:31 in slightly more detail in chapter 5.

159. None of this means, in my view, that "Paul accused *Judaism,* with himself as the paradigmatic example, of the attitude of boastful self-righteousness" (E. P. Sanders, *Law and the Jewish People,* 44, my emphasis). Paul's attack is against specific opponents, not against Judaism in general. His attack *appears* to be generalized in Rom 9:31 and elsewhere when he speaks of "Israel" wrongly pursuing righteousness, but several observations are important here: *(a)* In Romans 9–11, when Paul is dealing with the problem of "Israel's" refusal of the gospel, obviously he has primarily in mind those who have actively opposed his preaching by an insistence on the necessity of observance of law; *(b)* Paul is aware that though law-observance *can lead* to "boasting" (2:17-20) and a judgmental attitude (14:3), it can also be quite appropriate and indeed sometimes even necessary for the sake of the "weak" (14:13–15:1; 1 Cor 8:7-13); *(c)* Paul was surely as aware as is modern scholarship of a diversity of views within Israel in regard to Gentiles and law-observance; he attacks those Jews and Jewish Christians who, as he sees it, have wrongly insisted on law as the measure of true righteousness before God. "Boastful self-righteousness" is rejected when it appears, both within Israel (2:17-20) and the church (11:13-22); it is not exclusive to either one.

2:20 A Description of Life in Christ
Liberated from the Law's Illusion

I live, yet no longer I, rather Christ lives within me.
The life I now live in [the] flesh,
I live by faith in the Son of God who loved me
and surrendered himself for me

THE DEMISE OF SELF-ASSERTION

Verse 20 continues the thought begun in the purpose clause
of verse 19.[160] Specifically, it asserts and describes the Christological orientation of "living to God." The "I," again emphatic, is
perhaps occasioned, as Tannehill suggests, by the contrast with
"Christ."[161] That, however, cannot completely explain the matter,
for the participial clause also features emphasis upon "me" as opposed to "us" in 1:4 and 3:13. The motivation for the emphasis is
Paul's desire to focus the relationship of each believer with
Christ. This is also emphasized by the words "Christ lives in
me."[162] Reference to Paul himself is not to be dismissed, as 6:14

160. On the two instances of δέ ("but") in verse 20a, see Burton, *Epistle to the Galatians,* 137; Lightfoot, *Galatians,* 119; Mussner, *Galaterbrief,*
182. Both instances are slightly adversative, the first correcting the notion
that the "I" still has a life of its own ("yet not I"), the second introducing the
positive side of the preceding negative statement ("rather Christ lives in
me").

161. Tannehill, *Dying,* 57.

162. Pace Stuhlmacher, "Ontologischen Charakter" (note especially 4
and 22), who interprets texts like Gal 2:20 and 2 Cor 5:17 ("if anyone is in
Christ") in "generalizing" terms and emphatically *not* in terms of the individual. Balance has to be maintained here. Tannehill, *Dying,* 60, properly
comments that "'Christ in you,' in comparison to other formulations [e.g.,
'being in Christ'] . . . may express *a greater concern with each individual's
existence and action,* but the basic idea of the determination of the life of the
believer by the Master of the new dominion is the same" (my emphasis). A
balanced view is also provided by G. Schrenk, s.v. δικαιοσύνη, *Theological
Dictionary of the New Testament,* 2:206: Paul "is not referring to a communal justification but to a justifying action of God which seizes the individual.
To be sure, he does not think of individuals in the individualistic sense.

shows, where the apostle contrasts himself with the opponents. On the other hand, Paul's purpose is to present himself as the example for his churches to follow (4:12; cf. 1 Cor 4:16; 11:1), so it is mistaken to put the emphasis on Paul's mysticism as though he were reporting his individual experience.[163] The "I," which lives no longer, is the "old self" of every believer (Rom 6:6); Paul is reminding the Galatians of what became true for them also by faith.

The contrast between the "I" in Rom 7:9-25a and in Gal 2:19-20 is instructive for understanding the particularity of the two letters and the influence of the letter situation on the language of Galatians.[164] The "I" of Romans 7 is tortured; it endures a sort of living death under the power of sin, which, with the coming of the law, "revived" (ἀνέζησεν, 7:9) and caused the "I" to die (7:10). This "I" has no control; the good it wills it is unable to do because it is "fleshly, sold under sin" (7:14). It achieves the peaceful unity of willing and doing only when it is rescued by Christ (7:24). The "I" of Gal 2:19-20, on the other hand, like the "we" of 2:15-17, is not at all tortured and impotent within itself. This "I" is assured and confident, not unlike Paul's former assured self, which is described in Phil 3:4-6, or the self-assured Jew in Rom 2:17-20. It relies on "works of law" and believes itself on that basis to be "righteous before God" (Gal 3:10-11). This, as Paul sees it, is the confident mentality of separatist Judaism and Jewish Christianity, which characterized him in his

When the individual is justified, he becomes a member of the body of Christ as he previously belonged to Israel, the ἔθνη ["gentiles"] or humanity." See also Kümmel, "Individualgeschichte," 170.

163. On the "mystical" language of "death and rebirth" as having a wide provenance in the ancient world, see Segal, *Paul the Convert,* 133–38; also Betz, *Galatians,* 124 and note 93. The *traditional* language employed here shows that Paul speaks of an experience that is by no means unique to him.

164. Burton, *Epistle to the Galatians,* 137, is uncharacteristically simplistic on this point. He maintains that in both passages "the ἐγώ is the same, the natural man having good impulses and willing the good which the law commands, but opposed by the inherited evil impulse and under law unable to do the good." This is quite inadequate for Galatians 2.

"former life in Judaism" (1:13-14). What is common to both Romans 7 and Galatians 2, on the other hand, is that previous to faith, whether tortured by sin or confident under law, the "I" is always lost in illusion.[165] The law cannot avail the helpless victim of Romans 7, and it leaves its enthusiastic adherents in Galatians 2 lost in illusion.

It is no surprise, then, that the life of the believer "now," since "faith's coming" (3:23), is experienced and described by Paul as a radical departure from the previous life of the deluded and assertive "I." Having died to the law, the "I" does not, and must not, any longer have a life of its own, an indication of how completely law had come to define and rule the "I." But what was the result of this dominance of the law? The retrospect of faith recognizes that the "I" was dead under the power of sin (Rom 7:9-10; Gal 3:22), imprisoned and enslaved under law (Gal 3:23; 4:1-9; cf. Rom 8:1-2). But that, of course, was Paul's conviction, not the experience of the Judaizers. They were convinced that the law was necessary for true Christian faith and that, as adherents of the law, they enjoyed a status, even "in Christ," as yet denied to Galatian believers. It is these convictions, what he would recognize only as illusions, that Paul attacks.

In order to escape from these illusions nothing less is required than the death of the "I," for its life under law was characterized by two distinct but closely related illusions. The first was the illusion of righteousness due to performance of law, and the second was the illusion of privilege over the rest of humanity. The first was the basis of the second. The law not only deceived its adherents, it also cut them off from non-adherents. Paul criticizes the law on both points. The law demands obedience to its statutes and promises a blessing for the obedient and a curse for the dis-

---

165. The "I" of Romans 7 matches that letter situation in that there Paul blames not so much the law for humanity's plight but sin's domination (7:14c), perhaps because the harsh rhetoric of Galatians is being used against him and he must explain himself with considerably more nuance. In Romans, therefore, and specifically in Romans 7, Paul attenuates somewhat the attack on the law, but even there he portrays it as powerless and as a death-dealing instrument in the hands of sin.

obedient (3:10-12), thus focusing attention on itself and misguid-
ing its adherents at the cost of the divine-human relationship. Its
demands and concomitant promises and threats also promote divisions in humanity: "Jew [and] Greek, slave [and] free, male and
female" (3:28). The law, in this negative portrait, has become
completely detached from its function within the covenant. It has
become a power unto itself, threatening the bond between the
promises and their fulfillment (3:15-18).

Paul's attack on what he sees as the opponents' illusions becomes an attack on the law itself. This has to do, of course, with
Paul's evaluation of the opponents' interpretation of the law in
Galatia. Though in their teaching law remains "grace" for *them,*
it is not grace for the Galatians. Its prescriptions define who are,
and who are not, the "heirs of Abraham" (3:29) to the disadvantage of the Galatians. Paul will have none of this; for him, the law
has become a power of deception. It fosters a false understanding
of itself and a false understanding of humanity. The only way out
is the death of the "I," so that, in union with Christ, "I might live
to God" and no longer see the world as divided between "Jews
and gentiles." For Paul, true faith involves the awareness that
righteousness is not by law and that all humans stand before God
as "sinners," utterly in need of grace. What the "I" now knows is
that righteousness before God comes only by faith in Christ, and
the agenda of life "now" is derived only from this faith and not
from the law.[166]

166. It bears repeating that this negative view of the law by no means
encompasses all that Paul thinks about it. This harsh attack is shaped by the
demands of responding to the opponents' teaching of the law. The latter, Paul
knows, is persuasive because it was part of his own past (1:13-14; Phil 3:4-
6), but he is now convinced that such an understanding is erroneous. He attacks this erroneous understanding of the law as though he were attacking
the law itself. But that he has now (in Christ) come to a new positive understanding of the law and of how it was intended to function in Israel's life is
apparent from his appeal to the law as witness of the gospel and as "instruction" for the life of faith (Rom 15:4; 1 Cor 10:11; Gal 5:13-14). As God's gift
the law is about promise and grace, just as is the gospel.

LIFE IN UNION WITH CHRIST

The second part of the verse has in view this life with Christ,[167] and the first thing to be noted is that life ἐν σαρκί ("in [the] flesh") is determined not by flesh but by faith. The description of life "now" as being "in flesh" is not at all meant to temper the description of life "by faith." The opposite is the case.[168] It goes along with this that σάρξ ("flesh") here does not denote "the sinful nature," as in 5:13 "but simply the empirical mode of existence."[169] Paul concedes the realities of existence in the flesh but not the behavior of life *according* to the flesh. Furthermore, the "now" of verse 20b is the "now" of the time of faith; it is an eschatological "now." It contrasts with existence under the dominion of sin and law, not with the future "fulfillment" of Christian existence.[170] To be sure, Paul elsewhere is aware of the present limits of union with Christ in comparison to its fullness at the eschaton (e.g., Phil 1:23), but there is no indication that that is in mind here. And, indeed, the context militates against it. In this situation, where the Judaizers have belittled the Galatians' call to the gospel, Paul is at pains to emphasize the present fulfillment of the blessings of the eschaton.

167. The third δέ is continuative rather than adversative and is best translated as "and." See Burton, *Epistle to the Galatians,* 138; Schlier, Galater, 102, note 3.

168. See Tannehill, *Dying,* 60–61: "The sentence . . . asserts that this life in the flesh has the positive quality of life in faith."

169. Oepke, *Galater,* 63; see also Bruce, *Epistle to the Galatians,* 145; Burton, *Epistle to the Galatians,* 138. The use of σάρξ may also anticipate the invective against the "flesh" of circumcision in 3:3-5 (cf. 6:12). On this, see Jewett, *Paul's Anthropological Terms,* 95–97, and Lull, *Spirit in Galatia,* 31 and 104. Betz, *Galatians,* 125, says that σάρξ in 2:20 "may be polemical," aimed against "widespread enthusiastic notions, which may have already found a home in Christianity, according to which 'divine life' and 'flesh' are mutually exclusive." There is no indication, however, that enthusiasm is in mind here. Any polemic is far more likely aimed at the Judaizers' teaching of circumcision, as in 3:3-5.

170. Contra Oepke, *Galater,* 63. Better, in my view, is Lightfoot, *Galatians,* 119.

Of course Paul knows that "life in the flesh" can descend into life "according to the flesh" (5:13-24), since "the evil age," to which the Galatians are in danger of returning (4:8-9), remains a "present" reality (1:4). Accordingly, there is "an unmistakable tension set up by the coexistence of life in mortal body and life in Christ—by the fact that the life of the age to come ἐν Χριστῷ has 'already' begun while mortal life ἐν σαρκί has 'not yet' come to an end."[171] But the point of emphasis for Paul is that so long as believers remain ἐν πίστει ("in faith"), that tension is resolved on the side of faith. "Flesh" is determined by "faith," not the other way around; "those who belong to Christ crucified the flesh with its passions and desires"; by faith "the world was crucified to me and I to the world" (5:24; 6:14). "Faith" contrasts with "flesh" in such a way as to exclude the latter as determinative of the believer's mode of existence. And we have seen in the discussion of 2:19 ("I died to law") that "law" also is ruled out as determinative of the life of believers; the latter is determined radically and completely by "faith," guided by the Spirit (3:2-5; 5:16-25).[172]

Faith, however, is not left undefined. Paul describes faith's direction and content as faith in "the Son of God who loved me and surrendered himself for me." The choice of the title "Son of God" is deliberate. Paul refers to Jesus as "the Son [of God]" fifteen times, always with the definite article preceding "Son."[173] Schweizer's observation that for Paul the title has "the function of describing the greatness of the saving act of God who offered up the One closest to Him," is correct as a general description and is

171. Bruce, *Epistle to the Galatians,* 145.

172. E. P. Sanders goes to great lengths to establish his view that "Paul saw no incongruity between 'living by faith' and 'fulfilling the law.' Doing the commandments (1 Cor 7:19) is integral to living by faith." Foundational to this is Sander's assertion that for Paul "to some degree the law still functioned as law" (*Law and the Jewish People,* 114). In light of Gal 2:15-21 I do not see how this can be correct. Sanders is constrained to such statements by his failure to see the distinct ways in which Paul uses the word "law," as exemplified in Rom 3:21 and Gal 4:21.

173. Romans 1:3, 4, 9; 5:10; 8:3, 29, 32; 1 Cor 1:9; 15:28; 2 Cor 1:19; Gal 1:16; 2:20; 4:4, 6; 1 Thess 1:10. On the textual problems in this verse, see Betz, *Galatians,* 125, note 104.

particularly true of Rom 8:32.[174] More specifically, however, Lührmann notes that the title is particularly prominent in Romans (seven times) and Galatians (four times) and is used either in connection with the time of the law's demise (Gal 4:4; Rom 8:3) or with "the vocabulary of proclamation (Rom 1:9; 2 Cor 1:19; Gal 1:16)," noting that for Paul the "content of proclamation is nothing other than justification (Rom 1:17)." Among the Christological titles used by Paul, Lührmann continues, "'Son of God'. . . is the one which most closely corresponds to the theme of justification by faith." On Gal 1:16 (cf. 1:12) Lührmann notes: "The revelation, which stands over against tradition, is the revelation of Jesus Christ in his significance as the eschatological bringer of salvation, who annuls the time of the law with the time of righteousness without the works of the law."[175]

If we apply Lührmann's insight to Gal 2:20 we recognize that Paul is anticipating 4:4-5: "God sent his Son (τὸν υἱὸν αὐτοῦ), born of a woman, born under law, that he might redeem those under law, that we might receive adoption as children (υἱοθεσίαν)." In 2:20, therefore, "faith in the Son of God" means faith in the one who redeemed "me" *from the law* and who indeed for that purpose "loved me and surrendered himself for me." Confirmation of this is found in Paul's use of υἱός and υἱοθεσία in Galatians with reference to believers (3:26; 4:5-7). "Adoption" is applied to believers in the present in antithesis to their former "imprisonment" (3:23) and "slavery" under law (4:7-9; 5:1). To be "children" (literally, "sons") means to be free from the law. The title "Son of God," then, has a certain polemical thrust to it, for the Son came to set humans free specifically from the law. It is then all the more unthinkable that the Galatians should return to it.

The polemical edge in Paul's argument is most clear in his return to the formula of 1:4a. It is significant that to the formula Paul has added the aorist participle ἀγαπήσαντός ("loved"). The reference is to the act of love in Christ's death "for our sins." The

174. Schweizer, s.v. υἱός, *Theological Dictionary of the New Testament,* 8:384.
175. Lührmann, *Offenbarungsverständnis,* 76–78.

phrase "surrendered himself for me" simply specifies what the act of love was. It is also significant that Paul continues to speak in terms of "me," by which again he points to himself as an example of what is true of all believers.[176] The traditional language of the formula, like the baptismal language of 2:19, makes it clear that Paul is reminding the Galatians of what they ought already to know, that Christ's death became a power for life in them by faith. The formula expresses the conviction they hold but are threatening to compromise, indeed as Paul sees it, threatening to abandon. Return to law would be such, not because the law is evil, but because as taught by the opponents it shatters the relationship of radical trust that has been created by God's action in Christ and by the surrender of faith (5:2-4; 3:2-5). Paul's motivation here is his intention to call the Galatians to task for their threatened betrayal of Christ. His arguments therefore are not simply an appeal to reason. They are rather an impassioned recalling of the gospel he had proclaimed to them. His words have not slid away into theological musings; he has very much in mind the crisis situation in Galatia.[177]

2:21 The Polemical Summation of 2:15-20

> I do not deny the grace of God. For if justification comes
> by law, then Christ died for nothing

This final verse of the *propositio* summarizes the content of verses 15 to 20 in a distinctly polemical tone[178] and is also a pointed

176. Pace Schlier, *Galater,* 103, note 1, who interprets by way of Rom 8:32 and 4:25 and sees no stress here on the individual. Better is Bruce, *Epistle to the Galatians,* 146: "While Paul is still using the pronoun 'I'/'me' representatively, it is difficult not to recognize the intense personal feeling in his words."

177. Pace Burton, *Epistle to the Galatians,* 139–40, who properly recognizes "the deep personal feeling" in Paul's words but goes on to describe them as "a spontaneous and grateful utterance" rather than as having "an argumentative intent." I would maintain to the contrary, that the latter is precisely Paul's intention.

178. Properly maintained by Kieffer, *Antioche,* 78; Oepke, *Galater,* 64.

statement of the main theme of the letter. The first sentence harks back to Paul's indicting the Galatians for "deserting the one who called you in grace" (1:6) and anticipates the severe warning to those who accept circumcision: "You are cut off from Christ, . . . you have fallen from grace" (5:4). The conditional clause[179] echoes the principle of 2:16 that the law is excluded as a means of "righteousness" before God. The apodosis ("Christ died for nothing") corresponds antithetically to the formula of 1:4a and its restatement in 2:20. The separatist notions of the Judaizers have created a dilemma. For the Judaizers, of course, no dilemma exists, but for Paul in this context "the truth of the gospel" hangs on the alternative, law or gospel, law or grace. "Grace" here, as Mussner notes, is not only the event of Christ's death "for me," it is also a new "dispensation," which "stands over against another dispensation, the dispensation of law."[180]

These are two radically different ways of "living [in relation] to God," in other words, two different ways of seeking "righteousness." "Righteousness by law" is only part of the opponents' teaching, of course, and Paul was aware of that. In other circumstances he also would counsel believers to obey the law (Romans 14; 1 Cor 7:19). The difference is that in Galatia—at least as Paul understands the issue—the law is becoming *constitutive* of righteousness, and for Paul that is a crucial difference. For the apostle, the divine-human relationship cannot be defined in terms of the law's prescriptions and demands but only in terms of that radical

---

Betz, *Galatians,* 126 (cf. 114 and note 15), on the other hand, maintains that, in accordance with the nature of a *propositio,* this "concluding statement" is "the refutation of a charge." While this is possible and a tempting alternative, we shall see that the evidence does not favor interpreting the verse as though Paul was defending himself. It would appear rather that he continues polemically to expose the fault of the Galatians (see below).

179. Kieffer, *Antioche,* 78, takes the condition to be *irrealis,* which is possible, but Burton, *Epistle to the Galatians,* 141, properly cites 3:18 as a similar instance of a *conditio realis,* where what is supposed is contrary to fact. The condition is "real" insofar as it describes the teaching of the opponents; its content, however, in Paul's view, is false.

180. Mussner, *Galaterbrief,* 184.

surrender to God's grace that is faith. That is the qualitative difference between the principles of "works" and "faith" (Rom 3:27).

Paul's statements are clearly polemical, but to what is he reacting? Is it the Galatians' apostasy, or is Paul defending himself against the accusation that his gospel "denies the grace of God" as given in the law? A number of interpreters favor this latter view.[181] It is true, of course, that Jews considered the law to be God's most gracious gift to Israel (e.g., Deut 4:8 and passim; Psalm 119; Jubilees 2:31-33 and passim),[182] and an accusation of the kind mentioned might be seen behind Romans 3:31. Galatians, however, does not exhibit such a concern. Paul lays himself open to such a charge (e.g., 3:15–4:9; see especially 3:19-22), but nowhere is it apparent that he defends himself against it.[183] To the contrary he is on the offensive, denying that the law, as understood in Galatia, has anything to do with grace. Following on 2:20b, it ought to be clear that "grace" refers to the death of Christ "for me," not to the giving of the law. Furthermore, there is a striking correspondence of vocabulary between 2:21 ("deny the grace of God," "righteousness through law") and 5:4 ("fall from grace," "made righteous through law"). "Denying the grace of God" is Paul's description of the opponents' teaching and the Galatians' threatened apostasy. Paul, then, is on the offensive in light of the Galatian crisis.[184]

181. See Betz, *Galatians,* 126; Burton, *Epistle to the Galatians,* 140; Schlier, *Galater,* 104.

182. On this, see also Betz, *Galatians,* 126 and note 114; Schlier, *Galater,* 104, note 2; and especially E. P. Sanders, *Judaism,* 241–78, particularly 267 and 275–78.

183. Most interpreters similarly see Paul attacking the view being taught and accepted in Galatia rather than as defending himself: for example, Beyer and Althaus, "Galater," 21; Bonnard, *Galates,* 57; Brinsmead, *Response to Opponents,* 76; Mussner, *Galaterbrief,* 184 and note 80; Oepke, *Galater,* 64.

184. Bonnard, *Galates,* 57; Mussner, *Galaterbrief,* 184; see a reference to both Antioch (2:11-14) and Galatia at this point. This is not inappropriate, but the linguistic connections with 5:4 and the context in general argue for the Galatian crisis as being in the forefront of Paul's concern.

Most telling is the reason (γάρ) Paul provides why he will not, and the Galatians must not, "deny the grace of God" by recourse to law: "For if righteousness is by law, then Christ died for nothing."[185] From the opening statement of the gospel's content in 1:4a the argument has now come full circle with this reminder of the formula and the insistence that the heart of the debate has to do with what the Galatians believe about the death of Christ (see also 3:1-2). If the law remains at all determinative in the divine-human relationship, then Christ's death essentially changed nothing. Δωρεάν ("for nothing") in the apodosis is the antipode of ὑπὲρ ἡμῶν ("for us") in the formula, just as "law" is the antipode of "grace." Did Christ die "for our sins" or did he die "for nothing"?[186] "Law" or "the grace of God" is the radical alternative Paul wishes the Galatians to face.

The whole argument has to do with accepting *that* grace (that "love") as being *alone* sufficient for "righteousness"—the divine-human relationship in its entirety—as opposed to the com-

185. Even Ziesler, *Meaning of Righteousness,* 174, admits that "the main drift of the argument [vv. 20–21] is indeed forensic." As Betz, *Galatians,* 126, expresses it, "'Righteousness' . . . describes what the act of justification . . . is expected to produce: the status of righteousness before God." Ziesler (174), however, is not wrong to insist that "at the least v. 20 shows that 'a new form of existence under a new power' is also in Paul's mind, which is reflected in 'righteousness' in v. 21. Therefore, righteousness no more than justification is by the law, and this righteousness must surely be equated with the new life of faith of v. 20" (Ziesler's quote is from Tannehill, *Dying,* 59).

186. The apodosis ("Christ died for nothing") includes the thought that if the law were to function as the opponents insist, then it could fulfill what Paul claims has been fulfilled for "all nations" according to God's ancient promise (3:8) by the death of Christ. In other words, "if a law had been given which could give life, then indeed righteousness would be by law" (3:21), but in reality the law *as law* (i.e., as "commandment," Rom 7:7-10) was never given for such a purpose. For the apostle its purpose was always "the primacy of grace" (see E. P. Sanders, *Judaism,* 275–78) and not the definition of "righteousness" in terms of its prescriptions, as Paul's separatist tradition had taken it. Δωρεάν in the sense (as here) of "for nothing," is rare but is not impossible (Job 1:9; LXX Ps 34:7; John 15:25—Bauer, *Greek-English Lexicon,* 209); contra Gaston, *Paul and the Torah,* 67.

promise of the grace of Christ *along with* "works of law." This compromise is what Paul calls "denying the grace of God." What the debate comes down to is the question, Is the death of Christ "for our sins" truly a "rescue" from those sins and from the power of "the evil age" or is it not? If the death of Christ does not accomplish in believers what Paul claims for it, but if on the contrary the law *as law* continues to define and regulate that relationship, then the law still has dominion over the "I" of the believer, and the divisions in humanity fostered by that dominion have not been overcome. It is not that obedience to "works of law" is wrong, but as understood by the Judaizers "works" implicitly deny the salvific effect of the death of Christ, that is, they "annul grace."

"Grace" denotes God's gift, God's initiative of love for humanity lost in sin (Rom 5:6-8). The "righteousness" that corresponds to "grace" has nothing to do with "law" but comes only as God's gift. If the law and its prescriptions were definitive of righteousness, then grace would not be grace (Gal 3:18; Rom 4:14; 11:6) and Christ would have died in vain. Believers are "righteous" and so must exhibit goodness and, indeed, "fulfill the law" (Gal 5:14), but neither in its origin, which is "from God," nor in its fruition, which derives from the Spirit, is their righteousness subject to the definition of law. For Paul, of course, "*their* righteousness" is a misnomer. Any such claims to "my own righteousness" died when, in Christ, "I died to law that I might live to God." "Even we," Paul and other Jewish believers, have been revealed in the light of the gospel to be "sinners" (2:15-17). To be sure, by union with Christ believers have undergone real moral transformation, but the death of the "I" and Christ's life "within me" prevent that righteousness from coming under human control or becoming a human possession. Righteousness, like faith, remains primarily grace. Only in that way can it continue to be seen not as an entity to be acquired by "works" or by "faith" but as the *relationship* created by God in Christ, in which humans participate by the surrender of faith.

The Judaizers, the Galatians, and the faltering Peter did not see the issue in these terms. They did not recognize that so long as the law is permitted a determinative role in the relationship between God and humanity and within humanity itself, then the law represented the antipode to the grace of God in Christ. Paul saw this clearly. That is why he expresses the issue in such absolute terms. To compromise with grace is to deny grace completely. The Judaizers' fault is their illusion that the law has power to "give life" and that they, as its adherents, are "righteous before God." In 3:1 and following, Paul continues his attack on this illusion, but his focus again is not the opponents so much as the law itself. This is necessary because, as he sees it, it is "works of law" that have "bewitched" the Galatians (3:1-5). At least briefly, therefore, we must turn to Paul's arguments in chapter 3.

The Curse of the Law (3:10-13)

INTRODUCTION: THE IMPORTANCE OF THE EPISTOLARY CONTEXT

In the interpretation presented here 2:17-21 takes us back to Paul's radical understanding of the formula of 1:4a. There we saw that the sins for which Christ died were the sins of all humanity, Jew and Gentile alike. Paul returns to the formula at the end of the *propositio,* indicating that his whole argument hangs on the confession of Christ's death as a death "for our sins." The law played no part in the removal of sins, or better, as Paul says it, in believers being "made righteous" before God. On the contrary, as I shall now argue further, the law inflicts its curse on *all* who rely on it (3:10), just as it also cursed the crucified and set him apart from itself (3:13).[187] It is already clear that in Galatians the gospel fea-

187. The exegesis offered here is in various respects diametrically opposed to that of Wright, *Climax of the Covenant,* 137–156, and Donaldson, "Curse," 94–112 (see also Boers, *Justification of the Gentiles,* 69 and 74). Though they differ in several ways, a common key to these interpretations is "an exclusive reading" of "we" in 3:13 as referring only to "Jews," who alone, therefore, are truly "under law" (Donaldson, 97; cf. Wright, 143). In response to two of Donaldson's main points (97): *(a)* Christ's redemption is not for "Torah observers in particular" but for all who mistakenly rely on the law, imagining that it has a power it does not (3:2-5, 11–12, 21). *(b)* To say that "the status of [the] uncircumcised . . . is not under dispute here" flies in the face of the letter's context; the Galatians are being persuaded to accept

tures a distinctly destructive edge, and the primary target of this is the law and its claims. With its *positive* edge the gospel declares that δικαιοῦσθαι is determined only by God's deed in Christ ("grace") and by human acceptance of God's gift ("faith"). With its *negative* edge it destroys the stronghold of separatism, the law's claim to define who are the righteous. This negative edge is unsheathed in the threefold "not by works of law" of 2:16 and the assertion *"we also* were found to be sinners" of 2:17. But the harshness of the gospel's assertions against the law and its adherents, in Paul's analysis, needs careful definition. Specifically we must ask: How could Paul say that law-observant Jews had been "found to be sinners"? What is this "curse of the law"?

Εὑρέθημεν ("we were found"), as has been indicated,[188] corresponds to εἰδότες ("knowing") of 2:16a; both verbs presuppose a previously prevailing state of illusion from which "Jews by birth" were rescued only by becoming believers in Christ (cf. the lifted "veil" in 2 Cor 3:14-16). Jews of the mindset of the opponents, and of Paul when he was "in Judaism," were convinced by their possession and observance of the law that they were "righteous" before God and thus at a distinct advantage over Gentiles.[189] With regard to their own observance of the law the opponents believed the law's promise of life (e.g., Lev 18:5); with regard to the Galatians' neglect of it, its threat of curse (Deut 27:26). This is what the separatism of 2:15 was all about: humans are divided

---

the law in order to attain the same status as the opponents. It is *Gentiles* whom Paul is trying to persuade.

188. Under 2:17, above.

189. Note that this "mindset" is not to be equated with arrogance or legalistic self-righteousness. Such attitudes would undoubtedly be present in *some* Jews (see E. P. Sanders, *Law and the Jewish People,* 156), just as they undoubtedly were, and are, in some Christians, and in my view Paul was concerned with such attitudes among both groups (Rom 2:17-20; 11:17-24; Phil 3:4-9). In Galatians, of course, he accuses the opponents of base, self-serving motives (4:17; 6:13). Such accusations, however, are made in the heat of debate, and their rhetorical character has to be reckoned with. It is historically questionable, therefore, to presume the accuracy of Paul's harsh words even with respect to the opponents; it is even worse to see his judgments as descriptive of Judaism as a whole, as has too often been done.

in accordance with their stance toward the law, and present status will be reflected at the coming judgment. Thus separatism is not primarily a social distinction but a matter of eschatological urgency.[190]

The "knowing" that arises from faith,[191] on the other hand, recognizes that the law was never able to fulfill its promise (3:21)[192] and that the divisions in humanity which it fostered, both for now and the eschaton, have been destroyed "in Christ Jesus" (3:28). The separatist understanding of the law is awry; God's purpose for the law was otherwise (3:19-22). Jewish Christians "know" this, or at least they should. The impotence of "works of law" and consequently their own true status before God were revealed by the event of "being made righteous by faith." This notion that the law promises what it cannot give and thus leads its adherents astray, distorting the divine-human relationship with its demands and promises, is apparent in 3:10-22. The law is portrayed here as a power in opposition to God. The essential points can be established by careful exegesis of 3:10-13.

In the history of interpretation these verses have occasioned enormous difficulty,[193] but if the immediate epistolary context, the

190. See above, under 2:16, where I discussed my differences with Dunn on this issue. Here I wish only to emphasize, in light of my disagreement with Wright and Donaldson (n. 187 above), that for Paul the illusion of "righteousness by works of law" is a universal problem affecting Gentiles as well as Jews. Like those interpreters, Dunn also interprets 3:10 in an exclusive sense ("Works of the Law," *Jesus*, 226, and *Epistle to the Galatians*, 173).

191. On "knowledge" as an important aspect of faith see Bultmann, *Theology of the New Testament*, 1:318.

192. Bruce, *Epistle to the Galatians*, 163, says, "In the context of Leviticus 18:5 the promise of life to those who do what God commands is a genuine promise, but in Rom 10:5 as well as Gal 3:12 Paul indicates that, with the coming of the gospel, that way to life has now been closed, even if once it was open—and it is *doubtful if he would concede even that*" (my emphasis). Eckstein, *Verheißung*, 130, rightly says that for Paul the "Sinai-Torah . . . is excluded as a way of salvation not only as a matter of *fact*, but also as a matter of *principle*."

193. Particular difficulty attaches to Paul's use of the Scripture in these verses, most notably the tension between Hab 2:4 in verse 11 and Lev 18:5 in verse 12. This problem has given rise to several hypotheses about Paul's use

crisis situation to which Paul is responding, is kept clearly in mind, then some clarity can be achieved. In most interpretations this dynamic is almost completely ignored, as though Paul were writing abstract theology, which everyone agrees he is *not* doing.[194] In the discussion of the *narratio* and *propositio* we saw how Paul tailored his language to the circumstances of Galatia. It is reasonable to expect that a similar dynamic is at work here.

A clear interpretation demands answers to several crucial questions that can profitably be enumerated at the outset: (1) What is the relationship between verse 10a, the conclusion with which Paul begins, and verses 10b–12? Specifically, is verse 10a the conclusion *only* to verse 10b? (2) What is the origin of "the curse of the law" (3:13)? Is it God or the law itself? (3) Why is the curse inflicted? Is it because of disobedience or obedience or both? (4) Is the notion of the impossibility of keeping the law important to Paul's argument? (5) Why does Paul quote two Scripture texts (Deut 27:26 and Lev 18:5) that, on the face of it, contradict both the case he is arguing and the other Scripture text he quotes (Hab 2:4)? (6) Why is Paul's attack, here and throughout most of the letter, focused exclusively on the law itself, as opposed to the opponents and their "perverting of the gospel" (1:7)?

---

of Rabbinic methods of exegesis; for example, Schoeps, *Paul,* 177–78. Betz, *Galatians,* 138, notes 8 and 9, discusses Schoeps' hypothesis and several others. He properly rejects them all; the solution to the difficulty is not to be found that way. It is better to interpret in terms of the Galatian situation.

194. Theological interpretations having little or no reckoning with the Galatian situation are given, for example, by E. P. Sanders, *Law and the Jewish People,* 20–24; Bonnard, *Galates,* 67–68. Betz, *Galatians,* 144–48, takes the historical situation into account somewhat, but he fails to consider that the Scripture texts may not all have been introduced by Paul, an important issue in a debate largely concerned with the meaning of texts. Dunn's focus on the letter situation is diverted by his view that Paul in 3:10 is reacting to those who "were putting too much weight on the distinctiveness of Jews from Gentiles, and on the special laws which formed the boundary markers between them" (*Epistle to the Galatians,* 172; see "Works of the Law," *Jesus,* 228–29). He therefore underplays the obvious point that Paul is directly addressing the Gentile Galatians (3:1, "you stupid Galatians"!) and is warning them of *their* "desire to be under law" (4:21).

AN OVERVIEW OF 3:1-22

Like the rest of the letter, the first major section of the *probatio* (3:1-22) is carefully planned. In 3:1-9 there are two arguments: first, an appeal to the Galatians' experience that works of law had nothing to do with their receiving the Spirit (vv. 1–5),[195] second, an appeal to Abraham as the true anticipation and model of Christian faith.[196] They who aspire to be Abraham's children (3:29) must be like him in receiving "righteousness" by faith alone (vv. 6–9).[197] Verses 10–12 are the negative counterpart to the positive argument of verses 6–9. From the thesis that οἱ ἐκ πίστεως ("those who rely on faith")[198] are blessed, Paul moves to the antithesis that ὅσοι ἐξ ἔργων νόμου ("those who rely on works of law") are cursed.[199] "The curse of the law" (v. 13) is de-

195. See Lull, *Spirit in Galatia,* 54–56.

196. See Käsemann, "Faith of Abraham," *Perspectives on Paul,* 79–101, on the unique role assigned to Abraham by Paul as the prototype of Christian faith. This interpretation of Romans 4 has been contested by Cranford, "Abraham," 71–88, who largely follows Hays (see n. 50, above). Cranford (77f.) says that "if Paul were trying to invalidate reliance on good works in the light of human failure, Abraham would not be a suitable example . . . , since Abraham's obedience was proverbial." What Cranford misses is that Paul here, as in 9:11 and throughout Romans and Galatians, invalidates reliance on works "whether good or bad" on the principle that what matters is not human "desiring or striving, but God who has mercy" (9:16).

197. Verse 6 is best taken with verses 7–9, as in Nestle; Betz, *Galatians,* 137–38; Dunn, *Epistle to the Galatians,* 159, rather than with verses 1–5, as in United Bible Society and Matera, *Galatians,* 113. Donaldson, "Curse," 101, argues that in this passage (3:6-9) Abraham is not "a model of faith" to be emulated by "Jew or Gentile" but is "a representative figure" (see also Cranford, "Abraham").

198. Dunn, *Epistle to the Galatians,* 163, explains the phrase well: "'Those of faith' are those whose identity is grounded in faith, and whose relationship with God grows out of faith, is characterized and determined by believing and trusting . . . , *without reference to any 'works of the law'*" (my emphasis).

199. Bonneau, "Logic of Paul's Argument," 73 and note 33 (see also Westerholm, *Israel's Law,* 121, n. 40), rejects "rely" as appropriate in translation of ὅσοι γὰρ ἐξ ἔργων νόμου, (3:10) on the grounds that it "does not appear in the Greek" and it "intimates that one seeks justification by accom-

scribed in some detail in verses 10–12, the redemption from the curse in verses 13–14.[200] The antithesis between "the curse of the law" and "the blessing of Abraham" (v. 14) is followed in verses 15–18 by the antithesis between the promise to Abraham and the law's illegitimate intrusion[201] between the promise and its goal (Christ).[202] Verses 19–22 climax this section and prepare for the

---

plishing the law's requirements." And yet he characterizes Paul's opponents (quite rightly, in my view) as "those who believe that one must observe the works of the law in order to be justified" (75). In Rom 2:17 Paul characterizes his opposition as "relying on law" (ἐπαναπαύῃ νόμῳ), and in Philippians 3 "trusting in flesh" is synonymous with "having my own righteousness from law" and *contrasts* with "knowledge of Christ Jesus" and having "faith in [= "rely on"] Christ." Westerholm's reasoning is that "those of works of law" in 3:10 and those "under law" in 4:5 are "the same," and in 4:4-5 "the Jew's personal understanding, interpretation or distortion of the law does not enter the picture" (121 and note 40). But in fact, whereas 4:4-5 states objectively the plight of all humans "under law" whether aware of their plight or not, 3:10 refers polemically to those, like the Judaizers (and Galatians), who are (almost) convinced that the law is the way prescribed by God for the salvation of Jews and Gentiles alike. They have not lost sight of grace; they simply view it differently than does Paul. Thus "those of works of law" is not a purely objective description of their mindset. Paul sees them as "enslaved" (4:22-30), lost in their misunderstanding of the law, and thus as devoid of true faith in Christ (5:2-4). That is why he can also accuse them, perhaps unfairly, of arrogance (4:17; 6:13).

200. I should emphasize here what I will argue in detail below, that verses 11–12 are part of the description of the curse of the law (answering question 1, above).

201. Betz, *Galatians,* 155–56, describes the legal background and vocabulary presupposed in Paul's metaphor. Such an incursion of the law also seems to be presupposed in Rom 5:20 with the use of παρεισέρχομαι ("enter secondarily"), but significantly in Romans the negative connotations with respect to the law are muted in comparison to Galatians.

202. I would like to take up here the instructive discussion of Wright, *Climax of the Covenant,* 162–68, particularly his suggestion that Χριστός, the "one seed," in 3:16 should be understood "in a representative or corporate sense" (165). Such a view is also suggested in 2:19c ("I have been crucified with Christ") and is clearly Paul's understanding in 1 Cor 12:12. Wright makes no allusion to the latter text, but it supports his case well and is obviously reminiscent of Gal 3:28, which, as Wright properly notes,

coming eschatological arguments (3:23–4:7) with a discussion of the law's negative purpose in the time before faith. Of note here is the law's role to provoke transgressions and the distancing of the law's origin from God (see below).

In fact, what characterizes this entire section (3:1-22) is Paul's deliberate *distancing of the law both from God and from the gifts of salvation.* It had no part in the Galatians' coming to faith, nor in Abraham's faith, which "was reckoned to him as righteousness," and that must remain true for those who wish to be Abraham's heirs. Those who rely on the law receive not God's blessing but the law's curse. Indeed, in 3:13, the law distances itself from the crucified Christ, pronouncing him "cursed," and in 3:15-18 it is set apart both from the pronouncement of the promise and its fruition. It is not surprising, then, that in 3:21 Paul says that the law was never intended by God for the role of "giving life." In this portrait the law is a negative power that threatens to distort the promises of God.[203] These are harsh arguments, but in this letter Paul makes no retreat from them—Romans will be a somewhat different matter—and they are crucial for the interpretation of 3:10-13.

---

climaxes this section of Galatians, affirming that the church of Jews and Gentiles is "one" and is "therefore the seed of Abraham" (3:29). Wright, however, does *not* see the law as a hostile power in this context, as I do.

203. On the other hand, of course, the law is not "contrary to the promises" (3:21). This is true because the law and the promises have different functions in God's plan; they are not in competition (Burton, *Epistle to the Galatians,* 192–93). At this point Westerholm's "definition" (*Israel's Law,* 108) of "law" in Paul as "most frequently" referring to "the sum of specific divine requirements given to Israel through Moses" (= "Sinaitic legislation," 109) is correct and helpful; "law" in this narrow sense is to be distinguished from "instances in which the Pentateuch or the sacred scriptures as a whole are meant" (108). "Promises" *and* "law" are given by God and both have their role in salvation history. The negative function of the law, which yet has a positive outcome according to the divine plan, is portrayed in 3:22-25. The introduction of γραφή ("scripture") into the latter passage gives notice of Paul's difficult, paradoxical assertions about the law.

THE ORIGIN OF THE CURSE AND WHY IT IS INFLICTED (3:10)

As Sanders properly points out, Paul begins in verse 10a with his conclusion and then quotes a text that, in the apostle's interpretation, supports (γάρ) that conclusion.[204] The conclusion is evidently the negative antithesis to the positive thesis of verses 7–9. That thesis was supported by Scripture (Gen 15:6 and 18:18 in 3:6 and 8 respectively); so also is the antithesis. The conclusion in verse 10a is to verses 10–12 what verse 7 is to verses 6–9, that is, the major point Paul wishes to establish. Verses 11–12 fill out the description of being under the law's curse. If that were not the case, verse 13 could follow immediately. In other words, verse 10a is substantiated not only by the Scripture quote (Deut 27:26) but also by the antithetical argument of verses 11–12. "The curse of the law" has to do not only with Deuteronomy's pronouncement but also with the law's claim to confer "life," which does not hold true and consequently deludes the opponents (question 1, above). But before going further on this, we must consider the origin of the curse.

This is not a question that can be ignored.[205] Throughout this section, as I have indicated, Paul distances the interfering action of the law from the plan of God. His purpose in part is to distance

204. E. P. Sanders, *Law and the Jewish People,* 22; see also Betz, *Galatians,* 144. Schlier, *Galater,* 132–33, however, believes that the Scripture text is only intended to "emphasize *that* they who rely on law are under the curse." It does not intend, says Schlier, to "provide the reason why the curse falls" on such people, "since in that case the decisive thought would have had to be supplied: no one fulfills the law, i.e. no one can fulfill it." To say this Schlier has to disregard the γάρ ("because") following γέγραπται ("it is written"). Furthermore, the necessary thought to be supplied is not the impossibility of keeping the law but simply the *fact* of human transgression, as noted by Burton, *Epistle to the Galatians,* 164. Schlier skips from the one to the other far too freely. The fact of transgression is presupposed already in the formula of 1:4 and the argument of 2:15-17 and is confirmed in 3:19-22.

205. As does Räisänen, *Paul and the Law,* 94–96. So also does E. P. Sanders at first (*Law and the Jewish People,* 20–27), but later he seems properly to take it for granted that the law inflicts the curse (68–69). The importance of this question will become more apparent in the discussion with Hübner, below.

the *law's* definition of who are the sinners and who the righteous from that of God.[206] The law's curse, as the Judaizers see it, conforms to the judgment of God, but this is not true for Paul. Verse 13 confirms this in two ways. First, the genitive in the phrase, "the curse of the law," particularly in light of Deut 27:26 in verse 10, is best taken as subjective or, at least, as genitive of origin. Second and most decisive, Paul omits from Deut 21:23 in verse 13 the crucial phrase ὑπὸ θεοῦ ("by God"), which he would certainly have included if the curse, in his view, derived from God.[207] This exegesis is also confirmed by the fact that throughout Paul's letters Christ's death on the cross is "according to the will of our God and Father" (1:4c; see also Rom 5:8; 8:32) and was accepted by Christ in a decisive act of obedience (Rom 5:19), for in Christ's death God reconciles the world to himself (2 Cor 5:14-15, 19). In 3:13, therefore, it is clearly *the law* that is seen to curse the crucified, casting him out as an accursed thing but thereby exposing its own alienation from God (question 2).[208]

206. Burton, *Epistle to the Galatians,* 164–65, makes this point very well: "It is of capital importance for the understanding of the apostle's argument to observe that the sentence which he here quotes [v. 10] does not at all express his own conception of the basis of God's judgment, but a verdict of law. . . . It is necessary, therefore, throughout the passage, to distinguish between the verdicts of law and the judgments of God." See also Hooker, "Paul and 'Covenantal Nomism,'" *Paul and Paulinism,* 55: "The inadequacy of the law is seen in the fact that one who was *condemned by the law* has been *pronounced righteous by God.*" For a contrary view see Eckstein, *Verheißung,* 123–24.

207. Contra Hübner, 40 (and see below); Jeremias, *Central Message,* 35; Stuhlmacher, "Das Ende des Gesetzes," 29 and 33; Wilckens, "Aus Werken," *Rechtfertigung,* 91. That Paul used the LXX is clear both from his near-verbatim quotation and from the fact that only the LXX, employing a form of (ἐπι)καταράομαι in both Deut 27:26 and 21:23, provides the key word Paul needs to link the two verses; the Masoretic text uses a different word in each case (see Bruce, *Epistle to the Galatians,* 165). Thus the omission of ὑπὸ θεοῦ is clearly a matter of Paul's redaction (Bruce, ibid.). Contra Bruce, however, Paul does not leave "unanswered" the question by whom Christ was cursed (166).

208. See Käsemann, "Death of Jesus," *Perspectives on Paul,* 36. Further confirmation of this exegesis will come with the interpretation of 3:11, below.

But why, then, is the curse inflicted on humanity? According to the plain sense of Deut 27:26 the law pronounces its curse on *"everyone" (πᾶς)*[209] who transgresses its commands. In verse 10 there is no suggestion that *obedience* to the law might incur the curse. But the undeniable emphasis in verses 10 and 12 on ποιῆσαι ("doing")[210] leads Schlier to the view that the very *doing* of the law earns the curse.[211] Schlier's interpretation, like that of

---

Since Wright, *Climax of the Covenant,* 152, insists that the law's curse is "Israel-specific" and interprets 3:10-13 in terms of "the pattern of exile and restoration," he also insists that Paul's argument *"depends on the validity of the law's curse,* and on the propriety of Jesus, as Messiah, bearing it on Israel's behalf." In this view the redemption from the curse is very weak—the law is not shown to be wrong; it "merely did not have the last word." Furthermore, to be "under law" is part of the *human* condition (Gal 4:4).

209. "Everyone" must be stressed, because Paul sees the curse falling on all humans, Jews and Gentiles. As 4:4 says, even Christ was subject to the law and ultimately, as 3:13 says, to its curse. Christ's "becoming subject to the law" (4:4) is paralleled with his "being born of a woman" (i.e., entering the human condition) and took place "in order that he might redeem those subject to the law" (4:5). This and the near parallelism of "us" and "gentiles" in 3:13-14 ought to make it clear that Paul regards all humanity as subject to the law and its curse. Most interpreters would agree with this: for example, Mussner, *Galaterbrief,* 224; Reicke, "Law and This World," 273–74; E. P. Sanders, *Law and the Jewish People,* 81–83; Schlier, *Galater,* 193.

210. Contra E. P. Sanders, *Law and the Jewish People,* 54, note 26. With regard to the emphasis on "doing" in 3:10 see Kertelge, "Gesetz" (1984) 387; Mussner, *Galaterbrief,* 224; Schlier, *Galater,* 132–34 (see following note for some disagreement with Schlier).

211. Schlier, *Galater,* 133: "The quote [in 3:10] presupposes throughout that the law can be fulfilled and that it is fulfilled. This means that in what follows the only thought which is drawn from the citation is what has been mentioned, that the doers of 'what is written' are cursed." It is far more likely, however, that Paul presupposes human sinfulness than the actual or even possible fulfillment of the law. The fact of human sinfulness is one of Paul's basic presuppositions. On this point Schlier is undoubtedly under the influence of Bultmann's famous dictum (*Theology of the New Testament,* 1:259-69): "The way of works of the Law and the way of grace and faith are mutually exclusive opposites. . . . But why is this the case? Because *man's effort to achieve his salvation by keeping the law* only leads him into sin, indeed this effort in the end *is already sin*" (264). See also Bonnard, *Galates,* 68, following Schlier.

Bultmann (previous note), goes a step too far at the crucial point. There is no text of Paul that goes so far as to say that the very doing of the law is sinful. To be sure, the law *occasions* sin (3:19; Rom 4:15) in that its commands incite "covetousness," which humanity, "sold under sin," could not resist once its enticement was made known by the law's prohibition (7:7-17). But such sin has to do with the weakness of "fleshly" humans (7:14), not with any wrongfulness in obeying or attempting to obey the law. To the contrary, Paul presupposes that obedience to the law, *as dictated by the gospel,* remains the obligation of all (Rom 2:1-29; Gal 5:14). Obedience to the law, then, is not sinful, but on the other hand, neither does it lead to "righteousness."[212] Thus even the obedient, insofar as they rely on "works of law," come under the curse in that "by law no one is justified before God," as verses 11–12 establish (see below). Both the obedient and the disobedient ultimately come under the curse (question 3), but for now we need only stress that the *disobedient,* both Jews and Gentiles, are subject to it.

But this immediately raises the question whether Paul believed that obedience to the law was *possible.* Even Sanders, who answers this question in the affirmative, has to admit in his interpretation of 5:3 that Paul "did not forget that it [=Deut 27:26] said 'all.'"[213] Whether "all" in 3:10 is stressed or not,[214] the verse naturally *implies* that no one can in fact obey "all the things written."

---

212. Contra Wilckens, "Aus Werken," *Rechtfertigung,* 92, who presents the thesis that "only the one who fulfills the law perfectly will gain life thereby," but in fact "all Jews have sinned, so that the law curses them." The interpretation offered here lies between the extremes represented by Schlier and Bultmann on the one hand and Wilckens on the other.

213. E. P. Sanders, *Law and the Jewish People,* 21 and 27 respectively. Sanders has now decided against his earlier view that the law as Paul saw it could not be fulfilled (52, n. 21). The "all" (πᾶσιν) in question here is "all [the commands] written in the book of the law" (3:10, quoting LXX Deut 27:26).

214. Ibid., 21, says it should not be stressed. In general, as will become clear, I agree with Sanders on this in that the point for Paul is not the impossibility of the law. Wilckens, "Aus Werken," *Rechtfertigung,* 92, on the other hand, wants to stress "all" heavily because, as he sees it, the law would make righteous if all its commands were obeyed.

On the other hand, Paul does not actually use this argument, even though it easily lay to hand (cf. Acts 15:10). Our conclusion must be that the impossibility of obeying the law sufficiently is not Paul's major point in quoting Deut 27:26 (question 4). "The thrust," as Sanders says, "is borne by the words *nomos* ["law"] and 'cursed.'"[215] Paul's major point is the conclusion with which he began, "They who rely on works of law are under a curse." But if this is so, Räisänen's criticism of Sanders, that Deut 27:26 is "poorly chosen" if "Paul only wished to show that 'those who accept the law are cursed,'" is not to be ignored. As Räisänen goes on to say, "The text would seem to say exactly the opposite."[216]

This raises the issue of why Paul quotes two texts that fly in the face of what he is trying to say, and that brings us again to the matter of the influence of the letter situation on Paul's argumentation. In the hands of the opponents Deuteronomy as a whole was an obvious weapon to persuade ("compel") the Galatians to conform to the law's demands. Deut 27:26 is the climactic, all-inclusive curse of the Shechemite dodecalogue, which, with its sequel of blessings on those who obey the law, supports their argument rather well but Paul's rather poorly. The same has to be said of Lev 18:5. The unsuitability of these texts for Paul's argument is one of the reasons these verses are so difficult to interpret.[217] But then why does Paul quote them? The obvious answer,

---

215. E. P. Sanders, *Law and the Jewish People,* 21.

216. Räisänen, *Paul and the Law,* 95, note 13. For his part, Räisänen interprets 3:10-12 as offering "two different explanations of the curse of the law" (96): Verse 10 has in mind "the impossibility of fulfilling the Torah" (94, thus his disagreement with Sanders), verses 11–12 "that it drives man to *do* things" (ibid.). This goes along with Räisänen's thesis that Paul's theology is full of tensions and contradictions (11), a thesis of last resort, which I regard as unnecessary.

217. The difficulty is well illustrated by the various interpretations mentioned and rejected by Betz, *Galatians,* 145–46. His own interpretation stresses too much, as I see it, Paul's denial of "the *Jewish* concept of 'works of the Torah'" (146), which has Paul attacking some monolithic "concept" belonging to Judaism as such. What needs to be stressed is the way Paul is reacting to the opponents and *their* use of these texts and his desire to persuade the Galatians.

as Barrett has maintained, is that they were introduced into the debate by the opponents.[218] Paul's purpose is to show that the Scriptures actually support his view, not that of the Judaizers (question 5). In 3:10 he uses the connection of "law" and "curse" to portray the law as a negative, threatening power that stands over against God's intention to bless all nations in Christ. In quoting the law's threat of curse Paul is quoting not only Deuteronomy but also, and indeed especially, the opponents themselves. Furthermore, we may suspect that Paul's portrait of the law as interfering in the "covenant" (3:15-18) is colored to no small degree by the actions of the opponents. They are the ones who, contrary to God's eternal plan for the Gentiles (3:8), are imposing "deeds of law," compelling the Galatians to be circumcised and threatening them with the law's curse if they refuse.[219] Paul's rhetoric assimilates the Judaizers' threat to the law's curse and thus personifies the law—similarly as "sin" and "death" in other texts (Rom 5:12; 1 Cor 15:26, 54-56)—as a power in defiance of God.

Such rhetoric against the law itself was necessary in this context because of the Galatians' becoming enamored of the law as the means to "complete" righteousness (3:2-5). An attack on the Judaizers themselves was not enough; Paul had to disabuse the Galatians of their "fascination" (3:1) with the law (question 6). But such an attack is rhetorical, constructed for purposes of

218. Barrett, "Allegory," 6–7. See also Cosgrove, *Cross and the Spirit,* 59, with respect to Lev 18:5 as "a slogan of the agitators."

219. E. P. Sanders, *Law and the Jewish People,* 27, calls 5:3 "a kind of threat." This is applicable, in my view, to 3:10 also. In the Galatian context Deut 27:26, whether from the opponents or Paul, would be threatening. Of course in the opponents' teaching the purpose would be to encourage obedience to the law, but in Paul's rhetoric it illustrates the law's oppressive power from which there is no escape except through Christ. On verse 10 as a "threat" see also Stanley, "Under a Curse," 501. My one disagreement with Stanley is his stress on the "potentiality" (e.g., 509) of the curse, as though Paul did not see it as in fact realized due to human sinfulness. Paul's argument is rhetorical in that he aims to persuade by a one-sided, purely negative portrait of the law, but this does not mean that the curse for him is less than real, as 3:13 with 4:4-5 clearly shows.

persuasion. It is not an absolute rejection of the law in all its aspects; much less is it an attack on Judaism as such. It is in fact primarily an attack on what Paul sees as a misunderstanding and, more than that, as an abuse of the law, which in its origins, contrary to the opponents' claims, was not intended "for giving life" (3:21). Paul carries through this rhetorical attack against the law because of what it has become in the minds of the Galatians. Its demand for obedience to its prescriptions and its promise of "life" are undoubtedly compelling for them. In 3:11-12, to which we must now turn, Paul denies that the law has the power that the opponents claim for it. In Paul's portrait the law catches its adherents in a double bind, the first half of which is that the law curses all who transgress any of its commands; except by God's grace the disobedient will not escape. But what of the obedient? That is the second half of the double bind.

THE IMPOTENCE OF THE LAW (VV. 11–12)

In verse 10 Paul turns the opponents' (and the law's) connection of curse and law from an exhortation to obey the law to a portrayal of the law as a negative, threatening power that demands that all its statutes be observed. In verses 11–12 it is as though he moves from refuting the opponents' interpretation of Deut 27:26, with its threat of "curse," to refuting their interpretation of its sequel of blessings. Just as they would connect law and curse, so also they would connect law and blessing, or in the words of Lev 18:5, law and life. Again, in quoting Leviticus it is likely that Paul is following the opponents who introduced the text into the debate.

The δέ ("but") of verse 11a "introduces a matter in addition to a previous one ('furthermore')."[220] Verse 10 represents the first

---

220. Betz, *Galatians,* 146; Räisänen, *Paul and the Law,* 96. As Betz says, this means that "v. 11 is more than simply a 'parallel' to v. 10," contra Schlier, *Galater,* 133. Due to his interpretation of verse 10, Schlier sees nothing added by verse 11 except the Scripture proof. But actually, whereas verse 10 has in view the curse on the disobedient, verse 11 shows that even the obedient, such as the law-observant Judaizers, do not gain what they expect,

half of the law's double bind, verses 11–12 its second half. Verse 10 refers to the law's curse on the disobedient; verses 11–12 show that the law cannot "give life," not even to those who "abide by all that has been written." "It is evident," says Paul, "that no one is made righteous before God by law." The phrase "by law" (ἐν νόμῳ) stands starkly over against "before God" (παρὰ τῷ θεῷ). The law's verdict of life does not coincide with the judgment of God any more than its verdict of curse.[221] This further confirms that the origin of the curse is the law, not God. Paul supports his negative assertion ("no one is made righteous before God by law") by the positive statement of Hab 2:4 ("the one who is righteous by faith shall live").[222] He presumes that the Galatians will acknowledge the prophetic text as the Scripture's authentic witness to the truth of the gospel. This may indicate that he used this

---

and thus neither do they escape the curse. Wilckens, "Aus Werken," *Rechtfertigung,* 92, seems to interpret δέ as meaning "thus" or "therefore" ("So wird ἐν νόμῳ niemand bei Gott gerecht").

221. This is where I part company with Westerholm, *Israel's Law,* for example, 121, 156, 163, who, like Wilckens, "Aus Werken," *Rechtfertigung,* 92, sees the mere *fact* of human sin as the reason for the law's failure, suggesting that if only humans were completely obedient, then the law could be effective for salvation. The law's very insistence on obedience to its demands, which Westerholm (109–21) brings out so well, has convinced the Judaizers that the law's definition of righteousness is decisive, and it is that conviction that Paul tries to expose as an illusion. Paul's opposition is convinced that the principle of "doing" on which the law operates (3:12) is still operative in conjunction with "faith in Christ," as necessary in the divine-human relationship. For Paul that conviction, which, to repeat, is their interpretation of 2:16a, is an illusion produced by the law's demand for "works." To disabuse the Galatians of this conviction, Paul turns on the law itself.

222. In the present context, on the basis of ἐν νόμῳ οὐδεὶς δικαιοῦται (v. 11a) it is better to take ἐκ πίστεως with ὁ δίκαιος rather than with ζήσεται, so that the Habakkuk quote should read: "the one who by faith is righteous shall live" (see Westerholm, *Israel's Law,* 111). Fitzmyer, *Romans,* 265, with reference to Rom 3:20, argues that ἐκ πίστεως should be taken with ζήσεται which is not impossible, but Fitzmyer misses the significance of the contrast in Gal 3:11 between "made righteous by law" and "righteous by faith."

text in his preaching in Galatia (cf. Rom 1:17);[223] it certainly in-dicates that Paul can presume upon the authority of the confes-sion enshrined already in 2:16a that "all (Jews and gentiles) are made righteous by faith in Christ (alone), apart from the law," which is the evident foundation of Paul's argument here and in the rest of the *probatio.*

It is that same confession on which Paul relies in verse 12 in order to say *why* "no one is justified before God by law." "The law," he says, "does not depend upon faith," which also includes the thought that it is less than conducive to faith, as is already clear from 2:19 ("I died to law that I might live to God"). The law, to the contrary, depends on "doing" and defines human existence before God in terms of "works"; "the one who does them shall live by them" (Lev 18:5). Consequently, the law deludes its ad-herents into reliance upon itself. This is why even the obedient are under "the curse of the law." Their existence, or their "I," to recall 2:19-20, is based upon the law and its demand for performance as opposed to God's grace and the human response of faith in Christ. Such in Paul's view are the Judaizers and all who depend on their teaching. But this teaching is false, both because it flies in the face of the Christian confession that all are justified by faith alone and because, as Abraham shows, the ancient covenant ("the promise") is based on grace and faith, not on law. The law's claims and the opponents' convictions based on them have be-come a competitor to the gospel; in Paul's harsh portrait the law has become a power of illusion.[224]

223. This point is well made by Cosgrove, *Cross and the Spirit,* 55–57, who also points out that "the words of Leviticus 18:5 had become by Paul's day a common sentence–summary of the law," being reflected in texts as di-verse as "Neh 9:29; Ez 20:13, Lk 10:28; CD 3:16, and Pss.Sol 14:3," in none of which "is it introduced by any citation formula" (59 and n. 39), as is also the case in Gal 3:12 (cf. Rom 10:5).

224. The question arises of the relationship between Paul's rhetoric— his harsh metaphors, personifying the law as intruding between the promise and Christ (3:15-18) and so on—and Paul's theology—his serious and sober assessment of the law in God's plan of salvation. "Rhetoric" must serve "the-ology" but presumably does not run so far astray from theology that major

THE LAW AS A DECEPTIVE POWER OF THE EVIL AGE

On the face of it, then, Paul asserts that Lev 18:5 and Deut 27:26 are false statements, and he supports his assertion by appealing against them to Hab 2:4. As Beker would have it: "In a daring move, Paul opposes scripture to scripture (cf. Rom 10:5-9) and thus splits scripture apart, because Lev 18:5 is antithetical to God's will in Christ."[225] Rather more nuance than this, however, is required. Paul does not so much split Scripture apart as he refutes the Judaizers' interpretation of texts that, as he sees it, they do not understand. When they read these texts "a veil lies over their hearts" (2 Cor 3:15). Specifically, they ascribe to these texts an authority to embody the promise and its fulfillment that, in Paul's view, they do not possess (3:15-22). Paul is not rejecting the Deuteronomy and Leviticus texts as such; he rejects only an interpretation of them that makes "works of law" constitutive of the divine-human relationship. In another context (e.g., Rom 2:13; 1 Cor 7:19) Paul implicitly appeals to both of these texts—at least, to the principle they represent—in support of "[his] gospel," which does indeed require "doing goodness" (Rom 2:10, 16). It is what these and other texts have become in the hands of the Judaizers that has led Paul to attack the law itself. In Antioch, Jerusalem, and now Galatia the law was a weapon in the hands of those who opposed Paul's gospel. Indeed it was a powerful and effective weapon, persuading the hearts and minds of believers.

It should be no surprise, therefore, that in this letter the law is portrayed as a power of the "the present evil age" (1:4b). The further aspect of this portrait that now emerges is that the law is

---

assertions might ultimately be written off as "mere rhetoric." Nevertheless, it is surely not insignificant that the harshest metaphors of Galatians 3 (the "curse," the "intrusion," and the "angels"—the latter in conjunction with "the elements" [4:3, 8-9]) are not at all repeated in the more sober discussion of Romans, even though Paul's *theology* of the law does not essentially change from one letter to the other. More on this in chapter 5.

225. Beker, *Paul the Apostle,* 54. Beker calls the "logic" of Galatians "cryptic, intuitive and often inconsistent," and this is "because it is dictated by the crisis at hand" (58). As will become clear, I believe Galatians is rather closer to the heart of Paul's theology than Beker allows.

seen as a deceptive power that distorts the divine-human relationship and leads its adherents into illusion. In that sense the law is indeed "an antidivine agency."[226] The illegitimate intrusion of the law (3:15-17), the denial of its direct origin from God (3:19-20), its alignment with "the weak and beggarly elements [of the universe]" (4:1-9),[227] and the reiterated metaphor of the law as an enslaving power (3:23-25; 4:1-9; 5:1) confirm this. Its deception specifically has to do with its deluding of the obedient. That the law condemns the disobedient would require no argument, and it would be easy enough for the opponents to show that the Galatians had incurred this curse. Paul does not argue this point but, typically, attacks the opponents where they might think they are strongest. Not only are "sinners of the gentiles" under "the curse of the law," but so also are Jews, and Jewish Christians who are obedient to it. They also are "sinners," *not because* of their obedience but *in spite of it.* The law's promise that it can confer "life" is deceitful; it was never intended by God for such a purpose. This deception is the second half of the double bind in which the law holds humanity captive. "Life," meaning, of course, eschatological salvation, comes only by faith in Christ, and Christ knows no distinction between Jews and Gentiles.[228] That is why even "we

226. As Beker, *Paul the Apostle,* 54, merely says it "seems" to be.

227. On 3:19 and its statement on the law's inferior origins see Callan, "Pauline Midrash," 549–67; see also the discussion of Hübner, *Law in Paul's Thought,* 26–28, who says that the angels are "to be understood as demonic beings," which is certainly possible in this context. On the aligning of the law with "the elements," see Keck, "Paul as Thinker," 33; the discussions by Reicke, "Law and This World," 259–76 (n. 273); and Vielhauer, "Gesetzesdienst," 543–55 (n. 554), bringing out the harshness of Paul's language here.

228. This notion of the law as a deceptive power in Galatians has to answer some difficult questions from texts in Romans: Does not Rom 2:6-13 (cf. 7:10) represent the promise of *God* that those who "are doers of the law shall be made righteous"? How, then, can Lev 18:5 be seen as the *law's* deceptive promise? The answer lies in the differing contexts and purposes of the two letters. In Galatians Paul's attack, for reasons given, is directed against the law itself, and Paul therefore dissociates the law from God. In Romans, on the other hand, the attack turns upon the transgressions of the law's adherents. Thus in Romans 2 (quite unlike Galatians 2–4) Paul's purpose

Jews by birth" "were found" in the light of the gospel "to be sinners" no less than the Gentiles (2:15-17).

A POSSIBLE OBJECTION

The dissociation of the law's curse from God's judgment,
which has been an important part of the exegesis here, has to answer the objection of Hübner that "the curse pronounced by the
law in Deut. 27:26 is completely effective precisely because it is
God's curse, though of course pronounced by the law!"[229] The implication of this is that if the law's curse does not derive from
God, then in Paul's mind it could not possibly be effective. But if
this were true, how could Paul speak of the law as an enslaving
power? The latter requires that Paul envisaged the law as a power
in opposition to God, not unlike "sin" (Rom 5:12-21) and "death"
(1 Cor 15:26, 54-56). But that is precisely what we find in Paul,
especially in Galatians (2:19; 3:13-19; 4:4-5; cf. Rom 7:2-6;
1 Cor 15:56). The alternative is that Paul envisaged God operating in a virtually schizophrenic fashion, being forced to combat
his own authority resident in the law. And actually that is the view
to which Hübner has recourse: "The authority of the law is so
great that it is capable not only of putting all men under the curse
and promising real life but in addition of moving God himself to
react to the stipulations of the law."[230] But there is no need of such
extravagant notions.

The curse of the law is effective in precisely the same way
as "the evil age" and all of its powers are effective; it is at war
with the Spirit (5:17) and holds humans in bondage so that they
are unable to know God (4:8-9), making necessary Christ's liber-

---

is to show that the law is the gospel's ally, representing God's just demands
in the context of the "gospel" (2:16), indicting Gentiles and Jews as sinful
(3:9-19, 23), and "witnessing" to the gospel as the revelation of the righteousness of God (3:21b). More on this in chapter 5.

229. Hübner, *Law in Paul's Thought,* 39; his view is diametrically opposed to the one offered here: "The power of the law" for Hübner means that
it is not possible "to see the promise of life . . . at Lev. 18:5 as falsehood
and deception."

230. Ibid.

ating death (2:19-20; 3:13; 5:1, 24). Its power is known in its deluding of its adherents and in its dividing humanity according to
their allegiance to or ignorance of its commands. It is because of
such separatism that in 3:13-14 Paul envisages Christ's death as
"redeeming us from the curse of the law . . . so that the blessing
of Abraham might redound to the gentiles."

Accordingly "the curse of the law" is far more than simple
rhetoric. Although the Judaizers have been deluded by the law,
Paul is not combatting merely a misconception of their minds.
The fact that he directs the attack so much against the law itself,
personifying it as an illegitimate intruder, indicates that he views
the Judaizers' action as symptomatic of a power much greater
than them. The law itself has become a power of the evil age. This
is why Paul can approximate so closely his critique of the law to
the actions of the Judaizers. The latter are in the process of "perverting the gospel" (1:7) and thus of "bewitching" (3:1) the Galatians, but it is evident that they themselves are victims of the law's
deception. They are among those who "rely on works of law"
(3:10) and have believed the law's promise of life as well as its
threat of curse. The discovery of the illusion was only possible "in
Christ" (2:17)

V

Summation and Further Issues

Summary of Major Arguments

THE CONTEXTUAL METHOD

Throughout this book I have tried to show how interpretation benefits when the historical situation is taken into account as fully as possible. Paul's arguments, including his vocabulary and manner of describing events, were deeply influenced by the pressures of the Galatian crisis. The emphatic denials and assertions about his apostolate at the beginning of the letter answer the attack, whether explicit or implicit, that the opponents made against him. His description of the Jerusalem and Antioch incidents reflect the very vocabulary that he uses of the Galatian situation. His harsh portrait of the law, that its origins were inferior and that it functioned in a purely negative fashion in Israel's history, must also be viewed in light of his estimation of the opponents and the near apostasy of the Galatians. The fact that several Scripture texts actually run counter to Paul's argument indicates that they were probably favored texts not of Paul but of his opponents. The further observation that he portrays the law as a power that has led those who relied upon it into illusion suggests that this portrait has been made to fit the contours of the opponents' preaching. The law is an intruder in God's plan of salvation in a manner reminiscent of the Judaizers in Galatia. This unrelenting attack on the law itself is one of the primary distinguishing features of this

letter and, like the letter's other major features, cannot be understood unless its historical context is taken into account.[1]

THE ATTACK ON PAUL'S APOSTOLATE AND HIS RESPONSE

In order to achieve their primary purpose of discrediting
Paul's gospel it was also necessary for the Judaizers to discredit
his apostolate. To this end they contrasted Paul unfavorably with
the Jerusalem apostles and, indeed, may have denied Paul the title
of apostle completely. They certainly seem to have portrayed him
as a renegade pupil of Jerusalem, his primary fault being that he
did not maintain the law as they did. Paul's response to these assertions is found in 1:1–2:14.[2] In this narrative of the central
events Paul balances delicately between conceding, on the one
hand, that the Jerusalem apostles had any authority over him and
suggesting, on the other, that he did not value their authority and
importance in the church, as though there was opposition between
them and him. In the crucial final clause of 2:2, what Paul concedes is the "pillars'" ability to do harm to his missionary endeavors but not any authority to declare his gospel deficient.

It would have been impossible for Paul to concede the latter
because, as his positive statements in response to the opponents
make clear, he knew his apostolate and gospel to be by God's di-

---

1. There seem to have been three major factors in the Galatian situation that pushed Paul to his negative portrait of the law. He had to contend
with (a) the Judaizers' ability to quote the law against his gospel; (b) its considerable authority in the minds of the Galatians themselves, and (c) the supposed superiority of "Jews by birth" due to their standing within the law. Of
course, with only small adjustments these factors would also be operative
elsewhere (Jerusalem, Antioch, Philippi, Rome), so the issue of the law as
antithesis of the gospel must have been a reality for Paul during much of his
ministry, *at least* from the time of the Jerusalem Council in 48/49. His views,
then, in Galatians are by no means merely extemporaneous and rhetorical,
even though the question of the relation of rhetoric to theology in Galatians
does need to be asked.

2. Apart from 1:1–2:14 the only other explicit response by Paul to a
possible attack on his apostolate might be 5:11: "But if I myself am still
preaching circumcision, why am I still being persecuted?" On this very ob-
scure verse, see Betz, *Galatians,* 268-69.

rect commission. He was not content, therefore, only to refute the opponents' claims regarding his connections with Jerusalem; he was also intent to state in unequivocal terms his authority from God "to preach the gospel among the gentiles" (1:16). It was God, and God alone, who had taken Paul from his attachment to his "ancestral traditions" (1:14) and made him an apostle. It was inconceivable, therefore, that any human or even "angelic" authority should contradict the gospel Paul had preached.

THE "GOSPEL" OF THE OPPONENTS AND PAUL'S RESPONSE: THE SUPREME AUTHORITY OF THE GOSPEL

Although Paul's response to the attack on his apostolate can be distinguished from his response to the attack on his gospel, there is nevertheless an insoluble connection between them. The claim of the opponents that Paul is a renegade follower of the Jerusalem apostles and thus the implication that he has no divine commission to preach the gospel derives from their conviction that the content of Paul's preaching, particularly its neglect of the law, runs contrary to the will of God as clearly revealed in the Scriptures and in Israel's most sacred traditions. Their "gospel," not Paul, was their primary concern. That "gospel" was compelling because of the wealth of sacred tradition on which it could draw. The opponents had Paul at a disadvantage when it came to the use of sacred Scripture, for Scripture unquestionably demands circumcision of all Abraham's "heirs" (Gen 17:1-14). Furthermore, Scripture also demands that its statutes be observed and that those "who do not abide by everything written in the book of the law" (Deut 27:26) are under a curse. The law promises "life," as everyone knew, and therefore it is those who obey the law and believe in the Messiah the Scripture promises who are truly "righteous before God." It is not surprising that the Galatians were on the verge of capitulating to this gospel.

To refute these assertions was a far more challenging task for Paul than to refute the claims about the origins of his apostolate, for which it was sufficient to interpret history. But the *basis* of his refutation remains the same in both instances, namely, *the supreme authority of the gospel.* It is because of what the gospel reveals that Paul and other Jewish Christians "know that no one is made righteous by works of law but (only) by faith in Jesus Christ" (2:16). Paul's arguments derive from his convictions about God's eschatological action in Christ, "who gave himself for our sins" (1:4). It was the "revelation of Jesus Christ" (1:12), "the Son," which transformed him into an apostle "to the gentiles" (1:16) and exposed the inadequacy of the law, and which therefore lies at the heart of his varied statements aimed at denigrating the law.[3] The Galatian crisis was the cauldron in which Paul's arguments were formed, but the guiding principle in the formation of those arguments is the supreme authority of the gospel. It is that gospel, and the "new creation" that God is effecting by it, that exposes the law as a mere temporary and negative power in the history of the world.

This does not mean, however, as Sanders would have it, that it is merely "the Gentile question and the exclusivism of Paul's soteriology which dethrone the law,"[4] as though Paul did not discover the law itself to be at fault. The "weakness" of the law (Rom 8:3) has to do, especially in Romans, with its powerlessness in the face of "flesh" dominated by sin (7:7-14) and, especially in Galatians, with its operating in opposition to God as a power that leads its adherents into illusion. The Jewish-Christian confession (2:16a) becomes for Paul the basis for his argument that Jews and Jewish believers were mistaken in their former beliefs about the law and themselves as its adherents. These beliefs have (or should

---

3. See Dunn, "Light to the Gentiles," *Jesus,* 89–104, who argues persuasively that the most immediate significance of Paul's conversion was the commission "to the gentiles" and that other aspects of his thought, including the sharp antithesis between the gospel and the law, developed later (n. 98–99). I have argued above that James and Peter did not recognize, as Paul did, the radical implications of the confession of 2:16a. The major difference may well have been Paul's immersion in the Gentile mission and the wrestling with the issue of the law's role which that must have occasioned *particularly in light of the challenge of the Judaizers.* It was what the law had become in their preaching that pushed Paul to his harsh statements on the law in Galatians.

4. E. P. Sanders, *Paul and Palestinian Judaism,* 497 (see also following note).

have) now given way to the "discovery" under the gospel that the law cannot fulfill its promises and that the law's adherents never had the status before God that they thought they had. This is *not* a denial of Israel's election, which Paul affirms (Rom 9:4; 11:1-2, 28-29),[5] but simply the view that *the law* never granted the status that they imagined it did. To the contrary, they were "sinners" no less than the Gentiles. To the extent that the law convinced anyone that obedience to its statutes was the way to "life," it led them into illusion. Faith in Christ, therefore, has led Jewish Christians into abandoning the law as the basis for existence, and Paul has both proclaimed freedom from the law and has himself lived by that principle in Gentile churches such as Antioch. So also, for a time, did Peter and Barnabas and others (2:12a). But that has led to the accusation from Paul's opponents that Christ has been made "an agent of sin" (2:17c), an accusation that caused Peter and Barnabas to withdraw from eating meals with Gentiles.[6] But

---

5. Ibid., 551 (see also *Law and the Jewish People,* 47), seriously overstates the matter when he says, "Paul seems to ignore (and by implication deny) the grace of God toward Israel as evidenced by the election and the covenant. . . . Paul in fact explicitly denies that the Jewish covenant can be effective for salvation, thus consciously denying the basis of Judaism" (emphasis omitted). This flies in the face of Rom 11:11-36 (see also 11:1-2), which, for all of its tensions with other statements in these chapters (e.g., 9:6, 31; 11:7-10), envisages the ultimate salvation of "all Israel," "for the gifts and the call of God are irrevocable" (11:29; see also n. 41, below). Sanders pushes himself to such exaggeration because he cannot allow that "Paul polemicizes" against "the *means* of being properly religious," namely "works of law" (*Paul and Palestinian Judaism,* 551). Unable to allow that critique, Sanders focuses on Paul's "exclusivist soteriology" (550) and sees Paul as hostile to the covenant altogether. But if Paul could have simply dismissed the covenant, as Sanders believes, then his complex arguments about the law would not have been necessary. It is precisely because Paul knows that Israel is "the people of God," with all the gifts of election, covenant, and law (Rom 9:4-5), that his arguments are so tortured. Paul's polemic is not against the covenant but against the *law* and how his opposition sees the law functioning within the covenant.

6. I am not suggesting that 2:17c represents the exact words of the James delegation, but some such argument—conceivably, as articulated in Rom 3:8; 6:1, 15—must have been used to persuade Peter, Barnabas, and the rest to withdraw.

for Paul it is an offense *against Christ* for any believer to deny the effectiveness of the original decision of faith by reestablishing as the basis for life the law that was renounced by that decision (2:18).

The importance of the Jewish-Christian experience in coming to faith as an experience of moving from a life defined by law to one centered upon Christ becomes more apparent in 2:19-20 with the (probably) baptismal language of the death of the "I." The ἐγώ, by the decision of faith, "died to law at the hands of law." The law-dominated "I"—"we Jews by birth" of 2:15—was convinced of the law's definitive role in making humans "righteous before God." What the gospel has revealed is that that was a false conviction, and with the end of that conviction the "I" itself dies, and henceforth lives "to God." Far from bringing life, the law cursed both the crucified and those "crucified with" him, so that life now "in [the] flesh" is focused by "faith in the Son of God who loved me and surrendered himself for me" (2:20). The death of Christ as a death "for me," "for our sins," is the fundamental datum of the gospel, which makes reliance on the law unthinkable. Indeed, reliance on law for "righteousness" is a denial of "grace," as 2:21 makes clear.[7]

In 2:21 Paul sums up his opening theological statements and continues to attack the Galatians for their near denial of "the

---

7. In all of Sanders' references to Gal 2:21 in both *Paul and Palestinian Judaism* and *Law and the Jewish People* (see his indices) he never quotes or interprets its opening sentence, "I do not deny the grace of God," and therefore he never addresses the question, with respect to that verse, how denial of God's grace relates to "righteousness by law." It is, however, clear from Paul's letters that the Judaizers' affirmation of "righteousness by law," that is, by "doing" the law, is for the apostle the denial of grace, alternatively expressed as denial of the "promise" or "faith" (Gal 3:18; Rom 4:2-5, 13-14; 9:31-32; 11:6), as Westerholm, *Israel's Law,* 113-15, has shown clearly. Paul's rejection of the doing of the law as the way to righteousness does not *necessarily* lead to the criticism that "doing" involves "boasting" and "self-righteousness"—though such criticism is clearly apparent in Rom 2:17-20; 3:27—but the law's demand for "doing" is, contra Sanders, *Law and the Jewish People,* 159, a major part of "Paul's objection" to it and a source of the delusion that has led to the Judaizers' teaching.

grace of God." Their threatened apostasy contradicts the confession of the churches that "Christ died for our sins" and presumes that "works of law" are indispensable for "righteousness." Against them Paul brings forward forcefully Christ's atoning death as the only power necessary for the salvation of the world. Although the Judaizers intend nothing of the kind, their conjoining of faith in Christ with the demands of the law (*their* interpretation of 2:16a) so compromises "the grace of God" that in effect, in Paul's view, it is denied completely. By God's grace in Christ "righteousness" is possible for all humans equally by faith; it is a matter of "faithful hearing" not of "works of law" (3:2-5), "not of [human] desiring or striving but of God who has mercy" (Rom 9:16).

It emerges from 2:15-21 that δικαιοῦσθαι ("to be made righteous") is not merely a forensic and eschatological term but also has in mind all that Paul means by "new creation." In the study of 1:4 and its developments in the letter we saw that Paul's preferred way of describing the life of faith is with rich, positive terms—freedom, inheritance, and adoption—rather than with the vocabulary of the removal of sins, which he had from the tradition. The sequence of thought from 2:16 to 2:19-20 shows that the juridical language of justification leads naturally to the participatory language of union with Christ. Indeed, the latter provides the fullness of meaning of the former. And this description of Christian existence, in terms that go beyond mere removal of sins, answers very pointedly the problem in the Galatian churches. The Galatians had come to doubt that without the law they were truly "descendants" and "heirs" of Abraham; they feared that something essential was lacking in their relationship to God, which only the law could make good. This is why in Galatians Paul speaks so emphatically of the presence *now* of the gifts of the eschaton, so that even the Spirit is viewed not as the pledge of future blessings but as the fulfillment of the ancient promises. Within this positive vocabulary the δικαιο-root has a prominent place.

The reassurance of the Galatians has its counterpart in the undermining of the separatist thinking of the opponents. These are the positive and negative edges of the gospel, *both of which* are *essential* to understand the gospel as proclaimed by Paul in this letter. The Judaizers' separatist viewpoint is a major target for Paul's rhetoric. The defect of the law was not merely that it gave the Judaizers a false view of its own place in the divine-human relationship, but it also gave them a false estimate of themselves as its adherents and consequently built a "dividing wall" (Eph 2:14) between themselves and the rest of humanity. By their preaching of the law the Judaizers effectively "shut out" the Galatians and thus deny the grace of God in Christ. The destruction of that barrier is a major work of the gospel.

Galatians, then, is all about the contest between the law, conceived as a power of "the evil age," and the supreme authority of the gospel as revealed to, and preached, by Paul. The authority of the gospel, to repeat, is the basis both for Paul's apostolate and for his radical attack on the law. He could sweep aside the compelling appeal of the opponents to Genesis 17, Deuteronomy 27, Leviticus 18, and other texts because the gospel has revealed to him that the law was no longer "law" for Christians. Its function was completely other than Paul "and many of his contemporaries" (1:14) and forebears in Judaism had supposed; its meaning was not "law" but "promise." Unbelieving Jews, he was convinced, could not read those Scriptures correctly: "To this very day the same veil remains unlifted in the reading of the old covenant, for it is [only] taken away in Christ. Even until today, whenever Moses is read the veil lies over their hearts. But 'whenever someone turns to the Lord, the veil is removed'" (2 Cor 3:14-16). Paul's reference in that last verse is to Exod 34:34, but his rendering of it is typically free.[8] In Exodus 34 it refers to Moses himself removing the veil whenever he returned to God's pres-

---

8. LXX Exod 34:34 reads: ἡνίκα δ᾽ ἂν εἰσεπορεύετο Μωυσῆς ἔναντι κυρίου λαλεῖν αὐτῷ, περιηρεῖτο τὸ κάλυμμα ἕως τοῦ ἐκπορεύεσθαι ("Whenever Moses entered before the Lord to speak to him, he would remove the veil until he went out"), which translates the Masoretic text quite literally. Paul's use of this text is not so much quotation as allusion, but the context shows that the reference is certainly intentional (see also Nestle and United Bible Society).

ence; Paul applies it to the Jewish-Christian experience of coming to faith in Christ. As in Galatians, he quotes the "law" to defend his reading of the "law." This brings us to discussion of the coherence of Paul's views on the law in Galatians.

Νόμος, Νόμος and Γραφή in Galatians
("Law, Law and Scripture")

INTRODUCTION

It is crucial for interpretation to recognize that Paul uses νόμος in a deliberately dialectical fashion.[9] "Law" for him does not have one simple meaning. Throughout the first two-thirds of Galatians it bears a distinctly negative connotation, and yet he quotes it in support of his case and in 4:21 appeals to "the law" against the "law's" alluring fascination for the Galatians. Sanders insists that "when Paul uses the word 'law' or 'commandment' in connection with behavior, he never makes a theoretical distinction with regard to what aspects of the law are binding, nor does he in any way distinguish 'the law,' which Christians are to obey from the law which does not righteous (*sic*), which ties all humanity to sin, and to which those in Christ have died." Related to this, Sanders also maintains that in Galatians "the reader would not understand that Paul intends by 'law' in 5:14 and 6:2 a law which is entirely distinct from the other one."[10] Against this I

9. Paul's dialectical *treatment* of the law reflects his dialectical *understanding* of the law. The law is "dialectical" for Paul in that it both derived from God and was "good" and yet had become within parts of Judaism an opponent to God's purpose in the gospel. It is important to emphasize that this was a problem with which Paul *wrestled,* not a problem he *created,* any more than he created the conundrum of God as both Creator and Redeemer (see Westerholm, *Israel's Law,* 134–35).

10. Sanders, *Law and the Jewish People,* 96 and 98 respectively. Räisä-nen, *Paul and the Law,* 18, insists that attempts to distinguish between differing uses of νόμος in Paul "seem to be attempts of Paul's *interpreters* to create order in his theology of the law" and cites various scholarly attempts to make appropriate "distinctions" in support of his view that all such attempts are futile, since "Paul never alludes to any such thing." It seems to me

would maintain that unless such a distinction is understood the reader will not understand the passages in question at all. Paul's distinctions are certainly difficult and of course are not even *intended* as systematic or "speculative theology," but they can be discerned and, in my view, represent a powerful theological perspective on the value and dangers of religious law for adherents of *any* tradition.[11]

AN ANALYSIS OF Νόμος AND RELATED TERMS

Though difficult, the defining of Paul's uses of νόμος is eased somewhat by other terms Paul introduces, namely, γραφή ("scripture," Gal 3:8, 22; 4:30); γράμμα ("letter," Rom 2:27, 29; 7:6; 2 Cor 3:5, 7); and νόμος with various qualifiers such as τοῦ Χριστοῦ ("of Christ," Gal 6:2), τῶν ἔργων ("of works"), πίστεως ("of faith," Rom 3:27), τῆς ἁμαρτίας καὶ τοῦ θανάτου ("of sin and death," 8:2; cf. 7:23, 25), and τοῦ πνεύματος τῆς ζωῆς ("of the Spirit of life," 8:2).[12] The latter phrases from Romans cannot be discussed at length here but their antithetical character shows already that νόμος for Paul was a complex dialectical concept.

---

that the wordplays in Gal 4:21 and Rom 3:21, 27-31; 8:3-7, not to mention phrases like "the law of the Spirit of life" over against "the law of sin and death" (8:2), do indicate Paul's awareness of what he was doing. Winger's analysis (*By What Law?* e.g., 172–94, on Romans 7) strikes me as a strong challenge to Räisänen at this point.

11. "Speculative theology" is from Räisänen, *Paul and the Law,* 15, and is part of his less than enthusiastic endorsement of Paul as a theologian.

12. This, of course, is only a representative listing. First, there are other uses of "law" with a qualifier, all in Romans: "the law of God" (7:22, 25; 8:7); "the law of the mind" (7:23; cf. 7:25); and "law of righteousness" (9:31, see below). Also, "scripture" (γράφή) figures prominently in Rom 1:2; 4:3; 9:17; 10:11; 11:2; 16:26 (if the latter is genuine; see Käsemann, *Commentary on Romans,* 421–28), and especially telling is 15:4, which in its near parallelism with "God" is similar to the usage in Gal 3:8, 22; 4:30 (see also 1 Cor 15:3, 4). To these should be added several instances of the verb γράφειν ("write"), which is used most often in the formula καθὼς γέγραπται ("as it is written," e.g., Rom 1:17; 2:24). These formulaic quotations always presuppose a positive understanding of the law, which "was written for our instruction" (Rom 15:4; cf. 1 Cor 9:10; 10:11).

Νόμος πίστεως ("the rule, order, or norm of faith")[13] stands over against νόμος τῶν ἔργων ("order of works") just as "the 'law' of the Spirit of life" stands over against "the 'law' of sin and death" (8:2). The positive formulations in these texts do not designate the Mosaic law as such but rather stand over against it and expose its deficiencies.[14] The use of νόμος in such phrases brings into relief the leap with respect to it that has been made in the new age of faith. The law now has a completely new context, and its ancient purpose has now been revealed with a clarity not previously possible. It is in fact this eschatological leap in Christ that has all at once exposed the deficiencies of the law and given to it a radically new meaning.

But that new meaning is only perceptible to faith, and meanwhile there are many who insist that the status quo, in which the law functions to define "righteousness" and thus to divide Jews from Gentiles, is unchangeable. So much is this so that "law" has become, as Paul sees it, a competitor to God's claim on all humans in the gospel. This is the origin of his disparaging the law in Galatians 2–4. His shorthand term for the law in this mode is γράμμα ("letter"; see note).[15] This term does not occur in

13. Käsemann, *Commentary on Romans,* 103; see also Michel, *Römer,* 111; Westerholm, *Israel's Law,* 122–26.

14. Similarly, "the 'law' of sin and death" and "the 'law' of works" do not designate the Torah as such but, respectively, the principle or order of sin and death and of works. Nevertheless, such paradoxical formulations illustrate Paul's deliberately dialectical handling of the concept of law. The negative formulations show the connection in Paul's mind between law as an enslaving power and those other powers that must be vanquished in order to set humans free. On the other hand, the positive formulations forbid the complete demonizing of the law and recognize that as "scripture," as originally "proclaimed to Abraham" for the sake of "the gentiles" (Gal 3:8; see Rom 4:9-15), the law is, in spite of itself and in the context of the gospel, "the law of God," which believers "fulfill" by the Spirit (Rom 8:3-8). It should also be said here that "the law of Christ" in Gal 6:2 does not refer to the Torah, though again Paul's wording is deliberately dialectical. Sanders, *Law and the Jewish People,* 97, takes it as a reference to the Torah, but this is doubtful. On this issue, see Mussner, *Galaterbrief,* 281; Kertelge, "Gesetz," 389–91.

15. The translation of γράμμα as "letter" can be misleading. As Schrenk, s.v. γράμμα, *Theological Dictionary of the New Testament,* 1:767, says (in

Galatians but is nevertheless significant for our purposes in that it is an antithetical term standing over against πνεῦμα ("Spirit," Rom 2:27, 29; 7:6; 2 Cor 3:6)—not unlike "works of law" in Galatians 3:2-5.

The law as γράμμα is, first, the law as "commandment" (ἐν-τολή), which defines "the Jew" in terms of "circumcision" (Rom 2:27-29) and "righteousness" in terms of its own statutes (Gal 3:11-12).[16] The law as γράμμα "kills" (2 Cor 3:6), in that commandments, "written on stone tablets," assume a "lordship" over humans that catches them in a double bind. On the one hand it incites them to do what it forbids and condemns them for their disobedience. On the other it prescribes the "works of law" necessary for the divine-human relationship and promises "life" for their observance but can no more deliver on its promise of life than it can enable obedience to its statutes. Furthermore, as a function of its defining the divine-human relationship, it leads its adherents into the illusion that they are privileged before God over against those who do not know the law and thus separates Jews from Gentiles. Γράμμα, for Paul, is appropriate to designate these powerful but destructive features of the law because they derive from the law's character as a "written" code, which, deriv-

---

rejecting such a translation), "Any suggestion is to be rejected which would have it that the spirit of Scripture is here opposed to its letter, or its true or richer sense to the somatic body." Γράμμα "characterises the law in its quality of what is written or prescribed. The true meaning is 'prescription of the law'" (765), and this meaning is consistent with the usage of γράμμα in its larger background (761–64).

16. But this does not mean that "statutes" in themselves are bad, as 1 Cor 7:19 and Rom 2:6 and 13 show convincingly. Thus it is essential to emphasize that the antithesis of γράμμα and πνεῦμα is not simply the opposing of the external to the internal character of the law (preceding note). It is rather that γράμμα, though deriving from God at Sinai, has assumed a character and gained a power in the human sphere that now makes of commandments what God never intended for them. Schrenk, in *Theological Dictionary of the New Testament,* 767, insists rightly that the "killing" power of the law cannot "be attributed *only* to a false use of the Bible or the Law" (my emphasis), but "false use" does arise as a result of what the law has become in itself as a power of the evil age.

ing from Moses and the great events of Sinai, has assumed a near unassailable authority within the Judaism that Paul and his opponents had in common. "Law" as γράμμα—in Galatians, as ἔργα νόμου ("works of law")—stands as God's competitor and thus is personified as an illegitimate intruder into the world, which, like sin and death, God defeats by the cross of Christ.

Paul's specific vocabulary in Galatians bears out that, for the most part, he is intent on exposing the law as a power of the evil age but also continues to see the law as operating within God's eternal plan for the salvation of the world, Jews and Gentiles. He plays with the word νόμος (4:21), as he does in Romans (3:21, 28-31), and he uses νόμος qualified by τοῦ Χριστοῦ ("'law' of Christ," 6:2). A further aspect of this playing with the term is that he moves from an extremely negative usage of νόμος in chapters 2–4 to a positive usage that briefly emerges in 5:14 and 6:2. Finally, of crucial importance, he employs the positive term γραφή ("scripture"). Γραφή is used twelve times in Paul's letters[17] and is always a positive way of designating the law. Most often it is simply equivalent to the formula "as it is written" (καθὼς γέγραπται) and is followed by a Scripture quote (e.g., Rom 4:3; 9:17; 10:11; Gal 3:8), but this is not always the case (Rom 1:2; 15:4; 1 Cor 15:3, 4; Gal 3:22). In some texts where Paul uses νόμος he *conceivably* could have used γραφή. This is clearly the case, for instance, in 1 Cor 9:8-9, except that since γραφή is a near synonym for God (below), Paul would not speak of the γραφή *"of Moses."* In Romans 2 νόμος, though still denoting the "Sinaitic legislation," has, as I shall argue, a positive connotation as an authentic expression of God's just demands on humanity and thus prepares for νόμος as equivalent to γραφή in 3:21b. Understood in this way, νόμος is γραφή, whose demands serve "the gospel" (2:16) in exposing the "whole world" as "accountable before God" (3:19). Thus, in Romans 3:21*b* Paul could conceivably have written ὑπὸ τῶν γραφῶν ("by the scriptures"), but the actual ὑπὸ τοῦ νόμου καὶ τῶν προφητῶν ("by the law

17. Only eleven times if Rom 16:26 is excluded (see n. 12, above). The other instances are Rom 1:2; 4:3; 9:17; 10:11; 11:2; 15:4; 1 Cor 15:3, 4; Gal 3:8, 22; 4:30.

and the prophets") enables him to establish that his rejection of the law as the way to righteousness before God is *not* the rejection of the law as a means of knowing the divine will in the context of the gospel.

A similar pun on νόμος, and this is crucial, occurs in Gal 4:21.[18] Again, in 4:21*b* Paul could as well have written γραφή as νόμος, as 4:30 confirms. His pun, however, shows that there is a "law" that is to be shunned and there is a "law" that is to be heard and obeyed. Both have in view τὰ γεγραμμένα ("the written texts"), but each regards that corpus from a radically different perspective. The one "law" is an enslaving power whose "commands" dominate human existence and have become the be-all and end-all of God's covenant with Israel. The other "law" is the testimony of God's will, which believers "fulfill" not by adherence to individual statutes (γράμμα) but by the life of faith guided by the Spirit (πνεῦμα). When Paul breaks away from this dialectical usage of νόμος and wishes to designate the Scriptures according to their ancient meaning and present purpose, he uses

18. Romans 3:28, 31 are also clear instances of Paul deliberately playing with the different nuances of νόμος, and in verse 31 (though not v. 28) γραφή could conceivably substitute for νόμος. Romans 3:28 states almost verbatim the principle of 3:20a and Gal 2:16, but Rom 3:31, as Käsemann, *Commentary on Romans,* 105, says, "refers back to v. 21b in which the law is also witness to the righteousness of faith." Thus νόμος in 3:31 points to the coming "scriptural" arguments and is clearly distinct from the νόμος which prescribes "works." E. P. Sanders, *Law and the Jewish People,* 98, recognizes that "from the context one sees that 'the law' which is to be upheld is one which must be conformable to the equality of Jew and Gentile," but he insists that "the law" in 3:31 cannot "be defined and nuanced." Perhaps it is a matter of how much "nuance" one expects, but Sanders' own discussion shows that "law" in 3:31 bears a meaning *deliberately* different from that in 3:28. Sanders is quite right to insist, in his following discussion of Romans 8:3-4, that there is "no explicit distinction between the law of Romans 8:4 [which Christians fulfill] and the Mosaic law" (99). The "distinction" that Paul draws is in "the situation of the one whom [the law] confronts" (98). However, it is precisely the changed situation of humans in Christ that enables the recognition that the law cannot function as it was presumed to do in the tradition that Paul confronts. It is faith that exposes both the law's weakness and its proper function.

γραφή. Viewed thus, "law" is intimately linked with God's plan for human salvation. In Gal 3:8 γραφή could easily be substituted by θεός ("God"), and the parallel to the γραφή of Gal 3:22 in Rom 11:32 *is* θεός .[19]

PAUL'S DIALECTICAL UNDERSTANDING OF Νόμος

Paul's dialectical treatment of νόμος, however, is difficult for the modern interpreter and undoubtedly caused problems also in the early church (e.g., 2 Pet 3:15-16). Sanders' answer to this problem of "law and scripture" is that "Paul has found a canon within the canon. . . : those parts of the scripture which mention faith, righteousness, Gentiles, and love are in, as are those which accuse Israel of disobedience; parts which disagree with this interior canon, particularly the point about the Gentiles, whether explicitly or by implication, do not count."[20] But this employs a sledgehammer where a scalpel is required. In Gal 3:10-12, for instance, Paul is not intent on excluding Lev 18:5 from the canon. Texts such as 2 Cor 5:10 (see Rom 2:6, 13; 14:10c) indicate that in another context Paul might have quoted Lev 18:5 in *support* of

19. It goes along with this that in Rom 15:4-5 "the consolation of the scriptures" (τῶν γραφῶν) is paralleled with "the God . . . of consolation."
20. E. P. Sanders, *Law and the Jewish People,* 162; see also 100–105. Sanders insists that Paul makes "no theoretical distinction" (97 and passim) between the "law" to be obeyed and the "law" to be abrogated, even though he admits that Paul "did make de facto distinctions" (105). But the latter is proof of the existence of the former, as is the vocabulary of γραφή, γράμμα, and the puns on νόμος, which Sanders never discusses. He writes a brief section entitled "Law and Scripture" (160-62) but insists that they (νόμος and γραφή) are not used in a way "which leads to a clear distinction" (161). Sanders' refusal to follow Paul's distinctive uses of νόμος leads him to assert of Paul some completely non-Pauline viewpoints, as for instance when he speaks of "no theoretical distinction between *the law which governs Christians* and the law of Moses" (104; my emphasis). The italicized phrase here is explained as "the law which [Christians] fulfill." But, although the latter phrase derives from Paul (e.g., Rom 8:2; Gal 5:14), the former emphatically does not and, indeed, would be anathema to him (e.g., Rom 6:14; 7:1-6). Sanders eschews the very nuance that is required to do justice to Paul's complex thought.

his gospel.[21] Paul's problem with νόμος was not the obedience of its devotees but that obedience was made determinative of the divine-human relationship in a manner that compromised the sovereignty of grace and led its adherents into illusion about both its own power and their status before God and the rest of humanity. In the context of the Galatian crisis Lev 18:5 exemplified this power of the law, but in the context of the gospel it proclaims the indispensable corollary to the proclamation of divine grace, as is apparent in Romans 2. Νόμος becomes γράμμα when its prescriptions are made the arbiter of the divine-human relationship not only in terms of believers' "entry" into the "inheritance" of Abraham but also in terms of the *living out* of that relationship *and* of how humans are to understand God.[22] For Paul, in *any context,* "it is not a matter of [human] desiring or striving, but of *God who has mercy*" (Rom 9:16). Νόμος, on the other hand, is γραφή insofar as it embodies God's original "proclamation of the gospel to Abraham" (Gal 3:8) and functions for believers as διδασκαλία ("teaching") and νουθεσία ("instruction," Rom 15:4; 1 Cor 10:11), enlightening belief and conduct without binding humans to its individual prescriptions. In relation to the latter they are "free" (Gal 5:1-14). It is not the law that compels the behavior of believers, even though it may on occasion guide it; it is, rather, "faith in the Son of God who loved me and surrendered himself for me" (2:20).[23]

21. Käsemann, "Spirit and the Letter," *Perspectives on Paul,* 158, asserts that Lev 18:5 was important for Paul, as is shown in part by the fact that Rom 2:13 is "his [Paul's] paraphrased summing-up" of Lev 18:5; and as Rom 2:16b shows, Rom 2:13, with its focus on obedience to God's demands in the law, is an aspect of Paul's preaching of the gospel.

22. Sanders, *Law and the Jewish People,* 18 (and the ensuing discussion; see also 105, 157–59), strenuously rejects the view that "'*Nomos* means a way of life, a way of relating to God'" (157 and 158, quoting Keck) and insists that Paul's rejection of the law is simply his rejection of the opponents' teaching "that Gentiles must accept the law *as a condition* of or as a basic requirement for membership" (19). Against this, see the discussion under 2:20, above; also the telling critique of Gundry, "Grace, Works," 8–12, and following note.

23. In Sanders' view, although he knows that Paul did not require obedience with respect to "circumcision, Sabbath and the food laws" (*Law and*

Throughout almost all of Galatians Paul envisages and combats the law in the most negative terms he ever uses. It is characteristic of Galatians and a hallmark of this letter over against Romans that Paul so rigorously attacks the law but not unbelieving Jews. In Romans, as we shall see, Jewish ἀπιστία ("unbelief") is exposed mercilessly, but in Galatians, apart from occasional *ad hominem* remarks against the Judaizers, he confines his attack to the law. This attack presupposes that νόμος is a power that stands over against God, contending for the right to define the divine-human relationship. It is almost like a rebellious angel that dares to tell God how to be God. Such a portrait is possible precisely because of the level of opposition in Galatia and undoubtedly elsewhere among the churches. It is a portrait that is filled with emotion and with the characteristics of the Judaizers' actions in Galatia.

But this is not to say that the portrait is a mere ad hoc creation and that the abrogation of the law, which it represents, is not serious. That would do no justice to Paul. It is crucial, however, to recognize that this portrait is not all that he has to say about νόμος, not even in Galatians. In a manner that almost snatches the breath from his readers he shows that there is a way in which

---

the Jewish People, 102), the apostle did nevertheless expect Christians to obey the law (e.g., 84, 93–114). Further, he argues that Paul's "requirements of correct behavior still function *as law*"; indeed, "there is no distinction between the manner in which Christians are to fulfill Paul's requirements . . . and the manner in which Jews traditionally observe the Mosaic law" (113). This is wrong on several counts: *(a)* as Sanders himself knows (94–96), when Paul gave instructions on behavior he did not appeal to the law, even when it might have been easy to do so; *(b)* in Sanders' own descriptions of ancient Judaism (e.g., *Paul and Palestinian Judaism,* 107–205, 419–22) there is far more concern for obedience to law as *necessary for salvation* than there is in Paul, texts like Rom 14:10 and 2 Cor 5:10 notwithstanding; *(c)* Paul can think of evils that, in his view, may *exclude* from salvation (1 Cor 5:5; 6:9-10), but there are *no actions* that are necessary for it; *(d)* for Paul, not only human "working" but even human "desiring" for "working out salvation" is in fact "God working within you" (Phil 2:12-13). Excellent responses to Sanders on this point are provided by Gundry, "Grace, Works," 34–37; Westerholm, *Israel's Law,* 148–49.

νόμος properly serves God and can be faithfully interpreted: "You who wish to be under νόμος, do you not hear the νόμος?" Not only that, but in "love of neighbor" the "whole νόμος is fulfilled." The very fact that Paul so abruptly presumes a *positive* understanding of νόμος demonstrates that he knows such understanding to be already present in the community. Had he not already preached there and quoted from that same νόμος? What has been written, he says elsewhere, "was written for our instruction, upon whom the end of the ages has come" (1 Cor 10:11). For Paul, only those who have this perception of faith can understand "what was written." Thus it is not a question of reducing the number of statutes within the law that are to be obeyed,[24] it is rather that the law as a whole is now to be radically reinterpreted. It is only "in Christ" that the "veil" of misunderstanding is removed (2 Cor 3:14-16) and that the law can have any positive function.

To understand Paul's theology of the law in Galatians, then, depends upon understanding his dialectical thinking about it. It may bear repeating (see n. 9, above) that Paul *wrestled* with the problem of the law; he did not *create* it. But once faced with the dilemma of God's law functioning in a manner that defied the gospel, he set about the task of describing the relationship of "law" to gospel and in doing so was compelled to deal with the law dialectically. His dialectical thinking can be summarized by describing the two most important aspects in Paul's concept of the law. First, viewed positively, νόμος is equivalent to γραφή. It points to the entirety of "the scriptures" as "the documentation of God's will."[25] As such it bears witness to Christ and to the gospel

24. Pace Sanders, *Law and the Jewish People,* 101–3; also see preceding note.

25. Käsemann, *Commentary on Romans,* 88; see also 76, 87, 93–94, 102–3, and 104–5. Käsemann, 88 (his fullest delineation), speaks in terms of a "fluid interplay" between *three* aspects of "Paul's concept of law": "The documentation of God's will in scripture, . . . the function of the law given to the Jew as revelation, and . . . the law's inability to effect salvation." I do not entirely disagree with Käsemann's description, but the first and second aspects strike me as one and the same, and rather more, of course, needs to be added to the third aspect. Kertelge, *Rechtfertigung,* 205 (in the context of a full treatment of the issue, 195–206), succinctly expresses the distinction

and is to be used by believers as "instruction" for belief and conduct. It is never wrong to obey the law, including its prescriptions of circumcision, Sabbath, and foods (Romans 14), *unless* by that obedience one denies the reality of God's grace to Gentiles (Gal 2:11-14) or imagines that salvation is unattainable without it (2:16). Second, viewed negatively, νόμος is equivalent to all that Paul means when he uses the term γράμμα or, as Galatians 4:3 has it, τὰ στοιχεῖα τοῦ κόσμου ("the elements of the world"). This aspect arises from the power of the law in the hands of the Judaizers to "pervert the gospel" and cause believers to "fall from grace." It has the entirety of the Scriptures in view as the latter are, as Paul sees it, misinterpreted by the Judaizers, but it also abstracts from them and views the law as a power that opposes God's work in the gospel, particularly in the manner in which it holds its adherents in illusion and divides Jews from Gentiles. Obedience to the law so conceived is slavery and, no matter how successful, cannot effect salvation. The first aspect of law emerges in Gal 4:21b and 5:14. It is also apparent in the extensive use of the Scriptures and in νόμος as γραφή (3:8, 22; 4:30). It is, however, the second aspect that is the primary focus in Galatians.

It is not superfluous to repeat that the reason for this extremely negative portrait is the historical situation of the letter. Paul does not here lay the blame for the law's destructive power at the feet of unbelieving Jews, nor is he content to blame the Judaizers, even though he impugns their motives. To understand "law" in Galatians, it is essential to recognize that Paul finds it necessary to attack the law itself.[26] This suggests that Paul is not

---

this way: "One must distinguish in Paul a twofold concept of the law: the law as God's proper demand, which is directed toward good and 'life,' and the law as a factor of the former eon which has nothing to do with salvation." In his note 222 he points out that the majority of expositors of Paul's teaching on the law acknowledge such a distinction.

26. A probable part of Paul's critique of the Judaizers was their reduction of the law to those statutes they regarded as essential (see 5:3 and 6:13a), as Vielhauer, "Gesetzesdienst," 545–46, maintains. It is significant, however, that Paul does not choose this reductionism as the focus of his attack any more than he chooses, say, their moral failure. Nothing less is required,

fighting this battle for the first time. It also suggests, as does the careful construction of the letter, that Paul has thought out his views on the law. These are emotional, but they are not merely ad hoc formulations meant to stem for a moment the tide of fascination with the law. The fundamental notions belong inextricably to Paul's deepest convictions as an apostle. In Galatia it would have been insufficient to do less than expose the weakness of the law itself. Paul is convinced that the Galatians are not merely exhibiting momentary weakness in the face of forceful personalities (cf. 2 Corinthians 10–13); rather, they are virtually convinced of the "gospel," which insists that God's grace in Christ is of no effect unless received within the context of obedience to the law's prescriptions. The urgency of the situation, therefore, forced Paul to explain in uncompromising terms his views on the law as a power of the evil age. That under other circumstances he might stress more the failure of the law's adherents, have good things to say about the law, and omit from his abrogation of it his more scathing arguments is demonstrated in Romans.

Romans and Galatians

THEIR DIFFERING CONTEXTS AND EMPHASES

The many similarities between Romans and Galatians are in part to be accounted for by the fact that they were written within a period of about eighteen months.[27] But there are also some

---

apparently, than an exposure of the law itself as a power that has arisen in opposition to God's work in the gospel.

27. Kümmel, *Introduction to the New Testament,* 304 and 311, dates Galatians around "54 or 55 in Ephesus or Macedonia" (see n. 1, *(a),* above) and Romans "in Corinth . . . about the spring of 55 or 56." Lüdemann, *Paul,* 263, dates Galatians in the summer of 50 (or 53) in Macedonia and Romans in the winter of 51/52 (or 54/55) in Corinth. See also the lengthy note by Wilckens, "Aus Werken," *Rechtfertigung,* 84, note 16. Most interpreters follow similar dating. There would be a large gap only if Galatians turned out to be among Paul's very first letters—if not the first—as Bruce, *Epistle to the Galatians,* 55, believes.

major differences between them, particularly in that Romans makes some positive statements about the law that, viewed from Galatians, are very surprising. This is a major issue to which I shall turn presently. Also very different are the historical contexts, and it is essential for present purposes to make careful note of this and of the shifts in emphasis they have occasioned in the later letter.[28] In Romans Paul writes to a congregation he has never visited in order to solicit their aid for the Jerusalem collection (15:30-32) and for his future missionary endeavors in Spain (15:23-28). But that hardly exhausts his purpose, which by itself could not account for such a long, theologically involved letter. His further purpose is tied up in that theology. The situation is the more intriguing in that, unlike the earlier letter, Romans is not written to counteract the teaching of easily identifiable opponents, nor does Paul fear, as he does in Galatians, that the church in Rome may abandon the gospel. Nevertheless, opponents are in view (see 3:8), and even though they may not be on the scene nor wielding any great influence, there is reason to suspect that their critique has struck a nerve in the apostle and to some extent is the occasion for his lengthy explanation of his gospel.[29]

As we have seen, a distinguishing feature of Galatians is that it impugns the law itself as a power that led its adherents into illusion. In Romans, while the law itself does come under attack, what is especially noteworthy is Paul's scathing attack upon Jews who neither obey the law nor believe in the gospel. In general terms it is true to say that, while in Galatians it is the law that is found to be at fault, in Romans it is unbelieving Jews. Thus in Romans Paul attacks Jews as transgressors of the law (2:17-29) and insists that "doers of the law shall be made righteous" (2:13) and

28. On this see Beker, *Paul the Apostle,* 94–108; Davies, "Paul and the Law," 8–10; Stuhlmacher, "Purpose of Romans," 231–42, particularly 242; and especially Wilckens, "Abfassungszweck," *Rechtfertigung,* 143–49.

29. E. P. Sanders, *Law and the Jewish People,* 149, says, "It is possible that [in Romans] he had become aware of the fact that some of his statements were subject to being interpreted as leading to antinomianism (Rom 3:8, 6:1f., 15). This explanation would also account for the explicitly favorable statements about the law in Romans (3:31; 7:7, 12)."

that the law is "holy, righteous and good" (7:12; see 3:31b), statements that would have been impossible in the Galatians' context
and that, furthermore, appear on the surface of it to be contradictory of Gal 2:16 and 3:11.

The major theological problem posed by Galatians is precisely that its attack on the law is so absolute. It is no wonder that
it was the flagship of Marcion's canon. Scripture quotes aside,
most of Galatians might appear to verge on excluding the law as
sacred Scripture. It is quite apparent, of course, that this was not
Paul's intention, but it is not difficult to see that Paul's opponents
could have quoted him against himself, with Galatians as their
primary ammunition. It is thus quite probable that Galatians
caused problems for Paul that Romans intends to address, as the
defensive statement of 3:8 (also 6:1 and 15) suggests. If his opponents could portray him as a peddler of cheap grace who disavows the Scriptures and denies the divine election of Israel, then
his plans, both east (to have the collection received in Jerusalem)
and west (to visit Rome and gain their support for a mission to
Spain), would be seriously impaired. In such a context Romans
intends to explain Paul's theology of the law in more detail so as
to remove any misunderstanding that may have been caused by
the harsh statements of Galatians.[30] On the other hand, I should
emphasize that in my view Romans does not revoke Paul's abrogation of the law. The latter is also a part of Paul's theology in
Romans, but the nuances of this over against Galatians are instructive.

ROMANS OVER AGAINST GALATIANS ON THE ISSUE OF THE LAW

The most controversial aspect of my interpretation of Paul's
attack on the law in Galatians is the claim that Paul depicts the
law as a power of illusion, particularly in that I have posited this
as a coherent theme holding together various statements against

---

30. This thesis is developed in detail by Wilckens, "Abfassungszweck,"
Rechtfertigung, 142–43, who puts considerable emphasis on Paul's need to
explain himself to the leaders of the church in Jerusalem if he wishes to present himself there with the collection from the Gentile churches.

the law. In sum, the interpretation runs as follows: the performance of the law is well and good in itself, but it is not essential
for righteousness either for Jews or Gentiles. The law is a power
of illusion because it promises the obedient what it cannot give,
giving a false understanding of both its own authority and the status of its adherents. It condemns the disobedient simply by virtue
of their disobedience and because it holds them, too, under the illusion that its definition of "righteousness" conforms to God's intention. Thus what the sharp edge of the gospel reveals is both the
powerlessness of the law by itself to direct the divine-human relationship and the true status as "sinners" of those who relied
upon it. The issue now is how this compares with the treatment of
the law in Romans in light of the differing contexts of the two letters and particularly with respect to the theme of illusion. My purpose falls far short of a full exegesis of the relevant texts in
Romans. I wish only to point out major points of *contrast* on the
law between the two letters and also to describe what I see as an
essential inner *coherence* in Paul's thinking on the law.[31] In the

31. Beker's discussion of the law (*Paul the Apostle,* 235–54) is inclusive of various viewpoints and hardly serves to bring out any coherence in
Paul's view. At times, particularly on Romans 7, he agrees with Wilckens
that "Jews have sealed their doom because of their factual transgressions"
(239, no. 3), but in regard to Galatians he is very close to Sanders' position:
"The law is an outmoded and unnecessary reality for Gentiles because it was
not meant for them (Gal 3:6-14). . . . In other words, the basis for Paul's
indictment of the law is here the new lordship of Christ and not primarily the
sorry plight of the Jew under the law, as in Romans 7" (240, cf. 246). Beker
accepts Bultmann's view with its notion of "man" as "sinner" having a
"falsely oriented understanding of his existence" (quoted by Beker, 239–40),
not for Romans 7, but this theme is "certainly present in Rom 10:3 and Phil
3:9 (cf. perhaps Rom 3:27)" (on the latter, see 247). This argument only
arises, however, "after Paul has arrested the Jew in his actual transgressions
of the law (Romans 7), . . . [that is,] the Jew who has refused the gospel and
persists in a way that has been shown to be futile." In such a circumstance
"the Jew is caught in the illusion that works of the law are pleasing to God"
(240), the latter being, in my view, a serious misreading of the theme of illusion. Beker later seems to extend the notion of Jews being caught in illusion even *prior* to the gospel (246–47). Beker fails to carry through the
contextual approach here, and his interpretation becomes rather fragmented,

final section I will offer an answer to the problem of the apparent contradiction of Gal 2:16 in Rom 2:13.

The closest that Romans comes to speaking of the law as a power of deception is in 7:11 and its context. Only in a very qualified sense can this section as a whole (7:7-25) be titled "an apology for the law." It is true that "an apologetic motif is . . . evident at vv. 7a, 12, 13a, 14," but as Käsemann rightly insists, what is emphasized above all is "the effectiveness of sin." In other words, the "fleshly 'I,' sold under sin" (7:14c) is the main theme.[32] Even Dunn (see preceding note) admits that verses 14–25 are needed because verses 12–13 "could be said to have gone too far in reinstating the law, throwing the earlier more negative characterization of the law into possible confusion."[33] Verses 15–23 demonstrate the inability of the law, in the face of sin, to enable humans to do God's will.[34] They anticipate 8:3a concerning the law's "impotence, in that it was weak because of the flesh," and make more compelling the description of faith as a "dying to the law through the body of Christ" (7:4; cf. Gal 2:19). They describe in fact the "wretched-

---

but if one follows the theme of illusion as it is worked out—with differing emphases to be sure—in the two letters, then there is rather more consistency in Paul's view of the law than Beker recognizes.

32. Käsemann, *Commentary on Romans,* 192; see also 201–4 and 210. For the contrary view, see Dunn, *Romans 1–8,* volume 38A, 377. Beker, *Paul the Apostle,* 238–40, sees 7:7-13 as "an apology of the law," and verses 14–25 as containing "an autobiographical element," describing "Paul's Jewish experience . . . from a Christian perspective." In light of Paul's use of emphatic ἐγώ (see under 2:19) it does seem probable that Rom 7:14-25 includes some reference to Paul's own experience—*not,* however, to Paul's *present* experience as a believer (see below).

33. Dunn, *Romans 1–8,* 403–4.

34. On a "transferred sense" for "law," especially in verses 21 and 23, see Käsemann, *Commentary on Romans,* 199; Westerholm, *Israel's Law,* 124–25; Winger, *By What Law?* 183–89. Even "the law of God" in verse 22 probably envisages not only Israel's law but the will of God as that can be recognized even beyond Israel (see Käsemann, 205). Winger (186, n. 141) doubts that such a "general sense" would be recognized, but Paul's puns on the word invite varieties of meaning for it; Winger sees four meanings in the various phrases of verses 22–23 (185).

ness" from which humans are "rescued" by the death of Christ.[35] The whole section is necessary because of the unmistakable connection between sin and law, which Paul has posited already at several points (3:20; 4:15; 5:12-14, 20; 6:14-15; 7:4-6). In turn, those assertions reflect Gal 3:19-22 and suggest that Paul intends to explain the connection of law and sin more carefully but not retreat from his view that sin and law are allied in some way disastrous for humanity, and especially for those who regard the law as the way to live the divine-human relationship.

It is quite incorrect, therefore, to see Paul in this section as describing "a split in the 'I,'" and as being "aware as never before of the power of sin in his own life."[36] The "I" of verses 7–13, as Dunn acknowledges, evokes the story of Genesis 3. The "I" of 7:7-11 cannot be Paul.[37] The reader, therefore, is quite prepared for the "I" of verses 14–25 to be descriptive of the human condition (cf. 1 Cor 10:30; Gal 2:19-20) while also recognizing some reference to Paul's own experience (see n. 32). The present tenses of verses 14-25, which Dunn sees as signaling Paul's "personal testimony,"[38] are the same sort of timeless present as is common

35. I am agreeing, of course, with the view that Rom 7:7-25 is Paul's description, from the viewpoint of faith, of humans under law without Christ: see, for example, Beker, *Paul the Apostle,* 238; Käsemann, *Commentary on Romans,* 192. For a diametrically contrary view see Winger, *By What Law?* 168–71; see also Dunn, *Romans 1–8,* 377 (following note).

36. Dunn, *Romans 1–8,* 406–7. Dunn (377) believes that "the logic of the argument and the structure of the three chapters (7:7-25, parallel to 6:12-23 and 8:10-30) are sufficient indication that Paul has in view the eschatological tension of the present stage of salvation history, with both the 'I' and the law divided between the two ages of Adam and Christ in a period when these two ages overlap." A somewhat similar view, but seeing the "I" also in 7:7-13 as denoting Paul himself, is argued by Winger, *By What Law?* 169–71. Both Winger and Dunn here see Paul, as a believer, trying to obey the law. Winger admits (176–77) that this "seems to conflict with what Paul says of himself . . . in Phil 3:5-6" but insists that in the present context "it is not surprising."

37. Dunn, *Romans 1–8,* 404–5.

38. Ibid., 405; see also 387. Dunn does see some self-reference already in 7:7-13, but the transition to the present tenses, he says, makes it "sharper" (387).

in Paul (e.g., 1:18-20; 2:1-29; 8:4-39) and which he has just employed in the illustration of 7:1-3. They describe the plight of all
humanity under sin, and with particular poignancy describe the
plight of those who imagine that law can rescue them from sin's
power. Dunn denies that there is any reference here to "the pious
Jew. . . . [H]e himself had known none of that tension as a law-
abiding Pharisee . . . since his law-abiding stayed at the more superficial level of flesh and works."[39] But "superficial" is not how
Paul himself describes his law-observance (Gal 1:13-14), and
Dunn's interpretation takes "blameless" in Phil 3:6 too literally.
"Blameless" is quite consistent with some "anxiety" on the
simple assumption that Paul's obedience to the law included making full use of its system of atonement. Dunn's interpretation
leads to Paul saying in Philippians 3 that as a Pharisee he had no
anxiety about the law, but now as a believer in Christ he does so.
After Galatians and all he has already said in this letter, is Paul
now to be seen as telling the Romans that he is trying to obey the
law but in his present "wretched" state—in Christ!—he is unable
to do so? Paul does attenuate his attack on the law, but not to that
extent!

"Apology for the law" is not a good title for this section of
Romans. Paul softens the attack on the law by making "sin" the
major culprit in that it used the law as an unwitting instrument in
the deception and destruction of humans (7:9-11). Paul further attenuates the attack by exposing the weakness of humans who are
"sold under sin" (7:14) and thus cannot, before Christ's rescue,
obey the law. In Galatians, as we have seen, the "I" was dominated by law and the illusion of superior status. In Romans 7, by
contrast, the "I" is dominated by sin and tortured by sin's power
continually to deny it fulfillment of its earnest desire to do God's
will. The "I" of Galatians is lost *because of* the law, the "I" of Romans *in spite of* it, but in both letters it is mistaken to trust the law
as the way of righteousness. In fact, in spite of Paul's attenuated
attack in Romans there is not in the end a lot of difference between the Galatians' concept that *the law itself deluded* its adher-

39. Ibid., 394. Paul's observance of law as a Pharisee, says Dunn, had
been so "superficial" that he "had not even reached the stage of frustration!"

ents and the Romans' idea that *sin used the law to deceive* humans, who, due to sin's dominance, could not obey the law anyway. The law has not been reinstated in the later letter, even though its denigration is far more palatable.

In both letters the theme of illusion is apparent. What emerges from a comparison of the two letters with respect to this theme is that in Romans the illusion is primarily the fault of disobedience and unbelief rather than the fault of the law itself, as in Galatians. The main purpose of 2:17-29, for instance, is to convict Jews of sins against the law and thereby to place them in the same situation as Gentiles and deny any privilege by virtue of possessing the law. But along with the accusation of disobedience, there is also the notion of a reliance on the law that has been illusory and ineffectual. This is most apparent in verses 17–19, with its string of words denoting a conviction of superiority and privilege: "You (singular) *rely* on the law and *boast* in God; you *know* [God's] will and *approve* what is excellent, being instructed from the law; you are *persuaded* that you yourself are the *guide* for the blind, a *light* to those in darkness, the *instructor* of the foolish, the *teacher* of the simple, *having in the law the essence of knowledge and of truth.*" Such vocabulary intends not so much to expose his opponents' transgressions—the point of verses 21–24—but rather their illusion as they cherish a false estimation of their superior status due to law ("guide for the blind," etc.) over against the lawless Gentiles. The punch line is verses 27–29, which envisage the unmasking of the illusion in the coming judgment, but unlike Galatians there is no indication here that the law itself has functioned as a hostile power to produce the illusion; the fault lies simply with Jews who have both misunderstood and disobeyed the law.[40] What 7:7-25 adds to this is the explanation as to

40. Käsemann, *Commentary on Romans,* 72–74, rightly says that διά in 2:27 is best translated "in spite of"; see also Westerholm, *Israel's Law,* 211. Schrenk, *Theological Dictionary of the New Testament,* 1:765, says, to the contrary, that "it must also be given an instrumental significance. It is precisely through what is written and through circumcision that the Jew is a transgressor." In light of Rom 4:15; 5:13; and 7:7-11 it is not impossible that Paul would have an instrumental sense in mind here, but even if that were

why Jews—or anyone else!—could not in fact "be righteous" by the law. Within "the present evil age" it is more an ally of sin than of humans in their endeavor to obey God's will.

The next passage where the theme of illusion emerges is 9:30–10:4 and context. The preceding context first (9:1-5) speaks in emotional terms of Paul's desire for Israel's conversion and of the greatness of Israel's gifts. This does not prepare us for the following apparent exclusion[41] of unbelieving Israel from the "promise," until we recognize that in large measure unbelieving Israel's fault is precisely its *misguided* pursuit of what it should have received as *gift*.[42] As in 2:27-29, "true" Israel is defined by

---

the case it is significant that the idea is not developed into an attack on the law itself, either here or anywhere else in Romans. Further to Romans 2, see below.

41. I say "apparent exclusion" because, of course, as this discussion of Israel develops it becomes clear that Paul believes that "all Israel," in the "inscrutable" design of God, "will be saved" (11:25; see 11:33). How Paul gets from "not all" in 9:6 to "all" in 11:25 is reason for not a little scholarly ink. For recent discussion see Räisänen, "Paul, God, and Israel," 178–206; Cosgrove, "Rhetorical Suspense," 271–87.

42. Far more than elsewhere, Romans 9–11 presupposes a comparison between human endeavor and *what it cannot achieve* and God's initiative of grace and *what it accomplishes*. This is suggested already in the distinction between "children of flesh" and "children of promise" in 9:8 and becomes explicit in a whole series of contrasts, as the following diagram attempts to show:

	Human Effort	God's Grace
9:11	"Doing"	"Election"
9:12	"Works"	"Calling"
9:16	"Desiring, running"	"Showing mercy"
9:30-32	"Pursuing . . . not attaining"	"Not pursuing. . . gaining" (cf. 10:20)
10:3	"Seeking to establish their own righteousness"	"Being obedient to the righteousness of God"
10:5-8	"Doing"	"The word is near"
11:5-6	"By works"	"By grace"
11:7	"Seeks . . . did not attain"	"Elect(ion) attained"

This contrast is, of course, apparent already in 4:1-5, 17b, and, in my view, undergirds the foundational statements of 1:16-17 and 3:20-21. It is "promise," not by "flesh." Paul's radical reinterpretation of the quoted texts would never have been accepted by his opponents, and, again, the plain sense of the text favored them. But Paul, by the gospel, knows what they do not know, for they are still caught in the illusion of the law's demand for "works." That this is their fault, in Paul's view, is already suggested in verses 11–12 and becomes clearer with 9:16, 32, and 11:6 (n. 42). But in Romans, unlike Galatians, this does not lead to an attack on the law as the culprit. It is rather a question of an understanding of Scripture and of God's ways with Israel and the world, which unbelievers cannot fathom.

"Israel's" false understanding of the law is the major issue in 9:30–10:8. Caught up in their view of the law as being ἐξ ἔργων ("[a matter] of works") rather than ἐκ πίστεως ("of faith"; 9:32), Israel has failed to achieve its goal. The phrasing of verse 31 cannot be lightly passed over. Israel's διώκειν ("pursuit") was for νόμον δικαιοσύνης ("[the] law of righteousness"). This is not the description of Israel's fault; that comes with verse 32a. The "pursuing" was not wrong in itself, and "law of righteousness" means the law that demands and gives witness of righteousness.[43] Further-

---

significant, however, that it is in Paul's discussion of the problem of Israel's unbelief that the theme comes systematically to the fore, and it indicates that "Israel's" fault, for Paul—in addition to disobedience—is its misguided confidence in the effectiveness of "works of law."

43. In this respect I agree with Dunn, *Romans 9–16*, 581 and 592–93. However, it is one thing to say, with reference to Rom 8:4, that believers fulfill "the just requirement of the law"; it is quite another to say "the law is indeed the definition and measure of righteousness" (593). Such a notion is quite contrary to Paul's major thesis both in Romans (3:19-21) and Galatians (2:16; 3:11-12). Käsemann, *Commentary on Romans*, 277, takes "law of righteousness" to be "qualitative," and thus the phrase "indicates the demand or better, in context, the promise. The law is thus viewed as the witness of righteousness as in 3:21. . . . The point is," continues Käsemann, "that the will of God which calls for righteousness cannot be reached in the law, *this being misunderstood and made a summons to achievement*" (my emphasis). The italicized phrase here overstates the matter, in my view, in that it is not "achievement" (the *doing* of the law) that is faulted but simply the illusory idea that by its observance ("as though by works," v. 32) righteousness is

more, in verse 31b ("[Israel] did not reach the law") "law" has no negative connotation, so that now Paul's dialectic turns not so much on the law as on unbelieving Israel. If they had received the gift simply as gift they would by now, in Christ, have attained their goal.[44] The irony is quite deliberate. It is not the law that is at fault but Paul's opposition, which insists on viewing "law" "as though [it were a matter] of works" and thus misses the mark completely. Unlike Galatians, the law itself is not blamed for human illusion; on the other hand, neither is the law the way to righteousness.

The confirmation of this is found in 10:2-3. Ζῆλον θεοῦ ἔχουσιν ("They have zeal for God"), following as it does on Paul's heartfelt wish for Israel's "salvation," is in no sense a description of Israel's fault. It is equivalent to "pursuing the law of righteousness" in 9:31. The zeal in itself is well and good, but tragically it is οὐ κατ' ἐπίγνωσιν (literally, "not according to recognition"; *NAB* has "not discerning"). The best equivalent phrase in Paul is Rom 1:28, when he berates humans that "they did not see fit to acknowledge God" (τὸν θεὸν ἔχειν ἐν ἐπιγνώσει), even though "what can be known of God" ought to be "clear to them, since God made it known" (1:19). God's judgment in that case was to "hand them over" to their vices, so that their sin became its own punishment (1:24, 26, 28). Paul could have pursued the same line of thought here, but he remains comparatively restrained in describing the consequences of Israel's refusal, except

---

secured. Some interpreters (e.g., Barrett, *Epistle to the Romans,* 180; Michel, *Römer,* 250) understand "pursuing" as a description of Israel's *misstep,* but the parallel to this in 10:2a is not Paul's complaint against Israel but simply part of his lament that the effort is misdirected. The "striving" is not wrong, but its direction ("as though of works") is.

44. It is not, of course, the case for Paul that a true understanding of the gift of the law was possible prior to the gospel, so that if only the opponents had attained correct understanding they would have attained righteousness. On the contrary, Romans maintains, as does Galatians, that no human is justified by works of law. Paul's point in Romans is that Jews who refuse to believe in the gospel are blinded by an illusion *they* have produced, albeit as victims like all humanity, of sin's oppressive power. Galatians focuses the fault of the *law* for the illusion.

in 11:7-10 (see n. 46), which, however, immediately turns to the last phase of his argument (11:11-36), leading to the assertion that "all Israel will be saved" (11:26). It is with some pathos, then, that Paul describes the culpable illusion of unbelieving Jews: *"Disregarding* the righteousness of God and seeking to establish their own righteousness, they refused obedience to the righteousness of God."[45] Israel's pursuit of righteousness is not wrong in itself, but it is fraught with illusion, making the covenant a matter of "works" instead of recognizing its essence as "grace."[46] This has already been maintained not only in 9:32 but also in 9:16: "It is not a question of desiring or striving but of God who has mercy."

In 10:5-8 Paul comes as close as he ever does in Romans to the type of argument *against the law itself* that he employed in

45. Dunn, *Romans 9–16,* 587, rightly notes the appropriateness of translating ἀγνοοῦντες here as "disregarding," which therefore implies "some culpability." However, as for Gal 2:16 (see n. 49 in chap. 4), so here Dunn's interpretation in terms of Jewish "nationalism" fails to account for the letter situation in that Paul's concern is not merely, or even primarily, with Jews who try to "establish" righteousness as "theirs" exclusively (e.g., on Rom 10:3, Israel thought, says Dunn, "that God's saving power was extended to them exclusively," 595; see also 588, 593). Paul's concern was at least as much for *Gentiles* who were convinced that *they* must "establish their own righteousness" by "works of law." In other words, again it is the *universal* problem of fascination with "works" ("as if by works," 9:32) that Paul contends with. See the discussion of Westerholm, *Israel's Law,* 113–16, especially 115.

46. The same notion is repeated in different terms in 11:7-10, and there Israel's accountability for its fault is brought out sharply with a catena of Scripture texts. "What Israel seeks it did not attain." The reason is that "they were hardened" (cf. 11:25; 2 Cor 3:14); "as it is written: 'God gave them a stupefied spirit, eyes that they might not see and ears that they might not hear to this very day.'" The concluding Scripture text in the sequence turns the psalmist's curse upon his enemy against Israel and suggests, in Paul's context, that the very gifts of Israel (ἡ τράπεζα αὐτῶν, literally, "their table," with reference perhaps to the messianic banquet; see Bauer, *Greek-English Lexicon,* 832) have become "a snare and a trap, both stumbling block and retribution! May their eyes become so dim that they lose their sight!" *(NEB).* The harshness of the attack on unbelieving Israel is unmistakable, as is the notion of their being lost in illusion. That the illusion derives from the confusion of "works" for "grace" is apparent from 11:6.

Galatians. Indeed, in its antithesis of Lev 18:5 to the Deuteronomy texts[47] this passage is reminiscent of Gal 3:11-12, which opposes Lev 18:5 to Hab 2:4. As Paul elsewhere deals with the law and Israel dialectically, so here he deals with Moses. In the first instance, understood as representative of the law's insistence on "works," Moses is the antitype of Christ and the champion of unbelieving Jews, who likewise insist on "works of law" as the essential guide for the divine-human relationship. The folly of this insistence, for Paul, is that it effectively denies the principle of God's initiative of grace. The latter principle explains Paul's use of Deut 9:4, derived from a passage where Israel is warned against seeing its own "righteousness" as the reason for God's giving them the land. The focus on grace also explains the studied omission of ποιεῖν from Deut 30:12-14 (n. 47). As in Gal 3:12, so here it is what Paul sees as the false understanding of

---

47. The use of Lev 18:5, Deut 9:4a; 30:12b, 14b, c, is clear enough; what other texts, if any (Bar 3:29; 4 Ezra 4:8), Paul had in mind is not clear. Most significant is Paul's editing of Deuteronomy 30, leaving out its repeated emphasis on Israel's obligation "to do" the law. In context, the reason for Paul's omission is his consistent intent to deny that the "doing" ("works") of the law is constitutive of the divine-human relationship. However, Hays, *Echoes of Scripture,* 76, denies that there is any "antithesis" between 10:5 and 10:6 and interprets the passage in a radically different manner than here. In general, though many of the "intertextual echoes" he cites are powerfully instructive, his interpretation often depends on special pleading; the present passage is such a case. In light of the contrast between "by faith" and "by works" in 9:30-32, Israel's attempt to "establish its own righteousness" (10:3) obviously has to do with its misguided conviction about "works" as required for "righteousness." This sets up the obvious contrast Paul lays out in 10:5-6 between "righteousness by law," which, says Moses, requires "doing," whereas "the righteousness from faith" reveals that no doing ("going up" or "down" to find Christ) is necessary, since "*near* you is the word" (see note 42, above). Hays avoids the contrasts by trying to make "righteousness from faith" "*equivalent to* righteousness from Torah [and] *equivalent to* righteousness of God" (77, my emphasis). Thus we are to believe that Lev 18:5 says *the same thing* as Deut 30:14, contrary to the obvious contrasts that have brought us to this point and contrary to the plain sense of the texts, not to mention the precedent of Gal 3:11-12. Hays bends over backwards to avoid having Paul directly criticize Israel for its mistaken convictions about "works of law."

Lev 18:5 that has to be corrected.[48] He demonstrates how it is correctly understood by quoting from Deuteronomy. The latter text paradoxically represents Moses as the champion of the gospel. As in Gal 3:11-12, Paul quotes Scripture against itself and implies that Scripture has led unbelieving Jews astray. But, over against Galatians, this argument does not lead into assertions on the law as an illegitimate intruder and as deriving from the inferior power of angels. Here the argument leads into the question of human receptivity to "the word of faith which we preach" (10:8, 16-18), and that leads back into assertions of Israel's rejection of that word, that they are a "disobedient and contradictory people" (10:21). The purpose for the series of free quotes and interpretations of Deuteronomy is to describe the prevenient grace of God, which for Paul utterly forestalls seeing Lev 18:5 as making "works" determinative of "righteousness," and to announce again that grace brings both Jews and Gentiles together under the one merciful summons of God, so that faith, the obedient acceptance of the "word," which is "near," is the only appropriate and needed response to the proclamation of the gospel.[49] In the context of Galatians, Rom 10:5-8 would have been fully supportive of the idea of the law itself as a power of deception. In the Romans' context, however, that concept comes forward only marginally, and the primary focus, noting especially 9:30-32 and 10:2-3, stays on the disobedience and illusion of unbelieving Jews.

48. Käsemann, "Spirit and the Letter," *Perspectives on Paul*, 158, rightly says, with respect to 10:5-6, "The introduction to v. 6 clearly suggests that to interpret the text in this sense is to violate the meaning of scripture. For the statement in Deuteronomy 30 cited here is taken from the very same Moses who is quoted in v. 5. The apostle apparently sees in this no problem. The Word which is near to us and which as promise points forward to the gospel is in contradiction to Moses to the extent in which he embodies the 'letter.'" Thus, again, it is not that Paul wishes to exclude Lev 18:5 from the canon (n. 21, above) but that he insists on its being understood in the context of the gospel. To all intents and purposes he himself employs it in that fashion in 2:13 (see below).

49. Thus 10:9-15 describes the situation of *all humanity* in face of the preaching of the gospel (see v. 12), but verses 16–21, like 9:30–10:8, also struggle with the problem of Israel's rejection of the gospel and its motivation for doing so.

Once again, the theme of illusion is present in both letters, with the difference that Galatians sees the law as the culprit for the illusion whereas Romans blames Israel's misdirected zeal. Both agree completely, however, that by the doing of the law no one δικαιωθήσεται ("shall be made righteous"). The law was not given for that purpose. The gospel reveals the law's true purpose, which is to indict human sinfulness, bear witness to the gospel, and provide instruction for believers; but "by works of law no flesh shall be righteous before him" (Rom 3:20; cf. Gal 2:16; 3:11). But this seems to conflict radically with Rom 2:6 and 13, which state in no uncertain terms that God "will reward each person according to works" and that "the *doers* of the law shall be made righteous." How do these seeming contradictory assertions coordinate in Paul's mind? This issue must now be addressed directly.

THE APPARENT CONTRADICTION BETWEEN
GAL 2:16 (ROM 3:20) AND ROM 2:6, 13

This contradiction between Galatians and Romans is only such if the differing historical contexts and Paul's dialectical treatment of the law are not kept clearly in view. It is important to bear in mind that Romans was written in part to counter the views of "some" (3:8) who have impugned Paul's gospel as a gospel of cheap grace that unreservedly abolishes the law in a manner Paul does not accept (3:31). It is indeed possible that the cause of these criticisms was the letter to the Galatians, which his opponents have quoted against him. Be that as it may, it is certainly the case that in Romans, without going back on his earlier teaching, Paul shifts the emphasis from an attack on the law itself to an attack on Israel's historical failure both to obey the law and to understand its true intent.

It is in line with this that the purpose of Rom 2:1–3:20, as all would agree, is to indict Jews as being sinners "accountable to God" no less than the Gentiles.[50] This is a fuller explication of the

50. See E. P. Sanders, *Law and the Jewish People,* 123. I agree with Barrett, *Epistle to the Romans,* 41, that "it is not till v. 17 that [Paul] turns *specifically* to the problem of the Jews" (my emphasis), but the turn in the

principle that Paul enunciates far more briefly in Gal 2:15-17.[51] But the shift of emphasis from the earlier to the later letter is again to be noted. In Galatians 2 ἁμαρτωλοί ("sinners") is not primarily an ethical term but denotes first and foremost the *status* of humanity, Gentiles and Jews, as radically in need of grace. In Romans 2, however, the ethical failure of humanity, *especially* of Paul's Jewish opposition, is clearly in the foreground. This is signaled both by the vice lists (1:29-31 and 2:21-22) and by παράβασις (2:23) and παραβάτης (2:25, 27), which denote the "transgressions" of the law's adherents in addition to those of the "lawless gentiles." In other words, we see again that whereas in Galatians the law is the culprit that has done Jews, and all humans, a disservice, in Romans Paul indicts Jews for their transgressions of the law. Furthermore, in Romans it is the law that provides the "evidence" (3:9-18) to convict Jews as well as Gentiles of their sin and in so doing acts as the gospel's ally.[52] Thus in Romans the law not only bears witness, as in Galatians, to the revelation of God's righteousness in the gospel, it is also the instrument for the present revelation of "God's wrath" upon humans "who suppress the truth by wickedness" (1:18).[53]

---

argument of 2:1 is clearly ominous for the separatist mentality, which is convinced of its privilege and superiority due to knowledge of God's will in the law. Thus 2:1-11 leads to the key thesis, that "before [the judgment seat of] God there is no favoritism" (2:11), but this is true for "the Jew *first,* as well as the Greek" (2:9b, 10b; cf. 1:16). Thus Käsemann's view (*Commentary on Romans,* 53) that these verses are already "a polemic against the Jewish tradition," exemplified in Wisdom 15, is quite to the point.

51. See Wilckens, "Abfassungszweck," *Rechtfertigung,* 144.

52. I agree with E. P. Sanders, *Law and the Jewish People,* 124–25, that 1:18–2:29 is not "an objective description" but is rather "exaggerated rhetoric." Having made that point, however, Sanders goes on to say that "Paul's case" in this section is "internally inconsistent and . . . rests on gross exaggeration." But surely "rhetoric," like poetry, has its license. The interpreter's focus must remain on the point being made, not on rhetoric's exaggerations. See the excellent discussion by Westerholm, *Israel's Law,* 151–61; also see note 57, below.

53. In Romans the law is not, as in Galatians 3–4, God's adversary, interposing itself illegitimately between the promise and the promise's

Romans 3:21 picks up the thematic statement of 1:16-17 and encloses the indictment of the "whole world" (3:19) within it. The quote from Hab 2:4 in 1:17 is balanced and reinforced by Ps 143:2 in 3:20. The law bears witness to the gospel and in the service of the gospel brings the world to its knees before the Creator. But note how this use of Psalm 143 differs between the two letters. In Gal 2:16 it serves, in the harsh dialectic of that letter, to witness to the powerlessness of the law. In Rom 3:20, however, it simply reinforces the catena of quotations in 3:10-18, indicting the world for its sinfulness, not the law for its failure.[54] In Galatians 2 it leads to the negative assertion "I died to the law" (2:19). In Romans 3 it leads to the positive statement "we uphold the law" (3:31). The difference is that in Galatians Paul is already thinking of the *law itself* as the *enemy* to be defeated, whereas in Romans he *appeals* immediately to the law as his *ally*.

From the very beginning, therefore, Romans envisages a positive role for the law in the context of the gospel and backs away from indicting the law itself as the cause for human illusion. It is from the perspective of the law positively conceived that the statements in Rom 2:6 and 13 have to be understood. These statements, and this entire section of the letter (1:18–3:20), presuppose that its readers have accepted the gospel and have recognized that, though it reveals God's saving righteousness (1:16-17), it is also accompanied by the revelation of "God's wrath" (following note), which exposes all humans, including those who would take refuge "in law," as sinners (3:19-23). This revelation de-

---

fulfillment. In Rom 5:20 παρεισῆλθεν does not mean "sneaked in" but simply "came in secondarily" or, as Bauer, *Greek-English Lexicon,* 630, has it, "came in as a side issue." Romans 4:10-11—describing circumcision as the approving "seal" of the covenant with Abraham and, as a conclusion of that, asserting that it is not "through" or "from" the law that the promised is received (4:13-14)—is only mildly reminiscent of the biting metaphor of Gal 3:15-17, which *does* envisage the law as acting in an underhand, sneaky fashion.

54. See Hahn, "Gesetzesverständnis," 37, on the correlation between "the statement in 3:20a" and "the apostle's basic thesis enunciated in 1:17f." With somewhat different emphasis, Hahn, 59–60, also notes this difference between Romans 3 and Galatians 2 in the use of Psalm 143.

mands the obedience of all creation to the statutes of God. What those statutes are, however, can only be revealed by the gospel. The gospel demands obedience to the law *once the law is understood as only the gospel can reveal it.* That Paul, both in Romans 2 and elsewhere, demands obedience to the "commandments of God" so understood, is of course beyond all dispute (Rom 14:10-12; 1 Cor 7:19; 2 Cor 5:10; Gal 5:13–6:10). Bultmann expresses the point powerfully and must be quoted at length:

> The presupposition for understanding the proposition that not works lead to "righteousness," but only faith, is the acknowledgment that the law's demand is just, *that God is the Judge who demands good deeds of man* (Rom 1:18–3:20). The preaching of faith does not introduce a new concept of God as if God were not the Judge who requires good works but were only the Merciful. No, we may speak of God's "grace" only when we also speak of His "wrath." That is how it happens that Paul, in words that sound open to misunderstanding, can refer the Christian, who achieves "righteousness" not by works of the Law but by faith, to the judgment in which recompense is made according to works. . . . Though the Christian in a certain sense is no longer "under Law" (Gal 5:18; Rom 6:14), that does not mean that the demands of the Law are no longer valid for him; for the *agape* demanded of him is nothing else than the fufilment of the Law (Rom 13:8-10; Gal 5:14).[55]

It is not a denial of grace to remind believers that "it is a fearful thing to fall into the hands of the living God" (Heb 10:31); it

---

55. Bultmann, *Theology of the New Testament,* 1:262. Watson, "Justified by Faith," 209–21, properly insists that in order to understand these seemingly contradictory statements, due emphasis must be given "to the occasional nature of Paul's letters" (213). However, Watson seems to regard only the message of justification as "the gospel" (especially 219), with the message of judgment being Paul's corrective for those "whose faith had degenerated to a false security, that is, to Christians in their unbelief" (220). But the point of the parallelism of Rom 1:17 and 1:18 (on this interpretation, see Barrett, *Epistle to the Romans,* 32–34; Käsemann, *Commentary on Romans,* 35) is that along with the gospel, and indeed "in it" (ἐν αὐτῷ, 1:17), God reveals to humans the "truth" of their condition before God, which apart from the gospel they do not recognize. In that sense "wrath" and "judgment" (2:1-11) also have to do with "the truth of the gospel."

is rather an affirmation of what grace truly is. In the absence of wrath grace loses its meaning; indeed, it becomes perverted into cheap grace, the accusation of Paul's opponents (Rom 3:8; 6:1, 15). In this section of Romans Paul is intent to show that his gospel (2:16) in no way compromises God's power as judge (3:1-8).

In 2:1-29 the first thesis, as Käsemann says, is that God shows no partiality (2:11).[56] Jews stand in the forefront of the judgment because, due to the weightier measure of their gifts, theirs is the greater responsibility (2:10). But mere possession of the law, being "hearers" of it, does not secure the Jews any advantage over Gentiles. In this context (2:12-16) Paul highlights Jewish sinfulness by the foil of Gentiles who "by nature do not have the law" and yet are obedient to (parts of) it.[57] The whole

---

56. Käsemann, *Commentary on Romans,* 53.

57. On the notorious difficulties of this passage, see E. P. Sanders, *Law and the Jewish People,* 125–26. How can Paul envisage Gentiles being obedient to the law (2:12-16), and more difficult yet, who are the "uncircumcised" in verses 26–29, and in what sense can obedience to the law "be an advantage" (v. 25)? Sanders insists there is no basis in the text for the view that Paul speaks hypothetically or that the Gentiles are Christians, and at least on the last point he must be correct. It is apparent, however, that Paul's main point has *nothing to do* with the *identity* of these Gentiles. The "exclusive point," says Käsemann, *Commentary on Romans,* 62, "is that there is no escaping universal judgment." Like the prophets before him, Paul rhetorically holds up Gentile obedience in order to indict Jewish transgression (on this last point, see Westerholm, *Israel's Law,* 157–61). After 1:18-32 this is startling, but the sequence of Paul's argument is deliberate and telling. The universal principle of divine judgment on human disobedience (1:18–2:11) is followed by the assertion of Gentiles "sometimes" (ὅταν) doing "the requirements of the law" (τὰ τοῦ νόμου). Paul then indicts his Jewish opposition for the, to him, mistaken idea of privilege in the law and for disobedience to it. His conclusion (vv. 25–29), that uncircumcised ("by nature" lawless) Gentiles might exhibit obedience, which shows up Jewish transgressions and might even judge the Jewish transgressor, is the sharpest dart that Paul can aim at the heart of Jewish claims of privilege over against Gentiles. On φύσει ("by nature") in 2:14 as qualifying ἔχοντα ("having") and not ποιῶσιν ("do"), see Achtemeier, "Some Things," 258–59; the latter point, contrary to Dunn, *Romans 1–8,* 98 and 105; E. P. Sanders, *Law and the Jewish People,* 130 and note 45.

movement of the argument is ominous for the supposed privilege of those who are "in [the] law." What is distinctive about the passage, according to Sanders, is that it is imbued with "a Jewish perspective," in that it makes the law "the sole determinant of salvation."[58] That is undoubtedly true, and yet it radically undermines what that perspective means for Jews over against Gentiles in relation to God. "Synagogue sermon" or not (n. 58), this "Jewish perspective" enables Paul to attack his opponents *on their own ground,* where they feel strongest—not an unusual ploy for the apostle (cf. Phil 3:2-6; 2 Cor 10:3-6). Furthermore, it answers strongly those who would claim that Paul's gospel is a gospel of cheap grace while also maintaining Paul's characteristic polemic against the separatist privilege. Thus the phrase "according to my gospel" in 2:16 is part of Paul's assertion, against his opponents, that his preaching of the gospel does include the notion of judgment regarding "the demands of the law."[59] And, indeed, those opponents are put on notice that their

58. E. P. Sanders, *Law and the Jewish People,* 129. Sanders stresses this as part of his thesis that 1:18–2:29 is "a synagogue sermon" taken over substantially unchanged (see 123). This is an attractive hypothesis that might explain many of the passage's seemingly insuperable difficulties, and as Sanders points out (128), others also have seen "synagogue material" here. But the passage does not seem to me so devoid of the "Pauline imprint" (129) once one takes into account the context of this letter and what the apostle is trying to accomplish in attacking Jewish notions of privilege "in the law."

59. Of course, precisely what those demands are is quite a different issue for Paul than for his opponents, but what matters for Paul is to show that he has neither disregarded the law in general nor ethical considerations in particular (3:8; 6:1, 15). Verse 16 as a whole is sufficiently problematic that suggestions have been made either that it belongs elsewhere (after v. 13) or that it is a gloss or part of a larger gloss. For discussion, see Käsemann, *Commentary on Romans,* 66–67, who rightly takes the verse as is. Michel, *Römer,* 84, says that something needs to be supplied in order to make Paul's thought clear, and instructively paraphrases: "This secretive state of affairs will be revealed on the day of judgment when God will judge the secrets of humankind as I proclaim in my gospel through Jesus Christ." The gospel, then, is not the criterion of judgment (pace Dunn, *Romans 1–8,* 103 and 106); Paul is asserting the *content* of his gospel.

supposed privilege within the law is an illusion, for they are to be judged "first" (2:9-10).

Paul is not compromising here with his abrogation of the law as determinative of salvation, the point of 3:20 and Gal 2:16. In light of the attacks against him (especially 3:8), he shifts the focus of his attack from the law itself (as in Galatians) to the law's ardent adherents, and thus he defends his preaching of the gospel of grace. He does so aggressively by baring the gospel's sharp edge, its exposure of human sinfulness and its demand for goodness, in order to indict Jews as well as Gentiles and thus to unmask the illusion of superior status before God. But this adoption of "a Jewish perspective" is not mere rhetoric; it is also Paul's view, as an essential aspect of the gospel, that all humans, believers no less than unbelievers, must account to God for their deeds. In the context of Romans Paul is anxious to be seen as at one with the law in that regard. The difference, of course, between Paul and his opposition is that "works" and "law" have a totally different context and meaning for Paul than they have for the separatist viewpoint he opposes. Thus the principle of "works" enunciated here both *serves the proclamation of the gospel* and, for Paul, can *only be properly exercised and understood* within it. It ought to go without saying that Paul is not demanding nor is he expecting obedience to the individual prescriptions of the law.[60] It is, therefore, a matter of "rhetoric" that Paul argues from a position that he does *not* espouse *as it would be understood by its proponents.* Not unlike his sarcastic use of separatist vocabulary in Gal 2:15, which is then exposed as fallacious in 2:16-17, so here—also not with-

---

60. Nevertheless Sanders, *Law and the Jewish People,* 130, implies this. He also insists (129) that there is "no distinctively Pauline imprint in 1:18–2:29," and it has to be largely, though not wholly, conceded that this passage "at no point reflects specifically Christian thinking," except, as Sanders admits, 2:16. That exception, however, *and the context within which Paul places the passage,* betray Paul's *Christian intentions.* For Paul the passage is not an "appendix" (as Sanders deals with it); it is fundamental to his argument and his exposition of the gospel *in this context.* Thus in the passage's conclusion (2:28-29), particularly verse 29 (pace Sanders, *Law and the Jewish People,* 127), the spirit-letter antithesis is specifically Pauline and Christian, anticipating the thought of 7:6b.

out sarcasm (2:17-24)—Paul uses his opponents' viewpoint against them. He is critiquing unbelief from the perspective of belief and argues with belief's insights into the law's true intent as revealed by the "Spirit," which unbelief, dependent on "codified law" (γράμμα), can never possess.[61]

Viewed from this perspective there is no contradiction theologically between Gal 2:16 and Rom 2:13, just as there is no contradiction between Gal 2:16 and 5:14 or between Rom 2:13 and 3:20. At the level of language, of course, the tension will always remain between these statements, but if their contexts and purposes and Paul's dialectical handling of the law are kept in view, then it is apparent that they unite as announcements of the one gospel. In both letters Paul can and must assert the demand for "fulfilling the law," precisely because "righteousness by faith" is not a gospel of cheap grace. As Käsemann properly says, "The doctrines of justification and judgment are inseparably linked in Paul . . . , because the concern in both is the Creator's right as Lord of creation as this works itself out in the creature."[62] Romans 2, like Galatians, unsheathes the sharp edge of the gospel because the fallacy of separatism and privilege must be destroyed. By working with the presuppositions of his opposition but doing so in the context of the gospel, Paul is able to accomplish two things, both of which are essential in Romans: first, he demonstrates to those who may have been in doubt that his gospel does not mean what "some" have claimed against him (3:8), and second, he undermines the illusion of superiority within the law. If understood with these aims in mind Romans 2 coordinates well with the rest of the letter and answers those who may have used the harsh statements of Galatians against him.

---

61. On the antithesis of πνεῦμα ("spirit") and γράμμα ("letter") in 2:29, see especially Käsemann, *Commentary on Romans,* 76–77.

62. Ibid., 56.

Bibliography

Texts, Dictionaries, Grammars, Concordances

Bauer, Walter. *A Greek-English Lexicon of the New Testament and Other Early Christian Literature.* Trans. and adapted W. F. Arndt and F. W. Gingrich. 4th rev. & enl. ed. Chicago: University of Chicago Press, 1957.

Blass, F., and A. Debrunner. *A Greek Grammar of the New Testament and Other Early Christian Literature.* Trans. and rev. R. W. Funk. Chicago: University of Chicago Press, 1961.

Brown, Francis, and others, eds. *A Hebrew and English Lexicon of the Old Testament.* Oxford: Clarendon Press, 1979.

Buttrick, G. A., ed. *The Interpreter's Dictionary of the Bible: An Illustrated Encyclopedia.* 5 vols. Nashville: Abingdon Press, 1962.

Charlesworth, James H., ed. *The Old Testament Pseudepigrapha.* 2 vols. New York: Doubleday, 1983.

Elliger, K. and W. Rudolph, eds. *Biblia Hebraica Stuttgartensia.* Stuttgart: Deutsche Bibelstiftung, 1977.

Funk, Robert W. *A Beginning-Intermediate Grammar of Hellenistic Greek.* 3 vols. 2d corrected ed. Missoula: Scholars Press, 1973.

Kittel, G., ed. *Theological Dictionary of the New Testament.* 11 vols. Trans. and ed. G. W. Bromiley. Grand Rapids, Eerdmans, 1974.

Liddell and Scott. *An Intermediate Greek-English Lexicon.* Oxford: Clarendon Press, 1889.

Mandelkern, Solomon. *Veteris Testamenti Concordantiae Hebraicae atque Chaldaicae.* Tel Aviv: Shocken, 1978.

Martinez, Florentini Garcia, ed. *The Dead Sea Scrolls Translated.* 2d ed. Trans. Wilfred G. E. Watson. Grand Rapids: Eerdmans, 1996.

McKenzie, John L. *Dictionary of the Bible.* New York: Macmillan, 1965.

Moulton, W. F., and A. S. Geden. *A Concordance to the Greek Testament.* 5th ed., rev. H. K. Moulton. Edinburgh: T. & T. Clark, 1978.

Nestle and others, eds. *Novum Testamentum Graece.* 26th ed. Stuttgart: Deutsche Bibelstiftung, 1979.

Qimron, Elisha, and John Strugnell, eds. Text and trans. of 4QMMT, reprinted in *Biblical Archaeology Review* 20:6 (1994) 56–61.

Zerwick, Maximilian. *Biblical Greek Illustrated by Examples.* Trans. and adapted Joseph Smith. Scripta Pontificii Instituti Biblici, 114. Rome, 1963.

Commentaries Cited

Barrett, C. K. *The Epistle to the Romans,* rev. ed. London: A. & C. Black, 1991.

Betz, Hans Dieter. *Galatians: Commentary on Paul's Letter to the Churches of Galatia.* Hermeneia. Philadelphia: Fortress Press, 1979.

Beyer, Hermann Wolfgang, and others. *Das Neue Testament Deutsch: Die kleineren Briefe des Apostels Paulus.* Göttingen: Vandenhoeck & Ruprecht, 1970.

Bligh, J. *Galatians in Greek.* Detroit: University of Detroit Press, 1966.

Bonnard, Pierre. *L'Épitre de Saint Paul aux Galates.* 2d. ed. rev. and enl. Commentaire du Nouveau Testament, 9. Neuchâtel: Delachaux et Niestlé, 1972.

Bruce, F. F. *The Epistle to the Galatians: A Commentary on the Greek Text.* The International Greek Testament Commentary. Grand Rapids: Eerdmans, 1982.

Burton, Ernest De Witt. *A Critical and Exegetical Commentary on the Epistle to the Galatians.* The International Critical Commentary. Edinburgh: T. & T. Clark [1920].

Conzelmann, Hans. *A Commentary on the First Epistle to the Corinthians.* Ed. George W. MacRae and trans. James W. Leitch.

Hermeneia. Philadelphia: Fortress Press, 1975.

Duncan, George S. *The Epistle of Paul to the Galatians.* Moffatt New Testament Commentary. New York: Harper & Brothers [1934].

Dunn, James D. G. *The Epistle to the Galatians.* Black's New Testament Commentaries. Peabody, Mass.: Hendrickson, 1993.

_____. *Word Biblical Commentary: Romans 1–8.* WBC 38A. Dallas: Word Books, 1988.

_____. *Word Biblical Commentary: Romans 9–16.* WBC 38B. Dallas: Word Books, 1988.

Ebeling, Gerhard. *The Truth of the Gospel: An Exposition of Galatians.* Trans. David Green. Philadelphia: Fortress Press, 1985.

Fitzmyer, Joseph A. *Romans: A New Translation with Introduction and Commentary.* Anchor Bible. New York: Doubleday, 1993.

Haenchen, Ernst. *The Acts of the Apostles: A Commentary.* Trans. Bernard Noble and others. Trans. rev. R. McL. Wilson. Philadelphia: Westminster Press, 1971.

Käsemann, Ernst. *Commentary on Romans.* Trans. and ed. Geoffrey W. Bromiley. Grand Rapids: Eerdmans, 1980.

Lagrange, Le P. M.-J. *Saint Paul: Épitre aux Galates.* 2d. ed. Études Bibliques. Paris: J. Gabalda, 1950.

Lietzmann, H. D. *An die Galater.* Tübingen: J. C. B. Mohr, 1971.

Lightfoot, J. B. *The Epistle of Saint Paul to the Galatians* [1865]. Reprint ed., Grand Rapids: Zondervan, 1957.

Matera, Frank J. *Galatians.* Sacra Pagina 9. Collegeville: The Liturgical Press, 1992.

Michel, Otto. *Der Brief an die Römer.* Meyers Kommentar 4. 4th rev. ed. Göttingen: Vandenhoeck & Ruprecht, 1966.

Mussner, Franz. *Der Galaterbrief.* 3d. enl. ed. Herders Theologischer Kommentar zum Neuen Testament 9. Freiburg: Herder, 1977.

Oepke, Albrecht. *Der Brief des Paulus an die Galater.* Theologischer Handkommentar zum Neuen Testament 9. 2d. ed. Berlin: Evangelische Verlagsanstalt, 1973.

Ridderbos, Herman, N. *The Epistle of Paul to the Churches of Galatia.* Trans. Henry Zylstra. The New International Commentary on the New Testament. Grand Rapids: Eerdmans, 1953.

Schlier, Heinrich. *Der Brief an die Galater.* 5th ed. Meyers Kommentar 7. Göttingen: Vandenhoeck & Ruprecht, 1971.

Von Rad, Gerhard. *Genesis: A Commentary.* Trans. John H. Marks.

Rev. ed. The Old Testament Library. Philadelphia: Westminster Press, 1972.

Monographs, Articles, and Other Works Cited

Abegg, Martin. "Paul, 'Works of the Law,' and MMT." *Biblical Archaeology Review* 20:6 (1994) 52–55 and 82.

Achtemeier, Paul, J. *The Quest for Unity in the New Testament Church.* Philadelphia: Fortress Press, 1987.

_____. "'Some Things in Them Hard to Understand': Reflections on an Approach to Paul." *Interpretation* 38 (July 1984) 254–67.

Aune, David E. Review article in *Religious Studies Review* 7 (October 1981) 323–28.

_____. *The New Testament in Its Literary Environment.* Library of Early Christianity. Philadelphia: Westminster Press, 1987.

Barclay, J. M. G. "Mirror Reading a Polemical Letter: Galatians as a Test Case," *The Pauline Writings.* Ed. S. E. Porter and C. A. Evans. The Biblical Seminar 34. Sheffield, U.K.: Academic, 1995. 247–67.

Barrett, C. K. "The Allegory of Abraham, Sarah, and Hagar in the Argument of Galatians." *Rechtfertigung.* Festschrift für Ernst Käsemann. Ed. J. Friedrich and others. Tübingen: J. C. B. Mohr, 1976. 1–16.

_____. *Freedom and Obligation: A Study of the Epistle to the Galatians.* Philadelphia: Westminster Press, 1985.

Barth, Markus. "'The Faith of the Messiah.'" *Heythrop Journal* 10 (1969) 363–70.

Beker, J. Christiaan. *Paul the Apostle: The Triumph of God in Life and Thought.* Philadelphia: Fortress Press, 1980.

_____. "Recasting Pauline Theology: The Coherence-Contingency Scheme as Interpretive Model." *Pauline Theology I: Thessalonians, Philippians, Galatians, Philemon.* Ed. J. M. Bassler. Minneapolis: Fortress Press, 1991. 15–24.

Betz, Hans Dieter. "2 Cor 6:14–7:1: An Anti-Pauline Fragment?" *Journal of Biblical Literature* 92 (1973) 88–108.

_____. "Geist, Freiheit, und Gesetz." *Zeitschrift für Theologie und Kirche* 71 (1974) 78–93.

_____. "The Literary Composition and Function of Paul's Letter to the Galatians." *New Testament Studies* 21 (1975) 353–79.

Boers, Hendrikus. *The Justification of the Gentiles: Paul's Letters to the Galatians and Romans.* Peabody, Mass.: Hendrickson, 1994.

Bonneau, Normand. "The Logic of Paul's Argument on the Curse of the Law in Galatians 3:10-14." *Novum Testamentum* 39:1 (January 1997) 60–80.

Bornkamm, Günther. *Early Christian Experience.* Trans. Paul L. Hammer. New York: Harper & Row, 1969.

_____. *Paul.* Trans. D. M. G. Stalker. New York: Harper & Row, 1969.

Böttger, Paul C. "Paulus und Petrus in Antiochien: Zum Verständnis von Galater 2:11-21." *New Testament Studies* 37 (1991) 77–100.

Brandon, S. G. F. *The Fall of Jerusalem and the Christian Church.* London: SPCK, 1951.

Bright, John. *A History of Israel.* 3d. ed. Philadelphia: Westminster Press, 1981.

Brinsmead, Bernard Hungerford. *Galatians—Dialogical Response to Opponents.* Society of Biblical Literature Dissertation Series 65. Chico, Calif.: Scholars Press, 1982.

Brown, R. E. "Not Jewish Christianity and Gentile Christianity but Types of Jewish/Gentile Christianity." *Catholic Biblical Quarterly* 45 (January 1983) 74–79.

_____ and J. P. Meier. *Antioch and Rome: New Testament Cradles of Catholic Christianity.* New York: Paulist Press, 1983.

Bruce, F. F. "The Curse of the Law." *Paul and Paulinism.* Essays in honour of C. K. Barrett. Ed. M. D. Hooker and S. G. Wilson. London: SPCK, 1982. 27–36.

Bultmann, Rudolf. "ΔΙΚΑΙΟΣΎΝΗ ΘΕΟΎ." *Journal of Biblical Literature* 83 (1964) 12–16.

_____. *Primitive Christianity in Its Contemporary Setting.* Trans. R. H. Fuller. New York: World Publishing, 1956.

_____. *Theology of the New Testament.* 2 vols. Trans. Kendrick Grobel. New York: Charles Scribner's Sons, 1951–55.

_____. "Zur Auslegung von Galater 2:15-18." *Exegetica: Aufsätze zur Erforschung des neuen Testaments.* Ed. E. Dinkler. Tübingen: J.C.B. Mohr, 1967.

Byrne, Brendan. *Paul and the Christian Woman.* Collegeville: The Liturgical Press, 1988.

_____. *"Sons of God"—"Seed of Abraham."* Analecta Biblica 83. Rome: Biblical Institute, 1979.

Callan, T. "Pauline Midrash: The Exegetical Background of Gal. 3:19b." *Journal of Biblical Literature* 99 (1980) 549–67.

Charles, R. H. *The Greek Version of the Testaments of the Twelve Patriarchs.* Hildesheim: Georg Olms, 1908, 1966.

Conzelmann, Hans. *History of Primitive Christianity.* Trans. J. E. Steely. Nashville: Abingdon Press, 1973.

Cosgrove, Charles H. *The Cross and the Spirit: A Study in the Argument and Theology of Galatians.* Macon, Ga.: Mercer University Press, 1988.

_____. "Rhetorical Suspense in Romans 9–11: A Study in Polyvalence and Hermeneutical Election." *Journal of Biblical Literature* 115 (1996) 271–87.

Cranford, Michael. "Abraham in Romans 4: The Father of All Who Believe." *New Testament Studies* 41 (1995) 71–88.

Crossan, John D. *The Historical Jesus: The Life of a Mediterranean Jewish Peasant.* San Francisco: HarperCollins, 1992.

Cullmann, Oscar. *Peter: Disciple, Apostle, and Martyr.* Trans. J. E. Steely. Nashville: Abingdon Press, 1973.

Davies, W. D. *The Gospel and the Land: Early Christianity and Jewish Territorial Doctrine.* Berkeley: University of California Press, 1974.

_____. "Paul and the Law: Reflections on Pitfalls in Interpretation." *Paul and Paulinism.* (see F. F. Bruce, above).

_____. *Paul and Rabbinic Judaism: Some Rabbinic Elements in Pauline Theology.* 4th ed. Philadelphia: Fortress Press, 1980.

Dillon, Richard J. Review article in *Theological Studies* 50 (June 1989) 360–61.

Dodd, C. H. *The Parables of the Kingdom.* Rev ed. New York: Charles Scribner's Sons, 1961.

Donaldson, T. L. "The 'Curse of the Law' and the Inclusion of the Gentiles: Galatians 3:13-14." *New Testament Studies* 32 (1986) 94–112.

Doty, William G. *Letters in Primitive Christianity.* Guides to Biblical Scholarship. Philadelphia: Fortress Press, 1973.

Dunn, James D. G. "Echoes of Intra-Jewish Polemic in Paul's Letter to the Galatians." *Journal of Biblical Literature* 112 (1993) 459–77.

_____. *Jesus, Paul, and the Law: Studies in Mark and Galatians.* Louisville, Ky.: Westminster/John Knox, 1990.

_____. *The Partings of the Ways Between Christianity and Judaism and Their Significance for the Character of Christianity.* Philadelphia: Trinity, 1991.

_____. *Unity and Diversity in the New Testament: An Inquiry into the Character of Earliest Christianity.* Philadelphia: Westminster Press, 1977.

_____. "4QMMT and Galatians." *New Testament Studies* 43 (1997) 147–53.

Eckert, Jost. *Die Urchristliche Verkündigung im Streit zwischen Paulus und seinen Gegnern nach dem Galaterbrief.* Regensburg: Friedrich Pustet, 1971.

Eckstein, Hans-Joachim. *Verheißung und Gesetz: Eine exegetische Untersuchung zu Galater 2:15–4:7.* Wissenschaftliche Untersuchungen zum Neuen Testament 86. Tübingen: J. C. B. Mohr (Paul Siebeck) 1996.

Eisenman, Robert, and Michael Wise. *The Dead Sea Scrolls Uncovered: The First Complete Translation and Interpretation of 50 Key Documents Withheld for Over 35 Years.* New York: Penguin Books, 1992.

Feld, Helmut. "'Christus Diener der Sünde': Zum Ausgang des Streites zwischen Petrus und Paulus." *Theologische Quartalschrift* 153 (1973) 119–31.

Fitzmyer, Joseph A. "Paul and the Law." *A Companion to Paul: Readings in Pauline Theology.* Ed. M. J. Taylor. New York: Alba House, 1975.

Fredriksen, Paula. "Judaism, The Circumcision of Gentiles, and Apocalyptic Hope: Another Look at Galatians 1 and 2." *Journal of Theological Studies* 42 (October 1991) 532–64.

Furnish, Victor Paul. "On Putting Paul in His Place," *Journal of Biblical Literature* 113/1 (1994) 3–17.

_____. *Theology and Ethics in Paul.* Nashville: Abingdon Press, 1968.

Gaston, Lloyd. *Paul and the Torah.* Vancouver: University of British Columbia Press, 1987.

Giblin, Charles Homer. *In Hope of God's Glory: Pauline Theological Perspectives.* New York: Herder & Herder, 1970.

Grässer, Erich. "Das Eine Evangelium: Hermeneutische Erwägungen zu Gal. 1:6-10." *Zeitschrift für Theologie und Kirche* 66 (1969) 306–44.

Gundry, R. H. "Grace, Works, and Staying Saved in Paul." *Biblica* 66 (1985) 1–38.

Haenchen, Ernst. "Petrus-Probleme." *New Testament Studies* 7 (1961) 187–97.

Hahn, Ferdinand. "Das Gesetzesverständnis im Römer—und Galaterbrief." *Zeitschrift für Neutestamentliche Wissenschaft* 67 (1976) 29–63.

Hay, David M. "Paul's Indifference to Authority." *Journal of Biblical Literature* 88 (1969) 36–44.

Hays, Richard B. *Echoes of Scripture in the Letters of Paul.* New Haven: Yale University Press, 1989.

_____. "'Have We Found Abraham to Be Our Forefather According to the Flesh?' A Reconsideration of Rom 4:1." *Novum Testamentum* 27 (1985) 76–98.

Hill, David. *New Testament Prophecy.* New Foundations Theological Library. Atlanta: John Knox, 1979.

Holmberg, Bengt. *Paul and Power: The Structure of Authority in the Primitive Church as Reflected in the Pauline Epistles.* Philadelphia: Fortress Press, 1978.

Holtz, Traugott. "Die Bedeutung des Apostelkonzils für Paulus." *Novum Testamentum* 16 (1974) 110–48.

Hooker, Morna D. "ΠΙΣΤΙΣ ΧΡΙΣΤΟΥ." *New Testament Studies* 35 (1989) 321–42.

_____. "Paul and 'Covenantal Nomism.'" *Paul and Paulinism* (see F. F. Bruce, above).

Horn, F. W. "Der Verzicht auf die Beschneidung im frühen Christentum," *New Testament Studies* 42 (October 1996) 479–505.

Howard, George. *Paul: Crisis in Galatia: A Study in Early Christian Theology.* Cambridge: Cambridge University Press, 1979.

Hübner, Hans. *Law in Paul's Thought.* Trans. James C. G. Greig. Edinburgh: T & T Clark, 1984.

Hultgren, Arland J. "The Πίστις Χριστοῦ Formulation in Paul," *Novum Testamentum* 22 (July 1980) 248–63.

Jeremias, Joachim. *The Central Message of the New Testament.* Philadelphia: Fortress Press, 1965.

Jewett, R. "The Agitators and the Galatian Congregation." *New Testament Studies* 17 (1971) 198–212.

_____. *Paul's Anthropological Terms: A Study of Their Use in Conflict Settings.* Leiden: E. J. Brill, 1971.

Johnson, Luke Timothy. "Rom 3:21-26 and the Faith of Jesus,"

Catholic Biblical Quarterly 44 (1982) 77–90.

Kampen, John, and Moshe J. Bernstein, eds. *Reading 4QMMT: New Perspectives on Qumran Law and History.* Symposium Series. Atlanta: Scholars Press, 1996.

Käsemann, Ernst. *New Testament Questions of Today.* Trans. W. J. Montague. Philadelphia: Fortress Press, 1969.

————. *Perspectives on Paul.* Trans. Margaret Kohl. Philadelphia: Fortress Press, 1971.

Keck, Leander E. "Justification of the Ungodly and Ethics." *Rechtfertigung* (see C. K. Barrett, above).

————. "Paul as Thinker." *Interpretation* 47 (January 1993) 27–38.

Kennedy, George A. *New Testament Interpretation Through Rhetorical Criticism.* Studies in Religion. Chapel Hill: University of North Carolina Press, 1984.

Kertelge, Karl. "Apokalypsis Iesou Christou (Gal 1:12)." *Neues Testament und Kirche.* Festschrift für Rudolf Schnackenburg. Ed. J. Gnilka. Freiburg: Herder, 1974. 266–81.

————. "Das Apostelamt des Paulus, sein Ursprung und seine Bedeutung." *Biblische Zeitschrift* 14 (1970) 161–81.

————. "Gesetz und Freiheit im Galaterbrief." *New Testament Studies* 30 (1984) 382–94.

————. *"Rechtfertigung" bei Paulus: Studien zur Struktur und zum Bedeutungsgehalt des paulinischen Rechtfertigungsbegriffs.* Münster: Aschendorff, 1967.

————. "Zur Deutung des Rechtfertigungsbegriffs im Galaterbrief," *Biblische Zeitschrift* 12 (1968) 211–22.

Kieffer, René. *Foi et Justification à Antioche: Interprétation d'un Conflit (Gal. 2:14-21).* Lectio Divina 111. Paris: Les Éditions du Cerf, 1982.

Kilpatrick, G. D. "Gal 2:14 ὀρθοποδοῦσιν." *Neutestamentliche Studien für Rudolf Bultmann.* Biblische Zeitscrift für Neutestamentliche Wissenschaft 21. Berlin: A. Töpelmann, 1957. 269–74.

Koester, Helmut. "Gnomai Diaphoroi: The Origin and Nature of Diversification in the History of Early Christianity." *Trajectories Through Early Christianity.* Ed. J. M. Robinson and H. Koester. Philadelphia: Fortress Press, 1971. 143–48.

Kümmel, W. G. "'Individualgeschichte' und 'Weltgeschichte' in Gal. 2:15-21." *Christ and Spirit in the New Testament.* Studies in honour of C. F. D. Moule. Ed. B. Lindars and S. S. Smalley. Cambridge: Cambridge University Press, 1973. 157–73.

_____. *Introduction to the New Testament.* Rev. ed. Trans. H. C. Kee. Nashville: Abingdon Press, 1975.

Lambrecht, Jan. "The Line of Thought in Gal. 2:14b-21." *New Testament Studies* 24 (1977) 484–95.

Lohmeyer, Ernst. *Probleme Paulinischer Theologie.* Stuttgart: W. Kohlhammer, n.d.

Lüdemann, Gerd. *Opposition to Paul in Jewish Christianity.* Trans. M. Eugene Boring. Minneapolis: Fortress Press, 1989.

_____. *Paul: Apostle to the Gentiles: Studies in Chronology.* Trans. F. Stanley Jones. London, SCM Press, 1984.

Lührmann, Dieter. "Abendmahlsgemeinschaft? Gal. 2:11ff." *Kirche.* Festschrift für Günther Bornkamm. Ed. D. Lührmann and G. Strecker. Tübingen: J. C. B. Mohr, 1980. 271–86.

_____. *Das Offenbarungsverständnis bei Paulus und in Paulinischen Gemeinden.* Neukirchen-Vluyn: Neukirchener, 1965.

Lull, David John. *The Spirit in Galatia: Paul's Interpretation of PNEUMA as Divine Power.* Society of Biblical Literature Dissertation Series 49. Chico, Calif.: Scholars Press, 1980.

Lyons, George. *Pauline Autobiography: Toward a New Understanding.* Atlanta: Scholars Press, 1985.

Marshall, I. Howard. "Salvation, Grace, and Works in the Later Writings of the Pauline Corpus." *New Testament Studies* 42 (1996) 339–58.

Martyn, J. Louis. "Apocalyptic Antinomies in Paul's Letter to the Galatians." *New Testament Studies* 31 (July 1985) 410–36.

_____. "A Law-Observant Mission to Gentiles: The Background of Galatians." *Scottish Journal of Theology* 38 (1985) 307–24.

Marxsen, Willi. *Introduction to the New Testament: An Approach to Its Problems.* Trans. G. Buswell. Philadelphia: Fortress, 1968.

McLean, Bradley H. "Galatians 2:7-9 and the Recognition of Paul's Apostolic Status at the Jerusalem Conference: A Critique of G. Luedemann's Solution." *New Testament Studies* 37 (1991) 67–76.

Meier, John P. *A Marginal Jew: Rethinking the Historical Jesus.* 2 vols. New York: Doubleday, 1994.

Munck, J. *Paul and the Salvation of Mankind.* Trans. F. Clarke. Richmond, Va.: John Knox, 1959.

Neusner, Jacob. *Judaism: The Evidence of the Mishnah.* Chicago: University of Chicago Press, 1981.

_____. *From Politics to Piety: The Emergence of Pharisaic Judaism.* 2d. ed. New York: KTAV, 1979.

Quarles, Charles L. "The Soteriology of R. Akiba and E. P. Sanders' *Paul and Palestinian Judaism.*" *New Testament Studies* 42 (1996) 185–95.

Räisänen, Heikki. "Galatians 2:16 and Paul's Break with Judaism." *New Testament Studies* 31 (1985) 543–53.

_____. "Legalism and Salvation by the Law: Paul's Portrayal of the Jewish Religion as a Historical and Theological Problem." *Die Paulinische Literatur und Theologie.* Ed. S. Pedersen. Arhus: Forlaget Aros, 1980. 63–83.

_____. "Paul, God, and Israel: Romans 9–11 in Recent Research." *The Social World of Formative Christianity and Judaism.* Essays in tribute to Howard Clark Kee. Ed. Jacob Neusner and others. Philadelphia: Fortress Press, 1988. 178–206.

_____. *Paul and the Law.* Philadelphia: Fortress Press, 1983.

Redditt, Paul L. "The Concept of Nomos in Fourth Maccabees." *Catholic Biblical Quarterly* 45 (April 1983) 249–70.

Reicke, Bo. "The Law and This World According to Paul: Some Thoughts Concerning Gal. 4:1-11." *Journal of Biblical Literature* 70 (1951) 259–76.

Richardson, P. *Israel in the Apostolic Church.* Cambridge: Cambridge University Press, 1969.

Roloff, J. *Apostolat - Verkündigung - Kirche: Ursprung, Inhalt und Funktion des kirchlichen Apostelamtes nach Paulus, Lukas und den Pastoralbriefen.* Gütersloh: Gütersloher Verlagshaus, 1965.

Sampley, J. "'Before God I Do Not Lie' Gal. 1:20: Paul's Self-Defence in the Light of Roman Legal Praxis." *New Testament Studies* 23 (1977) 477–82.

Sanders, E. P. *Jesus and Judaism.* London: SCM Press, 1985.

_____. *Judaism: Practice and Belief 63 BCE–66 CE.* London: SCM Press, 1992.

_____. *Paul and Palestinian Judaism: A Comparison of Patterns of Religion.* Philadelphia: Westminster Press, 1977.

_____. *Paul, the Law, and the Jewish People.* London: SCM Press, 1983.

Sanders, Jack T. "Paul's Autobiographical Statements in Galatians 1–2." *Journal of Biblical Literature* 85 (1966) 335–43.

264   *The Gospel and the Law in Galatia*

Schmithals, Walter. *Paul and the Gnostics*. Trans. J. E. Steely. New York: Abingdon Press, 1972.

_____. *Paul and James*. Trans. D. M. Barton. Studies in Biblical Theology 46. Naperville, Ill.: A. R. Allenson, 1965.

Schoeps H. J. *Paul: The Theology of the Apostle in the Light of Jewish Religious History.* Trans. Harold Knight. Philadelphia: Westminster Press, 1961.

Schütz, John Howard. *Paul and the Anatomy of Apostolic Authority.* Cambridge: Cambridge University Press, 1975.

Schweitzer, Albert. *The Mysticism of Paul the Apostle* [1931]. Trans. William Montgomery. New York: Seabury, 1968.

Segal, Alan F. *Paul the Convert: The Apostolate and Apostasy of Saul the Pharisee.* New Haven: Yale University Press, 1990.

Smith, Christopher C. "᾿Εκκλεῖσαι in Galatians 4:17: The Motif of the Excluded Lover as a Metaphor of Manipulation." *Catholic Biblical Quarterly* 58:3 (July 1996) 480–99.

Smith, Morton. "Pauline Problems." *Harvard Theological Review* 50 (1957) 107–31.

Stanley, Christopher D. "'Under a Curse': A Fresh Reading of Galatians 3:10-14." *New Testament Studies* 36 (1990) 481–511.

Stowers, Stanley K. *Letter-Writing in Greco-Roman Antiquity.* Philadelphia: Westminster Press, 1986.

Stuhlmacher, Peter. "'Das Ende des Gesetzes': Über Ursprung und Ansatz der paulinischen Theologie." *Zeitschrift für Theologie und Kirche* 67 (1970) 14–39.

_____. "Erwägungen zum ontologischen Charakter der *kainē ktisis* bei Paulus." *Evangelische Theologie* 27 (1967) 1–35.

_____. "Erwägungen zum Problem von Gegenwart und Zukunft in der paulinischen Eschatologie." *Zeitschrift für Theologie und Kirche* 64 (1967) 423–50.

_____. *Das paulinische Evangelium.* 2 vols. Forschungen zur Religion und Literatur des Alten und Neuen Testaments 95. Göttingen: Vandenhoeck & Ruprecht, 1968.

_____. "The Purpose of Romans." *The Romans Debate.* Ed. K. P. Donfried. Peabody, Mass.: Hendrickson, 1977, 1991. 231–42.

_____. *Reconciliation, Law, & Righteousness: Essays in Biblical Theology.* Philadelphia: Fortress Press, 1986.

Tannehill, Robert C. *Dying and Rising with Christ: A Study in Pauline Theology.* Berlin: A. Töpelmann, 1967.

Tyson, Joseph B. "Paul's Opponents in Galatia." *Novum Testamentum* 10 (1968) 241–54.

_____. "'Works of Law' in Galatians." *Journal of Biblical Literature* 92 (1973) 423–31.

Verseput, D. J. "Paul's Gentile Mission and the Jewish Christian Community: A Study of the Narrative in Galatians 1 and 2." *New Testament Studies* 39 (1993) 36–58.

Vielhauer, Philipp. "Gesetzesdienst und Stoicheiadienst im Galaterbrief." *Rechtfertigung* (see C. K. Barrett, above).

Von Rad, Gerhard. *Old Testament Theology.* 2 vols. Trans. D. M. G. Stalker. New York: Harper & Row, 1962.

Walker, William O. "Why Paul Went to Jerusalem: The Interpretation of Galatians 2:1-5." *Catholic Biblical Quarterly* 54 (July 1992) 503–10.

Watson, Nigel M. "Justified by Faith; Judged by Works—An Antinomy?" *New Testament Studies* 29 (1983) 209–21.

Wegenast, K. *Das Verständnis der Tradition bei Paulus und in den Deuteropaulinischen.* Neukirchen: Neukirchener, 1962.

Westerholm, Stephen. *Israel's Law and the Church's Faith: Paul and His Recent Interpreters.* Grand Rapids: Eerdmans, 1988.

White, John L. "Introductory Formulae in the Body of the Pauline Letter." *Journal of Biblical Literature* 90 (1971) 91–97.

Wilckens, Ulrich. *Rechtfertigung als Freiheit: Paulusstudien.* Neukirchen: Neukirchener, 1974.

_____. "Statements on the Development of Paul's View of the Law." *Paul and Paulinism.* (see F. F. Bruce, above).

_____. "Zur Entwicklung des paulinischen Gesetzesverständnisses." *New Testament Studies* 28 (1982) 154–86.

Winger, Michael. *By What Law? The Meaning of Νόμος in the Letters of Paul.* Society of Biblical Literature Dissertation Series 128. Atlanta: Scholars Press, 1992.

Wright, N. T. *The Climax of the Covenant: Christ and the Law in Pauline Theology.* Minneapolis: Fortress Press, 1992.

Ziesler, J. A. *The Meaning of Righteousness in Paul: A Linguistic and Theological Inquiry.* Cambridge: Cambridge University Press, 1972.

Index of Authors

Abegg, M., 119, 121
Achtemeier, E. R., 134
Achtemeier, P. J., 37, 39, 248
Aune, D. E., 12, 13

Barclay, J. M. G., 7
Barrett, C. K., 41, 202, 240, 244, 247
Barth, M., 115
Bauer, W., 40, 41, 44, 70, 73, 95, 188, 241, 246
Beker, J. C., 2, 3, 9, 27, 34, 64, 69, 73, 74, 100, 113, 117, 140, 146, 167, 174, 206, 207, 231, 233–235
Betz, H. D., 5–7, 12–14, 66–75, 78–80, 84, 86, 88, 91, 94, 96, 97, 103, 104, 107, 116, 123, 148, 150, 151, 153, 160, 164, 165, 168, 171 179, 182, 183, 186, 187, 188, 193, 194, 195, 197, 201, 203, 212
Beyer, H. W., and Althaus, P., 14, 34, 59, 67, 97, 104, 147, 160, 168, 173, 187
Blass, F., and Debrunner, A., 41, 57, 150, 152
Bligh, J., 14, 36
Boers, H., 190

Bonnard, P., 32, 36, 39, 88, 90, 95, 96, 98, 104, 107, 147, 154, 168, 170, 187, 193, 199
Bonneau, N., 194
Bornkamm, G., 41, 58, 59, 79, 81, 82, 93
Böttger, P. C., 5, 89, 93, 122
Brandon, S. G. F., 37, 42
Bright, J., 110
Brinsmead, B. H., 12, 14, 27, 74, 103, 104, 151, 159, 168, 187
Brown, R. E., 37, 85
Bruce, F. F., 1, 9, 14, 38, 41, 44, 57, 69, 79, 82, 88, 90, 93, 94, 97, 104, 106, 107, 112, 147, 152, 159, 182, 183, 185, 192, 198, 230
Bultmann, R., 2, 21, 69, 106, 117, 124, 136, 140, 142–144, 146, 153, 154, 160, 172, 192, 199, 200, 233, 247
Burton, E. D., 33, 35, 36, 39, 44, 48, 59, 67, 73, 79–82, 87, 88, 91, 93–95, 97, 104, 107, 112, 116, 117, 123, 147, 148, 150–152, 156, 157, 159, 170, 171, 178, 179, 182, 185–187, 196–198
Byrne, B., 66, 84, 104, 156, 158

267

Index of Texts

Joshua
4:24   109
5:2-7   64

Judges
5:11   135

1 Samuel
12:7   135
24:17   134
26:23   134

Ezra
4:8   242
9:1–10:44   109
9:15   134
9–10   16
10:12   109

Nehemiah
9:29   205
9:32-37   134
13   16, 110
13:3-30   109

2 Chronicles
19:7   45

Job
1:9   188
6:29   135
9:2   136
13:18   136
27:5   136
32:1-2   136
33:32   136

Psalms
1:1-2   132
7:9   132
17:2   135
17:15   135
18:22-24   132
22:27-28   114

25:1   132
32   133
33:5   134
34:7   188
35:27   135
37:6   135
40:9   132
47:9   114
51:14   135
56:4   175
85   136
85:10-13   134
86:5   136
86:8-9   114
89:14   134
116:1   112
119   187
119:1   132
143   **130-132,** 143, 246
143:1   134
143:2   118, 246
143:11-12   134
147:19-20   109, 131

Proverbs
21:26   134
29:7   134

Isaiah
2:2-4   114
5:7   135
25:6-10   114
40–55   136
40–66   138
43:18-19   26, 60
43:25-26   136
45:8   137
45:20   137
45:20-25   136
45:21   137
45:22   137
45:23   137
45:25   137